TOO GOOD
to LEAVE,
TOO BAD
to STAY

Also by Mira Kirshenbaum

Parent/Teen Breakthrough: The Relationship Approach
(with Charles Foster, Ph.D.)

TOO GOOD to LEAVE, TOO BAD to STAY

A STEP-BY-STEP GUIDE TO
HELP YOU DECIDE
WHETHER TO STAY IN OR
GET OUT OF YOUR
RELATIONSHIP

MIRA KIRSHENBAUM

A DUTTON BOOK

DUTTON

Published by the Penguin Group
Penguin Books USA Inc., 375 Hudson Street, New York, New York 10014, U.S.A.
Penguin Books Ltd, 27 Wrights Lane, London W8 5TZ, England
Penguin Books Australia Ltd, Ringwood, Victoria, Australia
Penguin Books Canada Ltd, 10 Alcorn Avenue, Toronto, Ontario, Canada M4V 3B2
Penguin Books (N.Z.) Ltd, 182–190 Wairau Road, Auckland 10, New Zealand

Penguin Books Ltd, Registered Offices:
Harmondsworth, Middlesex, England

First published by Dutton, an imprint of Dutton Signet,
a division of Penguin Books USA Inc.
Distributed in Canada by McClelland & Stewart Inc.

First Printing, July, 1996
10 9 8 7 6 5 4 3 2 1

 REGISTERED TRADEMARK—MARCA REGISTRADA

LIBRARY OF CONGRESS CATALOGING-IN-PUBLICATION DATA
Kirshenbaum, Mira.
    Too good to leave, too bad to stay : a step-by-step guide to help you decide whether
to stay in or get out of your relationship / Mira Kirshenbaum.
    p. cm.
    Includes index.
    ISBN 0-525-94069-3 (alk. paper)
    1. Man-woman relationships.   2. Relationship addiction.
I. Title.
HQ801.K57   1996
646.7'8—dc20   95-53003
                                                                          CIP

Printed in the United States of America
Set in New Caledonia
Designed by Jesse Cohen

This book is printed on acid-free paper.

To my most important teachers: my patients. You have shared your lives with me over the years and I'm eternally grateful for everything I've learned from you; for your dedication to health; for how hard you work to find happiness; for your willingness to learn lessons I know are tough; for your trust.

To my mother. I know how much you've accomplished, and I know how hard you've struggled. I wish I could have helped you when you needed it most, but I was too young. Thank you for inspiring me to believe I could help others. Thank you for inspiring in me the desire to learn the truth about love.

And to my daughters. You're the best, and you deserve a world of love.

CONTENTS

ACKNOWLEDGMENTS

This is a book about truth and love. It would not have been possible without the work of Dr. Charles Foster. Every word here is the product of a fifty/fifty collaboration between us. His research, insights, and ideas fill this book. We are full partners in everything. Because of him, in every way this search for the truth has been a labor of love.

I'm profoundly grateful to all the individuals whose lives and stories went into the research for *Too Good to Leave, Too Bad to Stay*. They were amazingly open and helpful, and what we've learned from them constitutes the bricks out of which this book is built.

There are many people I must mention if I'm to thank them properly. The debt I owe each of them makes me wish I could do more, in this small space, than list their names. These people are, one way or another, colleagues, teachers, heroes, friends who've given something specific to me, personally or professionally, through the years here at Chestnut Hill and elsewhere. They may not even realize the value of what they've done for me, but it played some role in making these pages possible. To all of them I say thank you: Louise Bates Ames, Shaye Areheart, Lisa Bankoff, Susan Bickelhaupt, Ruth Bork, Mihaly Csikszentmihalyi,

Alexia Dorszynski, Barry Dym, Dorothy Firman, Roger Fisher, Betty Friedan, Diana Huss Green, Jennifer Hack, Jay Haley, Jules Henry, Kathleen Huntington, Allan Kaprow, Alfred Kazin, Michael Kirshenbaum, Mary Jo Kochakian, Rabbi Harold Kushner, Eda LeShan, Richard Marek, Amy Mintzer, Salvador Minuchin, Nancy Moscatillo, Eli Newberger, Maury Povich, Cynthia Roe, Izzy Rudski, Ann Ruethling, Kim Schaffer, Gitta Sereny, Myron Sharaf, Judith Sills, Ivy Fischer Stone, Richard Stuart, Walter Watson, Paul Watzlawick, Rosa Wexler, Robert White, Elie Wiesel, Beth Winship, and Harold Zyskind.

Some people are sadly no longer alive to hear my gratitude for what they've given me. But I feel I must nonetheless express my thanks to Fred Avery, Gregory Bateson, Herbert Berghof, Martin Buber, Paul Goodman, Walter Green, Don Jackson, Pearl Karch, Virginia Satir, and Isaac Bashevis Singer.

I want to thank my daughters, Rachel and Hannah, who cared so much about this project and who expressed their love and intelligence by letting me feel the full weight of every constructive criticism they could think of.

What incredible good luck to have a mensch like Howard Morhaim as my agent. Without his gifts and his belief in me and in this project, all the people who need it would be denied the help this book offers. I am profoundly grateful to him. And a thanks to his assistant, Kate Hengerer.

My editor, Deborah Brody, has wowed me with her intelligence and enthusiasm. I thank her for caring about this book and for her marvelous ability to translate her caring into effective action that's enabling this information to reach as many people as possible.

I'd also like to thank all the other terrific people at Penguin and Dutton who I know have helped and will help this book and me. I can't mention everyone's name but I would like to single out Marvin Brown, Judy Courtade, Arnold Dolin, Elaine Koster, and Peter Mayer. A thanks to Julianne Barbato for her excellent copy editing, and a thanks for the care she's taken with my work to Jennifer Moore. Finally, I know how important Lisa Johnson's inspired work on my behalf has been in the past and will be in the future, and I'm grateful for it. And a special thanks to Tracy Guest.

I'd like to thank all the readers of my previous book for their incredible support. It means so much to me. I'd like to particularly thank the countless numbers of people who called and wrote just to tell me how much that book helped them.

Last, but not least, I must thank those patients of mine who kept asking me to write this book. I can't mention your names, but you know who you are.

TO MY READER

You are not alone. There are 140 million Americans today in a relationship, and one-fifth of them—that's 28 million people—just can't decide whether to stay or leave.

You deserve the happiness you're searching for. I've dedicated years to developing a simple but comprehensive series of questions and guidelines that will help you see clearly, once and for all, whether it's best *for you* to stay in your relationship or leave it. The women and men you'll meet here have struggled with the same issues you have. Their experiences will help you discover what's real in your own relationship, regardless of how long you've been with your partner or how long you've been stuck in ambivalence.

This book contains only good news. If it's best for you to stay, you'll have the satisfying experience of facing all the issues and discovering that your relationship is truly too good to leave. You won't be settling; you'll know your heart is home.

And if you'll be happiest leaving, you'll get the reassurance that comes from finally understanding why your relationship has been too bad to stay in. When you end a relationship that deserves to end, you're liberating two people to move on to better lives.

Either way, because you'll see what's best for you, you'll be far happier than you've been. Everything in your life will be better. I've written this book to help you make this happen.

Part I
THE PROBLEM

1
Is You Is or Is You Ain't My Baby?

You've gone through a lot to get to this point.

You've hoped that love would be enough. And you've worked to resolve the problems in your relationship. And you've tried to accept things the way they are.

And you've agonized over the possibility of leaving.

But you just haven't known what to do. Now you're ready to face the choice that's been weighing on your heart. That's what this book is for—to help you discover which is best for you:

> *To stay in your relationship*, recommitting to it free of doubt, free of holding back, free at last to pour your love and energy into the relationship and get back everything there is to get from it

or

> *To leave your relationship*, finally liberating yourself from it, free of confusion, free of pain, free at last to get on with a new and better life.

Up until now you haven't found the kind of evidence that speaks to your heart and makes clear what's best for you. You haven't found a sign like one of the following:

Leaving. He wouldn't make her a sandwich. Heather had been working in the garden in the hot sun all morning, and Bill had been doing God knows what inside the house. Through the open kitchen window she'd heard him grab a beer, and she asked if he'd throw together a sandwich for her. "No, you do it," he said, as if she'd asked him to do something too hard, too inappropriate.

That's when it hit her, clear as day, once and for all, that his selfishness was undeniable and bottomless, that for her the relationship was over, that there was nothing here for her, and that she'd be better off getting out. And she did. And she's never regretted it for a moment.

Staying. What had happened to the sweet woman he'd married? Now, three years later, Steve felt that Lynn had turned into someone who did nothing but complain. Then one Friday coming home from work Steve heard a song on the radio—"When a Man Loves a Woman." Something about it got through to him, something about his having a responsibility to make sure she knew he loved her. They'd gotten so polarized, he saw, that he'd overlooked the possibility that she was unloving because he was unloving.

Steve spent that night and all weekend trying to show Lynn he loved her. It wasn't until Sunday that it got through to her. Then she just melted. Her old sweetness came back. It was suddenly clear to Steve how easily they could overcome the problems that had been making him think of leaving. Steve decided to put all thoughts of leaving out of his mind.

Good News

It's terribly frustrating to be able to do nothing but wait passively for signs like these. Fortunately, new hope is now entirely realistic for you. That's why I've written this book. You *can* find answers to the questions most important to you:

- Whether the two of you really do fit together or not
- Whether the things that bother you will get better or worse
- How you'll feel if they do get better and if they don't
- Whether you can improve the relationship on your own or with the best of therapists
- What you'll find if you leave and whether it'll be better or worse than what you have now
- How to balance the responsibility you have to yourself and to the people you care about

No matter how hard it's been for you to decide, now you *can* find out the truth about your relationship one way or the other, the whole truth, your own truth, the ultimate-reality-at-the-heart-of-everything truth. Now you *can* achieve the clarity that will enable you to feel confident making one of the most important choices of your life.

But finding clarity depends on whether you actually *want* to find clarity in the first place or whether the most comfortable place for you is staying up in the air the way you've been. Your relationship is *either* too good to leave *or* too bad to stay in. But it can't be both. So there are definite answers for you here, but if you really don't want to come to a decision, you'll find that out as well.

But What About Love?

We'll talk *a lot* about love here. The clarity you'll reach will also help you see how real your love is, and how strong. Love, which made everything so definite at the beginning, now makes everything more complicated. Sometimes things are terrible but your love still seems strong, and then what do you do about love?

Sometimes things aren't so bad but there's little love left to hold them together, and then what does love mean for you?

I just want to assure you that as you see what's right for you to do, you'll be able to put love into perspective among all the other things you care about.

THE HAPPINESS THAT LIES AHEAD

My mission is to do two things.

First, it's to share with you the experiences of people who've wrestled with the issues you're wrestling with and come out on the other side and to report what they discovered. For example, think about something that bothers you about your partner, that strongly weighs on the side of your leaving. Wouldn't you want to know how other people bothered by that felt once they left? You'll find that out here. And if something else pointed to a basic strength in a relationship that made people happy they stayed, you'd want to know that, too. And you will. And if yet another issue you've been stewing over really turned out not to make too big a difference one way or the other, you'd want to know that as well so you could stop stewing over it. And you will.

Second, my mission is to help you rediscover the value of your own experience. I'm not going to pull a rabbit out of a hat that has nothing to do with what you've felt and seen about your partner and your relationship. Just the opposite. We'll keep returning to the basics of your own experience. The problem isn't that you don't know what's going on; it's that you've had trouble sorting it all out.

The choice you discover will be one you feel good about after you make it, and better and better about as time goes by. It will be a choice that leaves you free of regret. Which is exactly what you were looking for in the first place!

TRAPPED IN LIMBO

If you've suspected that it's not good for you to stay up in the air, you're right. Staying ambivalent, in fact, can cause tremendous damage. Being stuck like this can end up killing you emotionally if you stay when you should be getting out. And it can end up killing your relationship if you keep thinking about leaving when it could be fixed if you only put energy into it. You can end up being deprived of joy and of freedom, of intimacy and of hope. And it's not as if waiting around is going to show you what's best for you. Ambivalence doesn't produce real answers. It's just a dangerous trap.

Doing the Limbo

Dee, a twenty-nine-year-old buyer, had lived with Keith for four years. There were good things about the relationship, like their strong sexual chemistry, but Dee was never really happy. They kept fighting about many things, like what Dee thought of as Keith's irresponsibility, which she was afraid would only get worse in the future.

After they broke up last year, Dee was happier. But she was lonely. Now they're dating each other again, partly because of her sexual needs, partly because she didn't meet anyone better, and partly because Keith promised to grow up. And so their relationship chugs on, no better than it was before, filled with the same mixture of familiarity and misery it's always had.

Dee's not on the verge of making a commitment one way or the other. She's on the verge of being stuck not knowing what to do with her relationship for a long time, possibly years.

Can you believe forty years? That's how long another woman, Kate, spent neither being in her marriage nor leaving it but miserably camped on the outskirts of it, waiting for a sign to tell her what to do.

Kate's Story

As you'll see in a moment, Kate's one of the most important women in my life; and the fact that she never broke through her ambivalence had an unhealthy impact on both of us. So it's not only professionally but personally that I've experienced the terrible price we all pay for not knowing what to do with our relationships, all the pain and wasted time millions of people suffer from staying endlessly undecided.

Kate had married on the rebound after getting divorced following a brief first marriage. Her second husband, now dead, had been a businessman, volatile, quirky, sometimes unpleasant, but in some ways a decent guy. They were able to put up a good front, and their friends envied what from the outside seemed like one of the better marriages in their circle. But it was hard for Kate to remember when they'd ever had much in common. They usually couldn't talk without fighting; when they weren't fighting there was usually nothing to talk about.

It wasn't the most terrible marriage in the world. There was just a lot of unhappiness in it flowing from distance and discord. On a scale of 1 to 10 (10 being best), Kate would've given it a 3. And yet she stayed in it, doing what she saw as her duty.

What do you think she should have done? Kate had two good alternatives. In spite of myths about women needing marriage, the evidence is now unmistakable that a woman like Kate could have been happy if she'd been on her own. And I believe she also could have had a chance at happiness if she'd stayed, working on the relationship more (perhaps going into couples therapy) instead of finding her energy sapped by thinking of leaving.

The Cost of Staying up in the Air. But Kate was terribly unhappy for forty years because she did neither. She waited for one milepost after another to pass—the kids starting school, her going back to work, the kids leaving home, her husband's retiring—hoping that she'd get a sign that would tell her what to do.

Just think about what it must have been like to spend all those years thinking about leaving. It meant spending years stewing over all the things that were wrong with him and all the things that were wrong with her for staying with him. You pay a price for feasting on negativity like this. Suppose that it would have been best for Kate to leave. To live with all that negativity and not leave could only destroy your sense of yourself as a valuable, effective person. Or suppose that it would have been best for her to stay. Then living with all that negativity could only pollute and ultimately destroy what would otherwise be a viable marriage.

Kate paid another price for a lifetime of not deciding. The tension and misery she felt, directly traceable to living stuck in ambivalence, put a strain on her relationship with her children that took years to heal.

The woman I call "Kate" is my mother, with some details changed to protect her privacy (as I've done with all the people you'll meet in this book), and her husband was my stepfather. In many ways, Kate's a heroine, as a Holocaust survivor and a self-made businesswoman. But in this important way she didn't know how to choose happiness. And in her ambivalence she's like far too many of our parents, far too many people in middle age, and far too many people just starting out. I wrote this book to save others, to save you, from going through what my mother went through.

THE AMBIVALENCE EPIDEMIC

You may be wondering if there's something wrong with you to feel so stuck. But the fact is that there's an epidemic of ambivalence about many things these days. We live in an age that promotes self-awareness but fails to show us how to use our self-awareness to arrive at good decisions. We learn more and more things about ourselves without learning ways to sort them out or to sort out the feelings they generate in us.

This is particularly true when it comes to our relationships. As one actress said on TV, being interviewed about her marriage, "You're supposed to reevaluate your relationship every day, aren't you?" Only if you want to confuse and exhaust yourself. We're told so many contradictory things: to be responsible to ourselves and to our partner, to be happy in ourselves and to be mature about our obligations, to fix our own lives above all else, and to fix our relationships no matter what.

Whatever love we feel for the other person feels so real, and yet we know we also have a responsibility to love ourselves. We see therapists on TV who claim they can bring any relationship back to vibrant life, but we know how difficult it is to change even the smallest thing in our own relationship.

No wonder so many of us have trouble figuring out what's best for us to do. But you *can* find the clarity you're looking for if you want to. And I believe you do want to, and that you have everything it takes to see what's best for you.

TAKING RESPONSIBILITY TOGETHER

What makes a book like this possible is the fact that an individual can be unique and yet still be similar enough to other people to learn from them. Without our similarities, medicine and psychology would be impossible. It's because we are similar that a diagnostic test or a wonder drug can help millions.

But it's because we're unique that medicine and psychology remain an art as well as a science. I know as a therapist that I can't meet my responsibility to you if I forget for a moment that you are an individual. Just because you're similar to other people in some respects doesn't mean there aren't profound differences as well. And I always have to take those differences into account.

But I also can't meet my responsibility to you if I fail to probe for the experiences that link people. That's the power that research and clinical practice give, not just mine but that of countless others, particularly Dr. Charles Foster, whose shoulders this book stands on.

Answers at Last

This book is based on an attempt to answer questions people have asked for a long time:

- Which iffy relationships will most likely be okay and which ones are virtually unfixable?
- What makes people happy they left a relationship? What makes them happy they recommitted to it?

Our research involved talking to people in the same situation you're in. They were asked about their ambivalent feelings and their partners' positives and negatives. They were followed over time, during which many tried to solve their problems (and many were successful) and many ended their relationships.

Then we tried to figure out what made some people say overwhelmingly *this* made me happy I left and made other people say overwhelmingly *this* made me happy I stayed. These answers evolved into the questions and guidelines that form the backbone of this book.

The ultimate test of all this is in one-on-one work with people like you. Only when these sturdy truths make sense for a wide spectrum of individuals can any of us feel confident that real help is available.

Trusting the Truth

To be fully responsible to your uniqueness, I have to be very careful about telling you what to do. But if I've found deep and powerful truths that hold up for large numbers of people, truths that have been validated over and over, don't I also have a responsibility to tell you these truths? I can't tell you what to do, but I can and must tell you what I know. I can't predict the future, but I can tell you the odds.

It's what trusted professionals in our lives do all the time. For example, about ten years ago I went to my dentist with a dull, intermittent toothache. He said I'd need a root canal to save the tooth and eliminate the source of the pain. He said that without a root canal the pain might go away for days or months or maybe even a year or two but it would come back and it would get worse. A root canal was the answer.

"How do you know for sure?" I asked.

"Well, I don't know *for sure*," he said. "Everyone's unique, but this is how things will probably work out in your case because, based on what I can see, it's how things generally work out for people in the kind of situation you're in."

I'm a show-me kind of person, so instead of following my

dentist's recommendation, I waited. I was betting that some quirky feature of my uniqueness would exempt me from the patterns my dentist knew so well.

Of course, he was right. I ended up in the worst pain of my life until I got the root canal I should've gotten earlier!

Our Contract

So here's the deal between you and me. I won't pull back from making definite recommendations about whether it's best for you to stay or leave based on your realities and my research and twenty years of clinical experience. In turn, you won't blindly follow my recommendations for people in a relationship like yours. You'll certainly want to make sure that you listen to yourself first, to make sure that the reality you've uncovered does ring true for you.

And if you have a therapist or other trusted advisor, you'll definitely want to run by them what you learn here. *Nothing in this book overrules what a good therapist you've been working with might tell you.*

At the same time, you know how easy it's been for you to stay stuck in ambivalence, and this book is about finding clarity in your situation and giving yourself permission to act on that clarity. So our responsibility to each other requires me to tell you the truth as I know it, as definitely as I can. And it requires you to face your truth and then do something about it.

The truths I've discovered here are the kinds of things we all recognize when we hear them. They make sense to people. Your responsibility is to give them a chance to make sense to you. Don't act on them before they make sense to you, but don't fail to act on them afterward. Your life is too important to you to waste any part of it stuck in ambivalence.

2

Dancing in the Dark

Issue: Relationship Ambivalence

If you're in a relationship that seems both too good to leave and too bad to stay in, every time something happens that clearly points to staying or leaving, you probably find yourself saying, "No, it can't be that simple. There's so much more for me to think about." Then a dozen memories and feelings creep in and you say, "I'd better not make a decision until I see what's best for everyone." But you never do see what's best for everyone.

This state you're in is called *relationship ambivalence.*

The Road to Ambivalence

We all feel doubts about our partners from time to time, and we all occasionally speculate about what it would be like to be on our own or live with a different person. But that's not relationship ambivalence.

I'm talking instead about what happens when the bulk of your attention shifts from being in your relationship to trying to figure out whether to stay in it or leave. This shift can take place at any time, from soon after you meet to the day after your twenty-fifth anniversary or even later.

Before that shift, there's a taken-for-granted quality to your thinking about the relationship, even if from time to time you get upset about things.

Then one too many things go wrong. New problems appear. Bad qualities in the other person or in the relationship get worse while good qualities dwindle or get lost. You find yourself complaining about things like the following:

- "He's made a million agreements about doing his share of the housework and never kept one of them."
- "She had this affair with a guy from work, and I really think it's been over between them for a year, but I'm having so much trouble letting go of the whole thing. And I don't know what to do about it."
- "This probably sounds like a Seinfeld episode but he's a noisy breather—I mean every breath in and out is like a sighing or a moaning. He sounds like Darth Vader when he breathes. Is he the most annoying person who ever lived, or am I the most petty, oversensitive person who ever lived, or what?"
- "Her family is so nosey and bossy and they control her with money—I sometimes feel she's got to get a divorce from them or I've got to get a divorce from her."
- "It's one thing for me to complain about him, but when I get embarrassed for my friends to see him or know about the stuff he does, that's really bad."
- "Aren't married people supposed to have sex? I mean, hello? How little sex can you have and then it's no longer a marriage?"
- "Is there a future for us if we can't even agree about where to go on vacation?"
- "We always have huge fights over money because I'm a saver and she's a spender."
- "He's such a strict and controlling father, and I think he gives our kids a sense that I'm a bad parent; but he's the

bad parent and I really think the kids and I would be better off if he just stayed out of it."

- "Sometimes I feel we're doomed because I'm a people person and I really need having people over to the house. But she's a real solitary person and resents our having people in our lives."

- "He was this successful older guy and it was sort of fun admiring him when we first got together, but what it turned into is from morning till night he judges me. I don't know how much of this you're supposed to take."

Once problems like these that make leaving seem desirable are added to all the forces that make you want to stay, you're in a state of relationship ambivalence. But there's more to the experience than just feeling all the pros and cons of your relationship.

Stops Along the Way

It's been a while since you first felt "jerk shock": the realization that the person you're with has feet of clay. But instead of giving up, you tried everything you could think of to improve the relationship: honesty and romantic vacations and how-to-have-a-great-relationship books and maybe even therapy. You've tried overlooking all the things that hurt or annoy you, and you've tried dealing with them. You've tried to make the other person happy, and you've tried to get the other to make you happy. You've tried . . . it's probably hard to remember all the things you've tried.

After working on the front lines as a therapist for more than twenty years, I've learned that almost no one gets to this point without having worked hard to make the relationship better. We take love too seriously to give up on it without a fight. At the same time, on almost the very first day that love isn't enough, we also feel hurt, and we withdraw and stand back, waiting and hoping for the other person to make things better.

Looking for the Exits

But thinking about leaving hasn't helped either. It's not that you don't know how to go about it, at least in general. It's just that you aren't sure you'll be better off leaving. Even when you're fed up with the person you're with, it's still not clear that leaving will be better than your entire current life with that person.

Every time you start trying to focus on leaving, thoughts creep in about how you'll find a place to live, and how you'll be able to afford it, and whether you'll find love again, and how expensive childcare or child support will be, and endless other details about how you'll live. Worries like these just make it harder to leave, and the more of these worries there are, the more you're willing to put up with a relationship that would otherwise be too bad to stay in.

And so imagining what your life will be like if you leave hasn't helped.

Friends Try to Help. And your friends haven't really given you the clarity you're looking for either. I'm not saying they haven't listened and been supportive and offered advice. It's just that as you've tried to sort out all the issues and figure out what's best for you to do, your friends haven't been able to convince you about what's best one way or the other.

I've seen cases where every friend a person has says leave, *leave, leave!* and yet somehow instead of it making everything clear it makes nothing clear. In spite of this passionate consensus, you might feel that your friends don't really know your partner or your relationship, that all they've heard most clearly are your complaints as you've used their shoulders to cry on.

And I've seen cases where every single friend says stay, and you just feel that for whatever reason your friends are somehow invested in your staying together, that they'll somehow be more devastated if you break up than you'll be.

And so all your wrestling with issues and trying to put them into perspective has given you little clarity. This confusion can be tormenting. I've had people tell me that they've prayed for their partner to do something really awful, just so they would get the clarity they need. But that clarity doesn't come.

And so here you are. You've spent what must feel like a very long time now dancing in the dark, flip-flopping back and forth about whether to stay or leave.

LOOKING FOR CLARITY IN ALL THE WRONG PLACES

I've talked about what's similar in what people go through, but the actual experience of relationship ambivalence itself varies widely. Here are some snapshots of what it's like for different people to be stuck in relationship ambivalence:

- One person goes through long stretches when things are really bad and she feels she's definitely going to leave, but then there's some mysterious atmospheric change and suddenly things are okay and she doesn't want to rock the boat by even thinking about problems, much less thinking about leaving. This lasts until the atmosphere changes back to terrible again.
- Another does everything he can to put the choice he's facing out of his mind. He asserts his right to complain about everything, and yet he stands next to this mountain of complaints and denies that he wants to leave. Occasionally one too many things go wrong or he spends just a little too much time with his partner, and then all his thoughts of leaving creep back in.
- Another talks to everyone, asking all the people who know her and care about her to tell her what to do.
- Another person obsessively and endlessly and constantly thinks about whether to stay or leave all day and half the night until her head's ready to explode.
- Another denies there's anything to be ambivalent about in the first place: he thinks it's not the relationship that's iffy, that the problem is just his fear of commitment.

- Another spends hours meditating alone, trying to remove all thought from his mind, so that he can allow an irrefutable signal to emerge all by itself and show him what's best.
- Another goes for the superrational approach, assigning a numerical value to every positive and negative, so he can add up the score and get a single number that will tell him what he'll be happiest doing, and he always gets some number but he never trusts it and never acts on it.
- Another keeps walking out, not because she wants to but because she's hoping that breaking up will make things clear. But then she keeps starting the relationship up again.

But while everyone expresses ambivalence a little differently, there's one thing people have in common: ambivalence in your heart goes hand in hand with distance in your relationship. When you feel ambivalent about your partner you make distance from your partner. You spend less time together. You talk less, and about less important things. You stop doing things together. There's a cool, formal, ritualistic quality to the relationship. You make distance from your partner because you're having an emotionally intense affair with your own ambivalence.

And like all the other things you do in your ambivalence, distance only serves to make it worse. Now your ambivalence has taken on a life of its own.

THE BALANCE-SCALE APPROACH

What is it about relationship ambivalence that gets us stuck in it and keeps us stuck in it? Good question! The people I've worked with over the years are a smart bunch, and for a long time it didn't make sense to me that women and men with all kinds of street smarts and academic smarts and every other kind of smarts could be so stuck.

I figured, wearing my researcher hat, that with all the differ-

ences among all these people there had to be something they
shared deep down that was responsible not for their feeling iffy
about their partners—we've all felt that from time to time—but
for their getting stuck in feeling iffy, so stuck that they couldn't
find their way out.

I discovered that everyone stuck in relationship ambivalence
shares an image so powerful, so controlling, that it shapes their
entire experience of deciding what to do about an iffy relationship: the image of a balance scale. You know—the kind of scale
the figure of Justice holds in her hand in front of the Supreme
Court, with a pan on one side and a pan on the other side, all set
up for weighing the evidence, pro and con. You might have used
a scale like this yourself in high school chemistry.

The image of the balance scale lies at the heart of how most
people deal with the stay-or-leave decision. It's what I call the
balance-scale approach. You try to figure out whether to stay or
leave by piling up all the evidence about your partner on a kind
of giant scale and seeing how it balances out:

On one side you pile up all the evidence *for staying* and *against leaving*: all the good things about your relationship, all the things you hope for, all the things that make leaving seem scary.	On the other side you pile up all the evidence *for leaving* and *against staying*: all the bad things in the relationship, all your fears, all your hopes for being on your own again.

All by yourself, you do what the opposing lawyers do at a trial,
each lawyer piling up evidence on one side or the other. Then after acting as lawyer for both sides, you act as the jury, looking to
see which pile of evidence weighs more. It's instinctive. It's universal. And it's guaranteed to drive you crazy.

Weighing the pros and cons of staying or leaving isn't like
weighing a can of tomatoes against a box of cornflakes. It's like
placing puppies on a teeter-totter: everything constantly moves
and shifts, nothing stays pinned down.

When it comes to relationships, the balance-scale approach is
the problem, not the solution. It gets us into trouble, not out of

it. How can you weigh the things you know about your relationship in the present against a huge uncertain future? How can you
weigh a problem that's bad for you against the knowledge that a
lot of people have this problem but don't seem to be breaking up
their relationships over it? How can you weigh a problem that
makes you want to scream today against the possibility that it
won't bother you so much tomorrow?

With the balance-scale approach pieces of evidence keep
sliding in and out of the picture. You try to add things up that
don't add up, to compare things that can't be compared. Like a
tenderfoot in the woods, the more you try to find your way, the
more lost you get.

Carol's Tale

Just look at the balance-scale approach in action. Here's how
Carol described it:

> Two weeks ago Tom was so nice to me. I wish it could be like
> that all the time. But then last week he went back to being the
> way he usually is, where he's so nasty and everything I do is
> wrong and he keeps putting me down and making my life mis-
> erable. How do I add those up? He leaves me alone to watch
> sports all the time and he yells at me if I want to talk about our
> problems, but sex is still okay with him. What does that add up
> to? To make it even more confusing, sometimes things are go-
> ing well with me and the things I have trouble with about him
> don't bother me so much.

There are more details, but Carol's provided a good sketch of
some of the pros and cons in her relationship. Is it clear to you
what she should do? I don't think it's clear to anyone. Weighing
the pros and cons just sucks you in to adding more and more
things to the balance, and every time you add something the picture gets more confusing.

Therapists do this, too. One way we get suckered into using
the balance-scale approach is that we try so hard to avoid playing

the blame game when people come to us for help. So whenever we see something "bad" that one person does, we look to see what the other person does to elicit it. For instance, if you say your partner's nagging drives you crazy, we'll say, okay, maybe your partner's nagging but maybe you're not listening.

But when you're helping one person decide whether it's best to stay or leave, you've got to look for the fly in the ointment, and it doesn't matter who put it there. The balance-scale approach doesn't work for anybody. I don't think you'd be reading these words if the balance-scale approach had worked for you.

So no more relationship ambivalence, starting right now. No more putting your relationship on trial. No more weighing huge, unwieldy piles of evidence pro and con. No more listening to the voices on both sides producing endless arguments and very little clarity. Fortunately, there's a much better alternative, one that will help you see straight through to the truth about your relationship.

Part II

THE SOLUTION

3

Enough Is Enough

Issue: Danger Signs

DIAGNOSTICS

Here's how to find your way out of relationship ambivalence. Don't put your relationship on trial the way lawyers do. Make a diagnosis the way doctors do.

That's what we'll do here. We'll ask one question at a time, step by step, responsibly searching for that one fact, that one piece of evidence about your relationship that makes clear what's best for you to do. And it's all based on what research shows are the experiences of other people in situations like yours.

It's like going to the doctor for stomach pains. If she can diagnose appendicitis after some questions and a few tests, you're all set. You don't need to go through every test and weigh every possible piece of evidence pro and con. If your answer to one question doesn't provide a diagnosis—"No, doctor, it doesn't hurt there"—you move on to the next question or test until you find the smoking gun that points to a specific ailment.

It works much the same way here. Instead of balancing pros and cons, we'll try to arrive at a diagnosis of your relationship. At each step you'll answer a question about an issue between you and your partner. In most cases it'll be a straightforward, easy-to-

answer, yes-or-no question. Depending on your answer, you may
be able to get a clear indication right then and there of whether
it's best for you to stay or leave. You'll have found out what's real
about your relationship without needing to go further.

One Step at a Time

The order of the questions is carefully arranged. The main principle, as with any diagnostic procedure, is to deal with the clear-
est, most obvious issues first. For example, if your TV is on the
fritz, the repairperson will check if you've forgotten to plug it in
or if the cable box is properly connected before looking into the
subtler malfunctions deep in the electronic bowels of the set.

In the same way, earlier diagnostic questions here deal with
clearer, more obvious issues, and later questions deal with more
nuanced issues. By the end we'll have dealt with all the major issues that might bother you—from intimacy to power, from affairs
to lying, from sex to money, from your hurts from the past to
your hopes for the future, from signs you really hate each other
to signs you really belong together. We'll investigate everything
that goes on in relationships from the point of view of what
makes them too bad to stay in or too good to leave.

By the end you'll know which is true for you.

All that needs to happen as you read is that you trust yourself, take things a step at a time, and think of each question as
an opportunity to find out what's real for you. Often you'll know
the answer right away, but sometimes you may have to sift
through your thoughts and feelings and memories.

Most people come up with their answers fairly easily, because
that's how these questions were designed. It's no more difficult
than when your optometrist clicks those lenses back and forth
and asks you if you can see better the first way or the second way.
Either one is better or the other is better or you can't tell the difference: they are all valid answers. The point is that with the
step-by-step approach all you have to do is come up with one answer to one question about one issue at a time.

The diagnostic questions here include everything that's important to pay attention to in deciding whether to stay or leave. If it's not in the questions, it's not so important in deciding what's best for you, and you can let go of worrying about it. So let's get started.

STEP #1: THEY WERE THE BEST OF TIMES

You've probably put a lot of energy into thinking about the bad times in your iffy relationship, but in this first step I'd like you to think about the good times for a moment. The best time, in fact. Try to remember when you felt most comfortable, most satisfied, most optimistic about the relationship you're in. It could have been the day you met, the time you took your first trip together, a special rainy weekend the first year you were married, a period when you were working together to achieve some joint goal. If you've been together a long time, don't worry about being too thorough. Trust your unconscious to throw a searchlight on a "best" time even if it's not the absolute best.

Now ask yourself:

Diagnostic question #1. **Think about that time when things between you and your partner were at their best. Looking back, would you now say that things were really very good between you then?**

This is a simple question. Were things between you actually very good when they were at their best?

What do I mean by "very good"? Some people, even in relationships that feel awful now, know that there was a time in the past when things were wonderful. They were in love, they were genuinely happy, they felt good about themselves when they were with the other—there was a kind of happy magic of warmth and connectedness. Their answer to question #1 is yes.

But other people realize that the "best" was never very good. Something was wrong. They're usually referring to an empty, distant, tainted, painful quality at the core of their relationship, even back then. Their answer to question #1 is no.

Here are some things people have said describing "best" times that weren't very good:

- "At the beginning I loved him very much and I thought we were close, but even then we'd have violent arguments every couple of days that completely drained me and spoiled everything."
- "Our best time was on our honeymoon. We were happy in a way, but I now realize that all the pleasure came from the activities we did, not from being with each other. It was like having a really great vacation with a stranger."
- "There was a period when we never fought, but we never spent much time together then or were close either."
- "For the first couple of years sex was great—it's how we got together in the first place—but we had nothing else in common and didn't really care about each other."

You probably have a pretty clear sense about whether, when things were at their best, they were actually very good or not. For most people whose relationships are iffy now, they were pretty good at one point. But for about ten percent of you, they were actually never very good.

Jennifer's Story

In a moment you'll see what your answer to question #1 means. But first, let's put all this in the context of someone who was going through something like what you may be going through now.

Jennifer was thirty-six. She was an attractive woman who acted like she could make quick work of any problem you gave her. When she came to see me she'd been married for eight years. And for the last six she'd been in a constant struggle about whether to stay with her husband or leave him for good.

For all the time and brain power she brought to thinking

about what to do—probing every strand and filament of feeling, every nuance of behavior, every hint of what the future might hold—she'd grown less and less clear over the past six years. And it was tearing her up inside.

With Jennifer's training and ability, you'd think she'd be smart and knowledgeable enough to avoid this dilemma. She'd graduated from medical school in the top quarter of her class, had started out on a promising career as an oncologist, and had switched to psychiatry when she got tired of seeing people die and wanted to help them find a way to live.

Finding a Balance. You might think being a psychiatrist would have given Jennifer an edge in figuring out relationships. But it didn't help: as you'll see, it produced only more confusion. She couldn't remember what started her ambivalence; maybe it wasn't anything specific. But for six years her heart was burdened by more and more considerations that piled up without ever sorting themselves out or producing a resolution.

I don't want to give short shrift to the mass of things Jennifer had to weigh, but this will give you the highlights:

- On the plus side, her husband, Don, was great with the kids, charming when he wanted to be, a good income earner as a computer executive; they shared some spiritual values, he said he cared about her, and he gave Jennifer the space she needed to do her work and be with her friends. She thought she still had some love for him.

- On the minus side, he was angry with her most of the time, picked fights with her, kept expressing his disappointment with her, kept trying to change her, had had an affair, and had once shoved her during a stormy argument after she'd shoved him. She didn't think she loved him enough.

Maybe you look at these two piles of evidence and it's clear to you which way Jennifer should go, but it was never clear to her. There were times when she vacillated minute by minute, and

long periods when she seemed to have made a final decision that
never turned out to be final.

Looking for Help. I was one of a long line of therapists Jennifer
had seen, and my goal was to be the last.

Jennifer had also spent countless hours with friends talking
about what to do. Most of her friends did what her best friend
Sarah would do: listen endlessly, commiserate constantly, and try
sincerely to be as supportive as possible. Sarah was never afraid
to speak her mind, and Jennifer valued her honesty.

The problem was that Sarah didn't have much to go on, and
Jennifer knew it. Sarah was a wise and honest friend, but of
course she knew less than Jennifer about what things were really
like inside the relationship. And the truth is that Jennifer se-
lected what she talked about. She shaded things. She made
things sound worse than they were when she needed sympathy.
She made things sound better than they were when she didn't
want to talk about them.

And Jennifer had done more than just talk to friends and
therapists. She and Don had gone on many vacations to try to
kindle a flame of caring and commitment. They'd made distance
to try and cool things off. And from time to time Jennifer had interviewed lawyers about the possibility of divorce.

Jennifer's Answer. Soon after she came to see me, I asked
Jennifer question #1. I was surprised by how quickly she said:

> Oh no, it was never really very good. We're just one of those
> good-on-paper couples. You know, we like the same things—
> books, music, movies—and we have similar opinions about
> things—politics, childrearing, spirituality. It wasn't a match
> made in heaven, just computer heaven. We never really got
> pleasure from each other. We thought we were enjoying being
> together because we did things we both enjoyed. We'd go sail-
> ing and have a great time, but I've gone for walks with my dog
> where I feel Champ and I have gotten closer than Don and I
> ever have. But I blamed myself. I just had this sense that my
> heart had always been closed to him and that something would

happen one day to make me open my heart and then my love would flow. But it's been so many years and I wonder what I'm waiting for.

When she heard herself saying this, Jennifer was hit by a kind of emotional shock. It was suddenly clear to her. All this time she'd spent trying to figure out what to do with a relationship so filled with pros and cons—there'd never actually been a relationship in the first place. There'd been a marriage and a joint history and children and friends and possessions and the dream of a heart one day opening up. But never a relationship. She started crying for all the years she'd spent trying to make a decision about something that had never existed.

What if what's true for Jennifer is true for you? The findings are very clear on this:

GUIDELINE #1

If, when your relationship was at its "best," things between you didn't feel right or work well, the prognosis is poor. I feel comfortable saying that you'll feel you've discovered what's right for you if you choose to leave. *Quick take:* If it never *was* very good, it'll never *be* very good.

If you fall into the ten percent of people in relationship ambivalence that guideline #1 applies to, I have to say to you what I say to everyone who answers no to question #1: it's your decision, but most people in your situation who end up leaving are glad they did.

"How Can You Tell Me to Leave?"

If you think about it, this guideline's not really such a leap. It's not as if everything were perfect except for your answering no to this question. You're in a state of relationship ambivalence right now! That means there are already plenty of negatives.

Beyond the fact that most people in your situation who leave are happy they did so, you've got to face the fact that if it was never very good at its best, then where are the good things going to come from that you have a right to look forward to in any relationship? You can wait, but it's unlikely you'll find them.

My years as a clinician plus a ton of accumulated research show that *you can often fix what was broken, but you can rarely fix what never worked in the first place*. There was a basic difficulty, present from the beginning, that prevented things from being good or prevented you from seeing that they weren't good. The satisfaction-producing core that's necessary for a relationship to take root was never there.

Professional integrity demands that I speak the truth as I see it. And the truth here is that a relationship that was never very good is unlikely to become good in the future. People can always surprise you, but in this case don't hold your breath. If your answer to question #1 is clearly no, then you've already found the truth about whether it's best for you to stay or leave.

Now let's look at the flip side. I'm *not* saying you should resolve to commit *to* your relationship if things were *good* when they were at their best—there's a lot more to consider before you do that. I am saying that people are generally satisfied when they choose to end their relationship if they realize that when things were at their "best" they weren't, in fact, good.

PERSPECTIVES: WHAT'S LOVE GOT TO DO WITH IT?

All the questions here are designed to probe for whether your relationship is basically alive or dead.

Here's an analogy. I've lived in a big old house in Boston for almost twenty years. When the real estate agent first showed it to me, students were living there and it was a mess. I took one look and said no way. Then for some reason I went back with a friend and she said, "Hang on a second, it just needs a cleaning and a clearing out of all this junk. Then it'll be great."

She was right. It turned out that with just some cleaning and paint the house was terrific.

That's the way it is with a lot of relationships. There's a surface of day-to-day experiences that might feel awful, but below the surface there's what I call a satisfaction-producing core. It's there as solidly and clearly as a sturdy well-built house might be there underneath some dirt and clutter. What makes a relationship actually too good to leave is when it has that satisfaction-producing core.

Now let's look at the other alternative. We've all known houses that look good on the outside, but there's structural damage due to a poorly laid foundation or major termite infestation or water damage or many other problems. These are houses that need a lot more than most of us are willing or able to put into them. They might look good, but they're really not worth the trouble. They will begin as a headache and end as a heartache.

It's that way with a lot of relationships. Any couples therapist will tell you about relationships where the surface might be nice and smooth and polite, even seemingly friendly, but below the surface there's what I call a basic discord. I'm talking about an emotional, psychological fracture or dislocation or disconnection. There's something rotten in the foundation, regardless of what the surface is like, and the only thing it's built for is distance and hostility. What makes a relationship actually too bad to stay in is when it has that basic discord.

The Truth of Love and the Love of Truth

How does love fit into all this? We'll talk about love plenty in this book. But for now let's remember what our job is here: to put love in perspective. Love is a mystery we have to respect. But I know this (and I hope you agree with me): *if love has any function it's as our servant, not our master.* Love is an important part of our lives, but we're not love's slaves. Most of all we're not love's fools.

To see the importance of putting love into perspective, just think about situations we've all known about personally and that I've certainly seen my share of as a therapist. I'm talking about those cases where some man or woman is horribly abused or neglected or maltreated and yet stays in the relationship. Why? "I can't help it," they say. "I love him [or her]." And we've all seen cases where it seems as though someone is in a perfectly good relationship with a thoroughly nice person and yet walks out. Why? "I couldn't help it. I just stopped loving him [or her]."

Love can too easily be the wild card in our relationships, taking on any value at any time for any reason. If we don't put it into perspective, it will make fools of us.

But it's time we told the truth about love. Love isn't blind and it isn't stupid. It can see and it can learn. If you allow your love to see the truth of your relationship, if you allow your love to take care of you, it'll respond appropriately.

Do you really want to open your heart to a love that will not let you show it the truth of your life? If the truth is that there's a basic discord in your relationship, that it's dead and will never work, what good is a love that refuses to see this?

The next question probes the one situation where more people have died of being enslaved to a blind love than any other. If the next question doesn't make clear why we must put love into perspective, nothing will.

Step #2: When It's a Matter of Life and Death

Another clear step may be possible right away toward discovering what's best for you to do. Answer this:

Diagnostic question #2. **Has there been more than one incident of physical violence in your relationship?**

Notice I'm not asking you if there was *only* one incident; I'm asking if there was *more* than one incident. Of course, if there's even one episode of physical violence that causes real injury or that makes you feel threatened with the real possibility of injury or death, there's nothing to discuss and you need to leave immediately for the sake of your physical safety.

Other than that, I'm a firm believer that everyone is entitled to one mistake, and it's hard to know what something means when it only happens once. I've seen a lot of situations where in the heat of an argument the man (it's usually the man) commits some first act of physical aggression. It had never happened before, and either he's horrified himself or she makes it clear that everything will be over if it ever happens again. And it never happens again. It's when acts of physical aggression repeat themselves that you can point to a pattern.

Facing Reality

You might wonder if this question is really necessary. With all the attention paid to spousal abuse in the media, doesn't everyone know that when there's physical violence you just get out as fast as you can?

People know this in general. But when it comes to their actual lives they face two kinds of obstacles. One is that as a practical matter it's often too difficult to get out, at least in the short run. People facing this obstacle fit the profile of the woman who's afraid for her life and knows to leave but who stays because of children, money, not having a place to go, fear of provoking her husband to still worse abuse, and other considerations that put her in the category of people who know what's best for them to do but haven't yet figured out a way to do it.

But the majority of women and a few men who stay in spite of the threat of violence are stuck because of something far different than the image promulgated in the media. The obstacle isn't that they can't get out; instead, it's that they can't decide what to do. As amazing as it might sound, while they know they're in a relationship that's too bad to stay in, they also feel it's too good to leave.

On the Inside

How can there be such ambivalence? From the outside we see someone physically abused to whom things should be very clear.

But from their vantage point inside the relationship, what people report overwhelmingly is the struggle to weigh a mass of evidence both negative and positive that keeps them in a terrible state of relationship ambivalence.

Here's how some people have described their lives as they actually experience them:

- "I admit I'm afraid of him sometimes, especially if things aren't going well for him at work, but things can be so great, too, and we can be so happy together."
- "Yeah, he slapped me some, and of course I hate that, and I know I deserve better, but most of the time I get a lot, too, because he's also very sweet and apologetic."
- "Forget about the times he hit me, which weren't that bad, but he's pulled his gun on me. It's just that he's a cop, and so in a way I really trust him. You might say I'm in denial, but he's a very solid, reliable guy, and he makes me feel safer than most guys have."

What millions of people like this in abusive relationships need is exactly what they themselves have been struggling so hard to find: a way to sort things out and decide what, in fact, is the best thing for them to do.

And here, too, experience and research speak with a clear voice. Slapping, punching, shoving, and other acts of physical violence, if they happen more than once, will not stop by themselves. They will escalate. The findings are very clear on this. Here's the guideline:

GUIDELINE #2

Abuse that happens more than once means you must leave the relationship. Otherwise it will happen again and again, and it will get worse, and your self-esteem will fall, and your sense of being trapped will grow, and you'll wish you'd started the process of getting out right now, however much you love the person and whatever the pluses in your relationship. The only exception to this is when the abusive partner is currently, actively, and motivatedly participating in a program designed to treat abusive partners and stays in this program for at least a year. *Quick take:* Physical abuse means love is dead.

Everyone who stays in a situation like this regrets it. Everyone who leaves feels better and better about it as time goes by.

Time for an Ultimatum

Here's how to put this guideline into effect. If you've been abused more than once, this is a time to issue your partner an ultimatum:

> Tell him he's got to find a program for abusive partners within the next two weeks. He's got to begin participating in it within the next four weeks. He's got to maintain active consistent participation for a full year, going to at least one meeting a week. If he's not willing to agree to this and keep to it, tell him that means to you that he's not serious about eliminating all threats to your physical safety, and that means your relationship is over. If he leaves the program before a year is up or if he ever hurts you or threatens to hurt you again, that means your relationship is over.

If you're afraid to even issue this ultimatum, that by itself means that your relationship is over and you must do whatever's necessary to contact women's shelters or spousal abuse resource centers to figure out how to leave your relationship both quickly and safely.

Simple Truths

If you're in a physically abusive situation, part of you probably feels it's more complicated than this. You love your partner and wonder how you can walk out on love like this. Your partner has most likely said how much he loves you during the period after he's abused you, when he's very sorry, and part of you may believe that his love is real even while he's abusing you. You're aware of his good qualities and of things you do that you feel provoke him. Perhaps the whole world thinks of him as a great guy, and so part of you feels crazy for thinking there's something terribly wrong with him.

And you feel that a good person like you couldn't love a bad person, so you think sometimes that he couldn't possibly be the monster he seems like, which means (you hope) that any day now he could wake up and your nightmare will be over. And you're sure your love can help you find a way to help him wake up.

I understand what your love means to you (and some of the questions coming up will help clarify how to deal with love that can make it so hard to figure out what to do). And I understand that most things in life really are more complicated than they seem on the surface. But if you answered yes to question #2, then it's certain you'll say you made the right choice if you decide to leave. It may *feel* more complicated than this, but in a situation where there's been repeated physical abuse, it *isn't*.

PERSPECTIVES: REGAINING YOUR SELF-TRUST

This is not only a book about figuring out whether to stay in your relationship or leave it. It's also about undoing some of the damage that occurs from being stuck in relationship ambivalence. And one of the most important kinds of damage is loss of your self-trust.

Think about what happens when you're stuck in relationship ambivalence: every day you give yourself the message that you're not able to figure out what's best for you. That's what destroys self-trust. And where do you go from there? How does a person who can't trust herself to figure out what's best for her, figure out what's best for her?

Let's go back to Jennifer. Six years of uncertainty had made Jennifer afraid that she actually wasn't smart enough—a doctor!—to figure out what to do with her relationship. And that's devastating. You might look at her and feel reassured by seeing how even certifiably smart people can be made to feel stupid in the face of their iffy relationships. But Jennifer became convinced she was stupid when it came to deciding whether to stay or leave, and that damaged her confidence that she could make the right decision.

And because she felt so ambivalent, Jennifer was also afraid she suffered from some grave psychological damage. Why would she be so ambivalent, she wondered, if she wasn't simultaneously suffering from a fear of intimacy where you're never happy staying and a fear of abandonment where you're never able to leave. Like a lot of psychologically sophisticated people, she sifted through events from her childhood, offering them to me as clues for why a decision kept slipping from her grasp. The longer it took her to see the truth about what to do, the more psychologically damaged she thought she must be.

But she was wrong.

From Ambivalence to Self-doubt

I think Jennifer was free of the kind of psychological damage that would leave a person truly unable to choose what to do about a relationship that others would have an easy time deciding about. Sometimes a cigar is just a cigar, most of the time in fact, and sometimes relationship ambivalence is just relationship ambivalence, without any history of deep psychological damage.

"I'm stupid." "I'm psychologically damaged." "I'm afraid of being abandoned." "I don't know how to handle intimacy." These are ways in which not knowing what to do about a relationship undermines self-trust. And your undermined self-trust helps keep you stuck.

You're not the problem. The method you've been using is the problem. It's trying to balance pros and cons that damages your self-trust. How could you trust yourself when you used a method virtually designed to produce confusion? The diagnostic step-by-step approach we're using now is designed not only to uncover your truth but to do so in manageable chunks.

The Ambivalence Trap. Let's look at what losing self-trust does to you. Back when she first met Don, there was a race inside Jennifer between love and doubt, the way there is for all of us in that period before you commit to somebody. Love usually wins, otherwise you wouldn't make the commitment. But love's victory doesn't annihilate doubt. Doubt lurks in the bushes, waiting for you to come back from your honeymoon.

And for Jennifer, as it does for so many of us, doubt crept back in as Don revealed more and more of his shortcomings. At the beginning she'd trusted herself to recognize that love was speaking the truth to her, and now she desperately wanted to trust that she'd known what to do then and knew what to do now.

But she didn't know what to do now. And the less certain she was, the less she trusted herself. The less she trusted herself, the harder it was to find her way back to certainty.

This is a psychological process called the Ambivalence Trap. The more we try to weigh the mountain of facts and feelings we've accumulated, the more confused we get. The more confused we feel, the less we trust ourselves. The less we trust ourselves, the more we feel we have to wait, allowing more confusing evidence to pile up. This is where relationship ambivalence becomes a self-perpetuating trap.

The Way Out. Imagine being thrown into a deep sandy pit with a small shovel. All a shovel can do is dig you in deeper, eroding the very walls you need to climb out. That's what self-doubt does: it erodes whatever happens to be solid under your feet. To climb out you need a completely different kind of tool, a ladder let down to you that you can use to climb out step by step.

This book is your ladder. Clarity waits for you on the other end. It may be that your self-trust has received many blows, but in fact it's not really been damaged. You were simply using the wrong tool.

A week after she answered question #1 and realized the truth about her relationship, I saw Jennifer happier than I'd ever seen her. It was clear to her that she wanted to end her relationship with Don, and she felt better about her decision with each passing day. Jennifer has been on her own for four years now, and she's never regretted her choice for a moment. Whatever alternative turns out to be right for you, I know you'll feel the same way.

NEXT STEPS

There's a chance you've already found the truth you were looking for if you answered no to question #1 or yes to question #2. You can feel secure with this truth. Nothing's going to change it. The guidelines here won't contradict themselves.

But it's more likely that you'll find your truth as I keep asking questions and discussing what your answers mean. Some answers, like the ones I've talked about so far, will allow me to recommend you get out. But you'll be happy to know that other answers will allow me to point to important strengths in your relationship you might have overlooked. These strengths permit me to feel comfortable saying there are resources in your relationship that can overcome a number of risk factors.

What if you've found your truth already? If this were one of my workshops, I'd make an offer no one ever takes: "If you're clear already about what's best for you to do, feel free to go." And they're right to stay. Sometimes, even though you see the truth with your mind, you don't feel it with your heart. Sometimes you feel the truth but you just need confirmation. And you'll find it as you keep going through the questions and guidelines. So even if you know your truth right now, you'll benefit by answering all the questions.

Take whatever time you need. I want you to feel confident that, as long as you're honest with yourself, you're on a path that'll lead you to the best, most responsible decision for you.

4
It's Too Late, Baby

Issue: If You've Already Decided to Leave

We've all known people who got married and one or two things went wrong and *bang* they ended the relationship. But there's a deepening sense that divorce shouldn't be so easy and automatic. People today just don't feel comfortable with hair-trigger divorces.

But the other end of the spectrum is growing. I'm talking about people who've made it too hard for themselves to leave, not too easy. Instead of a hair-trigger divorce, for these people the bullet's already left the gun and yet they're still afraid to pull the trigger. Deep down they've *already decided* to leave the relationship and yet they're sticking around anyway. If they could admit it, they'd say, it's too late, baby, to their partner—this relationship's not been good enough for me to stay in for quite a while, and now it's over.

These "stuck stayers" are a minority of people in relationship ambivalence, but if you fall into this minority, you deserve help fast because you're not really ambivalent at all.

There are many reasons for not knowing it's over when it's over. You might feel guilty. You might still think you're in love. You might not be willing to face the post-breakup choices that await you. You might be afraid of freedom. You might be afraid of loss. And you might (this is just as true for women as for men) be having a hard time connecting with the bedrock of how you really feel about the relationship. The next two questions are designed to help you get over these obstacles if deep down you've already decided to leave.

STEP #3: ACTIONS, NOT WORDS

Sometimes the best way to figure out your truth is to look at what you do, not at what you say. Here's an example.

We've all had the experience of spending all day Friday looking forward to going out that night. But when we get home from work we dawdle and laze around and have trouble making up our minds about exactly where we want to go. Soon it's nine, ten, eleven o'clock, and at some point it hits us that from the moment we got home we were too tired to go out at all. We'd made the decision to stay in the moment we got home, but it took us all evening to realize we were implementing that decision.

It works the same way for a lot of people in relationship ambivalence. Here's the question to ask yourself:

Diagnostic question #3. **Have you already made a concrete commitment to pursue a course of action or lifestyle that definitely excludes your partner?**

What do I mean by this? What follows is a clear example.

Ruth's Story

Ruth had been married for ten years to the same person. Spike was a rock-and-roll musician, and the first several years of their relationship were filled with a sense of promise about his career. There was always the band that was going to take off, the recording contract just around the corner. Ruth worked this whole period as a nurse, and for long stretches her income was their sole support.

Ruth was proud of being a nurse and found satisfaction in helping people, but after a while the work started feeling routine, and she yearned for more meaning, variety, even excitement. Meanwhile, Spike's aging-rocker routine was getting old. It kept looking less and less likely that the lightning of success would strike his career, and frustration was making him increasingly bitter and blue.

The fairy-tale version of this would be that he let Ruth know she was the one good thing in his life. The real-life version, as you might guess, is that he took a lot of his frustration out on Ruth. If misery loves company, Spike seemed determined to take Ruth down with him.

Ruth was a self-aware woman, and she knew exactly what was going on. But she was kind, generous, and loving. Besides, you know how it is: the more you make an emotional investment like Ruth's, the harder it is to pull out. She thought about leaving, and even threatened to leave if Spike didn't change his act. But she never thought she would.

Training to Leave

Here's what Ruth actually did. As an outlet for her search for a sense that she was really helping people, Ruth volunteered for an organization working with refugees with health problems who were newly arrived in the States. These were refugees from such places as Thailand, Cambodia, Guatemala, Haiti, the former Yugoslavia, Russia, Liberia, and Rwanda. Ruth didn't speak any of their languages but she had one special qualification besides being a nurse: she was the daughter of refugees herself.

The organization's main mission was to recruit people like Ruth to go abroad for long periods of time for little or no pay to work in refugee camps in some of the worst places in the world. The training they provided Ruth was geared for sending her to those places.

Ruth acted as though working with these refugees here at home was as far as she wanted to go, but for two years everything she did deepened her ties to this organization that would take her out of Spike's life.

When I saw Ruth, she was agonizing over whether to stay with Spike or leave him. When I first asked Ruth question #3—Have you already made a concrete commitment to pursue a course of action or lifestyle that definitely excludes your partner?—she said she didn't think so. But after she told me more of her story I asked her to look again at what she'd actually done and take another crack at question #3.

She sat silently for a long time and then said, "How am I going to tell Spike?" The bullet had left the gun a long time before she was ready to pull the trigger. Deep down she'd already decided to leave him eighteen months earlier.

So here's the guideline:

GUIDELINE #3

If you've actually made a concrete commitment to pursue a course of action or lifestyle that excludes your partner, then on some level you've already decided that you'll be happier if you leave your relationship. Most people who've done this are not happy when they stay. It's as if you'd already advised yourself to leave. *Quick take:* If you look like you're leaving your relationship and act like you're leaving it, you're leaving it. You know best.

Let's be precise about what this guideline says and what it doesn't say. The emphasis is on doing something concrete to change your life in a way that excludes your partner. This does *not* mean experimenting, fantasizing, speculating, or merely screwing up, and it does *not* mean doing things that will allow you to keep on having the same kind of life with your partner that you've been having. Here are a couple of examples to make this distinction clear:

- Checking out apartments you might move into does *not* mean you've already decided to leave. Actually renting an apartment and paying for the first month plus a security deposit *does* mean you've decided.

- Applying for jobs far away when you know your partner can't relocate does *not* mean you've already decided to leave. Accepting an offer for such a job *does* mean you've decided (unless you've both agreed to a temporary arrangement like this).
- Consulting a divorce lawyer, even a whole series of such consultations, does *not* mean you've already decided to leave. Filing divorce papers after a careful consultation *does* mean you've decided.

Some of these might seem obvious to you. But to stuck stayers, they're far from obvious.

Actions, Not Accidents

What about affairs? Are they expressions of a "concrete commitment to leave"? Let's talk about affairs for a moment here. Later we'll get into the issues behind affairs that make relationships too bad to stay in, but for now I'm only going to look at how affairs relate to guideline #3.

As a result of years of clinical work with couples, I've learned not to jump to conclusions about what it means psychologically when someone has an affair. Sure, the person who's been cheated on (the "cheatee") often sees the relationship as over when she discovers her partner's affair. But just because it means it's over to the chea*tee* doesn't mean it's over to the chea*ter*. Whatever the cheatee feels, it wasn't necessarily the intention of the cheater to create those feelings.

If you're in an iffy relationship, the fact that you've had an affair could mean many things. It could mean you were experimenting to see if things could be better with someone else. It could mean that you just made a stupid mistake. It could mean you were very angry. In and of itself, it doesn't necessarily mean that you're setting in motion a chain of events designed to take you out of your relationship.

Here's where your having an affair does mean you've "made a concrete commitment to leave": If you stop caring whether your partner finds out or not, then an affair is a sign of your having taken practical steps to set in motion some course of action or lifestyle that definitely excludes your partner. I'm talking about transparent lies. Trips for which you don't bother to give an excuse. Mysterious late night phone calls or gifts or lipstick stains you don't try to hide.

If your answer to question #3 is yes, you'll know it by now. It's not that you've just "done something," it's that you've done something to burn your bridges behind you or to pour the foundation for a bridge to a new future that excludes your partner. You don't have to decide to leave. You've already decided.

A woman once asked me about this. "I slept with a guy at work. It's over now, but my problem is that I feel so guilty and mad at myself that I can't get beyond those feelings and that makes me wonder if it isn't too late for me."

My answer is this: you have to treat feelings carefully. They're real and important but they can also be complicated and misleading. If your relationship is really over, you'll find that out through answering this series of questions. But having had an affair can make you feel guilty, grief-stricken, fearful, enraged, self-satisfied, empowered, and a lot of other emotions that can lead you to think you've done something to end the relationship when you really haven't. You've only done something to end the relationship when you've done something that actually ends the relationship. In and of itself an affair is not necessarily that.

PERSPECTIVES: HOW TO GET OVER THE LOSS OF LOVE

The theme right now is your facing up to the possibility that the relationship is already over, that it's just been hard for you to face the fact that you've decided it's best to leave.

Why would you be so blind?

It's hard to give up on love, to say good-bye to love, to move into a future where for sure you don't have the love you used to have. After all, even in the worst of relationships there's a little love left somewhere. And for people in relationship ambivalence there's usually more than just a little love left. Leaving means saying good-bye to this love, and that's very scary for a lot of people.

This is particularly an issue for women. In one area of life after another, from love to money, women are often more motivated by fear of loss than men are, less willing to take risks. When offered the choice between the bird in the hand and two in the bush, more women than men will choose the bird in the hand and more men than women will go for one of the birds in the bush.

I don't want to overemphasize the difference. There's no huge polarity. It's not that all men love risk and all women hate risk. But when it comes to staying in a bad relationship more women are motivated by fear of loss and loneliness than men.

The last thing someone in your situation wants is empty reassurances. So I won't tell you that if you've found someone once you can find someone again; and if you've loved someone once you can love someone again; and the more love you have to give, the more likely you are to find someone.

Instead, let me tell you what most people in your situation say when they've left a relationship that was clearly too bad to stay in: over and over, they say they feel relief and hope, supported by a newfound sense of self-respect and self-reliance.

Women particularly say they're surprised at how much they like living on their own, able to do what they want when they want. They'd like to fall in love but *almost never* are they willing to settle again for the kind of relationship they left.

What's their advice to you? Don't worry, they say. If you made your choice in a responsible way, you will get over the loss of a particular partner. In the meantime, the keys to happiness are doing things you care about and staying connected to people.

Step #4: "If It Were Up to God ..."

Some people have already decided to leave their relationship even though they've taken no action to get out. The obstacle for them isn't acknowledging something practical, it's acknowledging something emotional.

What's missing for them is a sense of permission. They might feel guilty about leaving a partner who needs them. They might feel publicly shamed if this relationship can't work. They might feel worried about what leaving will do to their children. They might dread the sense of failure that'll come with ending the relationship, perhaps because other relationships have failed. They might be unwilling to acknowledge the death of love. They might be feeling all of these and more in some unique combination I've never seen before. Every part of them knows it'll be best to leave—they just need permission before they can see their truth.

Michael's Story

Lots of people have shed tears in my consulting room, but I never saw a flood of tears like the one poured forth by Michael, a locally prominent couples therapist, who'd come to me for help. After I worked with him for a bit I started to smell a rat. This talented, knowledgeable, highly motivated guy shouldn't have had such a tough time seeing what was going on in a relationship so clearly filled with terrible problems.

So I asked Michael what I'll ask you:

Diagnostic question #4. **If God or some omniscient being said it was okay to leave, would you feel tremendously relieved and have a strong sense that finally you could end your relationship?**

That's when his tears flooded forth.

We've all seen films about wild chimpanzees in which there's the heartbreaking scene of a mother chimp carrying around the corpse of her dead baby for hours, even days. That's what it had been like for Michael: he'd been carrying around the corpse of a dead relationship for a long time for the simple reason that he couldn't give himself permission to acknowledge that it was over. He sobbed in sudden mourning for a loss he'd been living with for a long time.

Why was it so hard for him to give himself permission? Partly it was because he was a therapist: if his relationship was over, didn't that mean he was a fraud and a failure? And lots of non-professionals have the same feeling, too. Women feel it because we believe that making a relationship work is ultimately our job, our skill, our talent even. But men feel it as well.

There were other reasons why it was hard for Michael to give himself permission to leave. Most important was the sense he'd had that if he really were a good person he'd stay and work harder at it. Only a bad person, he thought, would walk out on a partner and all the hopes they'd had for the future, to say nothing of what this would do to their children.

This "I don't want to be a bad person" factor is often overlooked these days because so much emphasis is placed on our sense that there are too many divorces. Perhaps there are too many. But for every divorce brought about by people who should feel more responsible to themselves and their partners, there's a relationship not ending because someone feels too responsible.

Let's deal with question #4 itself. Here's the guideline:

GUIDELINE #4

Imagine how you'd feel if God or some omniscient being said you had permission to leave your relationship if you wanted to. If this suddenly gives you a strong sense that it's all right for you to end your relationship, you'll most likely feel you've discovered what's best for you if you choose to leave. *Quick take:* If God's saying "Hey, whatever you want is okay with me" is all you'd need to feel it's okay to leave, it's okay to leave.

Your answer here is only meaningful if a clear, definite yes came through without hesitation or confusion. If you have to stop to analyze your feelings to see if your answer is yes, it's not yes.

You won't need such an overwhelmingly resounding yes to count as an answer to other questions, but you do here. If the sense of total relief at the thought of getting total permission to leave doesn't immediately clarify the fact that you've already decided to leave, you need different kinds of information to get you out of relationship ambivalence. You'll get that information later, but you haven't gotten it yet.

My World Is Empty Without You, Babe

Every once in a while someone has an unusual response to question #4. Instead of feeling either tremendously relieved or not feeling anything strongly one way or the other, they're astonished to find they feel dismayed or indignant. They feel a kind of loud No! rise up in them. They discover that they very much do not want to hear that it's okay to leave. They're aching for some sign that there are buried treasures in the relationship that make it too good to leave.

What does it mean if you felt something like that? It might mean that you'd pinned a lot of hopes on this relationship and that you're convinced your life will be empty without it. If that's the case for you, then you've got to face the possibility that there are a lot more negatives for you in this relationship than for someone who's just as ambivalent as you are but isn't so hopeful. With all of your hopes, it would take that many more negatives to make you feel so ambivalent.

So as you read through the material to come, don't let your hopes blind you to the realities in your relationship. If it's too good to leave, that should only be because it *is* too good to leave, not because you want it to be too good to leave.

On the other hand, your being that incredibly hopeful even though you're stuck in relationship ambivalence might mean you're a candidate for couples therapy if you haven't tried it already. If that's the case, you might find the following Perspectives especially helpful.

PERSPECTIVES: A NOTE ABOUT COUPLES THERAPY

I rarely see people in relationship ambivalence who haven't worked hard to make things better. And that means there's a good chance you've already tried some kind of couples therapy or workshop. So I'm reluctant to urge people who've already worked on their relationship to work still more on it. At some point enough is enough.

If you *haven't* worked on your relationship, though, that changes things. All the recommendations I make here are based on the current realities between you. I'm saying that if a specific reality is true at this moment, then other people for whom that's true felt they were better off breaking up. But I'm *not* saying that it *must* be true, that it *can't* change.

A really good couples therapist can sometimes change things between you that seemed horrible and unchangeable. So if some reality in your relationship points to your leaving, you always have the option of going to a couples therapist to see if you can change it.

But you want to avoid falling back into relationship ambivalence. Here's the test. If your experience with the therapist is "Gee, she's really good" and yet there's no change after nine months in whatever it is that makes your relationship too bad to stay in, then you can feel confirmed in your sense that it's most likely unchangeable. You'll know you've done everything you could do. And that can make it easier to accept that you'll be happier leaving the relationship.

When I'm working as a couples therapist, for a couple, I feel that it's my mandate to always work to save the relationship, to never give up, to always search for a sign of life. A doctor shouldn't give up until death wins, because that perseverance often enables a doctor to achieve victories over death. I feel the same way about the death of a relationship.

But I'm also a therapist for individuals, who have to make decisions about what's best for them as individuals. And that's my function here with you, to help you get out of the pain and waste of relationship ambivalence. So if you haven't tried to make the relationship better, then by all means do so. But if you have tried and there's no change after working nine months with a good therapist and your answers to the questions in this book point to leaving, then you can feel comfortable that you've been smart and responsible if you decide to leave.

5

Let's Do It, Let's Fall in Love

Issue: Preconditions for Love

FITTING LOVE INTO THE EQUATION

I've never met anyone in a state of relationship ambivalence who wasn't trying, in one way or another, to find a way to fit love into the equation. One of the biggest issues that keeps coming up is whether love exists between you at all. This is a question most of us have been asking ourselves since junior high school. "Do I love him/her?" "Do I *really* love him/her?" "How can I tell if I love him/her?" "Am I *in* love with him/her or do I just love him/her?" "Can I love him/her if I feel so frustrated and angry so much of the time?" It can be very confusing.

There are ways out of this confusion. The way we'll look at right now is to see if the preconditions for love still exist in your relationship. The issue of love is endlessly mysterious, but it certainly helps to know if love is possible. If it's not even possible, then it sure can't exist.

You know how in some cartoons the character runs off the edge of a cliff but stays suspended in midair until he looks down? Only when he sees there's nothing under him does he start to fall. It's like that for a lot of us in iffy relationships. We're up in the air because we haven't looked down to see that there's nothing under our love to hold it up. If we hadn't fallen in love with this person in the first place, we wouldn't be in love now.

So if you're trying to find the truth about whether you'll be happier if you leave or stay, it's important to explore the foundations for love in your relationship. Wouldn't it be great to know that love was possible? Wouldn't it be great to know that there was a foundation for your love to rest on?

Then you'd have something you could point to to say yeah, let's do it, let's fall in love.

STEP #5: STAYING ALIVE

Sometimes things look dead and they're not. I remember years ago when I was a kid growing up in New York City on the Lower East Side. We moved to a new apartment and there was what looked like a dead tree outside our door. New York is a tough place for trees, and this tree looked really dead. I must have some kind of an instinct about life and death because when some neighbor said she was going to call to have the tree removed I found myself insisting it was still alive. I made a bet with her—I'd give her free babysitting for a year if that tree didn't bring forth leaves in the next spring.

Of course the tree did sprout leaves. Somewhere under the dry, peeling bark and the brittle branches was some current of life.

I think about that tree from time to time when people come to me for help figuring out what to do about their relationship. Like my neighbor, they're sometimes pretty sure it's dead and are looking for my advice about removing themselves from it. And yet they're asking my opinion. That tells me they're still ambivalent. They suspect that maybe there's a current of life, of love, still flowing through their relationship. They're hoping I can point to it, show it to them, hold it up to them right under their noses so they can smell it.

Jack's Story

A few years ago a man came to see me because a lot of things weren't working in his life. Jack was a corporate consultant and trainer and seminar leader. With the busy, dizzy pace of his life, Jack had grown emotionally estranged from his wife, and that bothered him. He felt the two of them should be connected, the way they'd been years ago because, he said, when things between them had been at their best they'd been very good indeed. Disconnected as he was from his wife, he wondered if he didn't owe it to himself and to her to leave the relationship. It's not that it was too bad to stay, but he couldn't see how it was too good to leave. "What should I do?" he asked. I felt he was asking me to find a sign of life in his relationship. I asked Jack the question I'll ask you to answer for yourself:

Diagnostic question #5. **In spite of your problems, do you and your partner have even one positively pleasurable activity or interest (besides children) you currently share and look forward to sharing in the future, something you do together that you both like and that gives both of you a feeling of closeness for a while?**

Instead of answering right away, Jack made me justify every bit of what I asked. Frankly, I think he was stalling for time and, on a deeper level, he was making it hard for me because he was scared I'd provide some illusory and ultimately disappointing piece of reassurance.

First thing he said was, "What do you mean 'besides children'? What's wrong with children bringing people together?"

The short answer is that children aren't glue and shotgun weddings don't work out. You probably know people who had kids in the hopes that it would pour some cement into the shaky foundation of their marriage. We all root for that to work, but we all know how often it doesn't. Children will keep you connected, that's for sure, but it's not the kind of connection that has much to do with your love for each other. People fall in love and make a bond before there are children and they have to stay in love after the children have left home; if you want to look for a sign of life you've got to look beyond the children for it.

Beyond Sex

Jack was silent for a moment. He and his wife did have children and they had similar values and, on the rare occasions when they had the time, they shared family time together. But now I was asking him for another positively pleasurable connection between him and his wife. He still had trouble wrapping his mind around what I was getting at. "Do you mean sex?" he asked. "I like sex. Does that count?"

Maybe, I said. Orgasms alone don't count. Good sex alone doesn't count. Sex counts for question #5 only if it's something you really share. You know it counts, I said, if it's something you both anticipate with pleasure, if it not only feels good but makes you feel close, if that glow of closeness is real and lasts for a significant period after sex, and if you keep seeking it out.

I could almost see the wheels working as he tried to take in the distinction between sex that superficially felt good and sex that produced a real close connection that felt good on every level. Then I saw discouragement spreading over his face.

"Look," he said, "I've never had bad sex. But I can't honestly say that Laura and I really connect through it. Sex happens but we don't go out of our way to make it happen and when we do, for me, it's basically about sex. So does that mean that I've struck out on this question?"

Not at all, I said. We've just begun. It doesn't matter how you connect as long as there's something you do together that feels good and you look forward to doing together and that makes you both feel close. I'm not saying that if you don't have this things are over between you. But if you do have it, that's an indication of life in your relationship, a foundation for love.

"So help me out," Jack said. "What are you talking about?"

It's different for different people, but here are some activities

that people have told me give them a close, pleasurable connection, that give these particular people an experience of being in
love again:

- Cuddling in bed together before turning off the lights
- Having friends over for dinner
- Gossiping about those friends after they've left
- Laughing together at the same zany comedy
- Going dancing
- Going away together
- Talking politics
- Playing tennis
- Sitting around on Sunday morning with the *New York
  Times* and a pot of coffee
- Kissing each other
- Checking out the antique shops
- Gardening together
- Walking home from church
- Holding hands and going for long walks in the country or
  on the beach
- Running around in the park with the dog and a Frisbee

It's not that activities like these make everything great or that
they'd mean anything to anyone else, but for at least one particular couple one of these things made them feel close and made
them feel good about feeling close. Whenever they did these
things—and they did them at least once a month—they not only
felt their love, they felt their love was real. For a few moments
they could forget all the things that made their relationship feel
too bad to stay in.

Now You're Cooking

Jack closed his eyes and drifted off in thought to see if he could
find something like this in his life with Laura. "Does cooking
count?" he asked.

It depends. What are you talking about?

"The thing is," he said, "that we don't have to cook at all, not together the way we do, but every couple of weeks or so on a Saturday afternoon or something we'll really get into making some special meal and we'll go into the kitchen and we sort of mesh the way we work together. We'll talk, we'll even sing, or we'll be silent for a period. I know some couples get into fights the minute they're both in the kitchen together, but for us it's a kind of tension-free zone, and I have no idea how it happens but I think we really feel close, like we're enjoying something together we're not supposed to enjoy."

Jack had found it, and it had been under his nose all the time. That's how it works for some people with this question and with other questions later on that point to the possibility that a relationship really may be too good to leave. Pain throbs, but the current of life in a relationship is all too invisible. No wonder it so often dies of neglect.

So here's the guideline I was able to provide for Jack:

GUIDELINE #5

If there's even one thing you and your partner experience together and look forward to (besides children) that reliably feels good and makes you feel close, there's the possibility you'll be able to clean out the crap between you and have a viable relationship. If you had just met, there'd be the possibility of your falling in love. *Quick take:* Real love needs real loving experiences.

This guideline doesn't refer to things you do together that just feel okay or that enable you to stop fighting or hating each other. It refers to things that provide regular, positive, pleasurable connections, that you both look forward to and you both make happen.

But remember that Jack was a tough customer. "If all this gives me is just the possibility that I've got a viable relationship, what's the big deal about it?" he said.

Every sign of life is precious. A yes answer to question #5 is a sign that love is possible. It gives you what strong, deep roots give a plant that's been hit by drought. There's reason to hope. There's reason to press on. There's reason to keep cultivating the relationship and looking for more signs of life. It might still turn out that later on in this book you'll learn something about your relationship that makes it clear that you'll be happier if you leave, but for now it's clear you're not there yet.

PERSPECTIVES: A NOTE ON HOW THE GUIDELINES WORK

Because this book works just like medical diagnostics, positive and negative guidelines don't exactly have equal status. A guideline that says your relationship is too bad to stay in overrules any guidelines that say your relationship is too good too leave.

Why is that? I know that sounds negative, but it isn't. It's just how diagnostics work. Let me explain.

Suppose you were trying to decide whether to stay in your house or move. An incredible view or an ideal layout might make your house too good to leave and might outweigh a lot of negatives. But they don't counteract your house being sandwiched between a slaughterhouse and a cement factory. They don't counteract your house's foundation having been completely eaten away by termites. They don't counteract your living in a floodplain.

It's a kind of rule in life. A lot of good stuff might make us willing to put up with some bad stuff. But any *really* terrible stuff has veto power over a ton of good stuff.

So any guideline that says *this* makes a relationship too good to leave is provisional only. *It's true only as long as nothing else comes along to make it too bad to stay in.*

Guideline #5 is absolutely basic. Even some couples in the worst possible shape trying to work out the greatest difficulties have discovered they can answer yes to this question, and that positively pleasurable connection, however small, has provided a basis for working their way back to each other.

But guideline #5 has a special importance for people who are in what clinicians refer to as dead or devitalized or roommate marriages, where the really bad thing that bothers them is that there doesn't seem to be anything really good. Guideline #5 is a test for whether this is really the case. Some relationships are more cool and distant than others. But if there's a positively pleasurable connection and you answered yes to question #5, then your relationship may not be as lifeless as you think.

What If Your Answer's No?

If you've been holding your breath this whole time because you answered no to question #5, you can relax. With diagnostic questions, usually one of the answers to a question is more meaningful than the other. You know how it is. If you can jog a mile without getting completely out of breath, that's a sign you're in decent shape. But if you can't, if you have to stop and catch your breath, it doesn't necessarily mean you've got a medical condition—you just might be out of shape.

In the same way, when it comes to question #5, if you answered no there's still the possibility that you've got a viable relationship. It's just that you've got to work together to find something that you both look forward to doing together that feels good and makes you both feel closer. It might be something you used to do together. It might be something you've never done together. If nothing else is seriously wrong, there's still a chance you can find it.

STEP #6: THE NASTY-STUPID-CRAZY-UGLY-STINKY FACTOR

There's an even more elemental precondition for love than having something you do together that makes you feel close. It's so obvious I'd be embarrassed to mention it except for the fact that it's proved so helpful and reliable for people. You can't fall in love with somebody you find repulsive, loathsome, and, as Daffy Duck would say, despicable. So if you want to know what to do about your relationship, it's time we took a look to see if we can rule out what I call the nasty-stupid-crazy-ugly-stinky factor.

Diagnostic question #6. Would you say that to you your partner is basically nice, reasonably intelligent, not too neurotic, okay to look at, and most of the time smells all right?

This is an unpretentious question. I'm sure that you, like most people stuck in relationship ambivalence, are all too aware of all kinds of unmet needs and unsolved problems. But you can't let this blind you to a basic issue: suppose you got everything you want and all the problems were solved—would your partner still give you the creeps?

You're not looking for the most wonderful person in the world with this question. You're not applying anyone's standards but your own. You're not trying to live up to any expectations but the most basic. You're just looking for animal compatibility, and I use the word *animal* in the nicest sense of the word.

So would you say that your partner's essentially a nice person? Not the biggest-hearted person in the world, or even someone who goes out of his way to be kind. But do you have a sense that your partner is the sort of person who doesn't always grab the last piece of cake for himself?

And would you say that your partner is smart in ways that matter to you? Not that she's a genius or smarter than you are or even particularly smart in most ways. But would you say that there's some vein of wisdom or cleverness or common sense that you can tap into and that you respect in your partner?

And would you say that your partner's reasonably sane (or at least no crazier than most of us)? Indeed we're all a little crazy in our own ways, so I'm not asking if your partner has no emotional hangups or psychological quirks. But if you remember Jack Nicholson in *The Shining* or Glenn Close in *Fatal Attraction*, would you say that your partner's not like that?

And would you say that your partner still looks pretty good to you? Of course most of us start heading downhill once we hit twenty-four. But the human heart is very forgiving and the human eye can find attractions everywhere, so would you say that on balance you like the way your partner looks?

And would you say that your partner still (believe it or not) smells good to you? Smell is the most emotional of the senses. It's not that any of us smell like perfume, and as comedian Monica Piper says, "Who wants to smell like a man?" But when your partner's reasonably clean, do you like the way he smells?

Now suppose your answer to question #6 is yes. Let's talk about the yes answer. Yes is good.

GUIDELINE #6

If you can say that right now you feel your partner's reasonably nice, smart, sane, not ugly, and okay smelling to you, you've removed an important obstacle to your finding your way back to each other. When people say yes to this question, the possibility of love still exists. *Quick take:* You just can't love someone who's mean, dumb, crazy, ugly, or stinky.

I know we fall in love with people because we feel there's something special or wonderful about them, some deep connection, some magic chemistry. But before all that can happen, even when it's a case of love at first sight, there's at least a moment—an absolutely necessary moment—of what you might call pre-love. It's a kind of almost animal-like filter where you determine the other person's basic okayness for you. It's so basic that we tend to forget it. Question #6 is a reminder.

What if your answer was no? In most cases, that's not necessarily a bad sign. When I ask people this question, their no's are often misleading. Remember, they're stuck in a state of relationship ambivalence. They've built up a huge backlog of negatives about the other person. In fact, in most cases when people say their relationship is too good to leave but too bad to stay in, the negatives usually outweigh the positives because it takes an awful lot to make us think of giving up on love.

So, when people say no to question #6, it's very often an angry, disgruntled, grievance-filled no. It's a no that's tainted with hurt and disappointment. They may feel the other person's not nice because they've just had a huge fight, stupid because he doesn't understand how she feels, crazy because his feelings seem to make no sense, ugly because he's so angry and damn it because he said he'd lose weight and he didn't, and stinky because he . . . well, because he's been acting like a stinker. This is not a diagnostically meaningful no. There's a high probability that negative feelings are clouding your lens and your no answer isn't a useful indicator for you right now.

A Dead-Certain No

Every once in a while, though, someone answers question #6 like this: They think about it for a while, taking enough time to make sure that they're not being controlled by the moment. Then suddenly it's very clear. There is a resigned but dead-certain no. This kind of careful, thoughtful, unmistakable no only happens a small percent of the time with this question, but when it happens it's a definite sign that there's a basic discord. If you look your relationship in the face, if you can see it unclouded by superficial hurt and anger, and the nasty-stupid-crazy-ugly-stinky factor stares back at you, then it's most likely you'll feel you've made the right decision if you leave.

Linda's Story

Let me tell you about Linda. I worked with her when she was married to a very rich man. To put it bluntly, this guy had enough dough to make a lot of people stick around in an otherwise unsatisfying relationship with him. Linda was a person like this. I asked Linda question #6 and she knew without the slightest doubt that for her this guy was a mean, dumb, weird, ugly, smelly bastard. But while she was unhappy with him, there was frankly too much money there for her to want to get out.

But when a major business deal of his went sour and his net worth dipped below 5 million dollars, Linda finally left him. As Linda said, he just wasn't rich enough anymore to put up with. It takes more than 5 million dollars to make it bearable to live with someone when you answer no to this question.

It's a crude story, but isn't clarity great?

6

You've Got a Hold on Me

Issue: Power—When the Other Person Is Bossy, Controlling, Domineering, Overwhelming . . .

"Because I just can't deal with her."

"Because he's impossible."

"Because I have a terrible knot in my stomach every day while I'm waiting for him to come home from work."

These are some of the most common things I hear from people who are wondering if their relationship is too bad to stay in. There's something about their partner that frustrates and confuses and overwhelms them and makes their life unbearable. And that something has to do with power. Everyone intuitively understands there's such a thing as being in a relationship with someone whose personal power is so overwhelming and destructive that you've just got to get out. That's what we'll deal with here.

HURRICANE SEASON

Have you ever been outside during a hurricane? I have. The wind was so powerful that it was almost impossible to walk in the direction I wanted to. Most of the time I could barely manage to avoid being blown over or carried away in the direction the wind wanted to take me. I didn't want to conquer the wind. I just wanted to go where I wanted to go. But it felt as if the wind wanted to conquer me.

Imagine falling in love with that wind before it turned so powerful, while it was still a gentle tropical breeze. That's what a lot of our relationships are like. Almost no one shows their true capacity for power when things are just starting out. Even young women who get involved with rich, influential older men find that generally in the early stages guys like that soft-pedal their ability to throw their weight around. They're even careful to show how sensitive and considerate they can be. It all feels so good. Then with time the winds start picking up.

There's a beautiful illustration of this in the movie *Citizen Kane*. When Kane first meets sweet young Susan Alexander, the incredibly powerful Kane is as cute and vulnerable as he can be. But before you know it, he's ruling her life and everything in it.

When I ask people in relationship ambivalence to talk about the things that make them feel maybe they'll be happiest leaving, the issue of power comes up a lot, one way or the other, even if the word *power* is never used. Everyone's experience is a little different, of course, but here's what one guy said that really captured the essence of what a lot of people have to deal with:

> My friends tell me that years ago I said I wanted to marry a strong woman, and I'm sure I did. But Gwen's more than I can handle. She's so passionate about everything, and it keeps shading into rage or craziness. Plus she's got this whole set of tricks up her sleeve I mean, she'll make a scene in public if it looks like she's not going to get things her way, or she'll win by making me feel like a jerk for wanting what I want. And she's always got so many arguments for her side that half the time I feel like an idiot for even bringing things up.

It can be exhausting and demoralizing to live with someone like this. But if you're in a state of relationship ambivalence, you know it can be very hard to see when the other person crosses the line from being *just* difficult to deal with to being *too* difficult to deal with. It's not knowing where that line is, not even being able to see it, not feeling you have a right to draw that line that keeps you stuck in relationship ambivalence.

That's what we'll sort out here, so that you can discover whether your partner's power is something you just have to deal with the way everyone else does or whether there's something about power in your relationship that's so bad that most people in your situation ended up feeling happy they left and unhappy they stayed.

Let's begin with an example that'll give us a frame of reference we can keep coming back to.

Rosemary's Story

Rosemary and Vinnie came to me seeking help because of what they said was Vinnie's unwillingness to "consider" Rosemary, as if this were one of those typical cases of the insensitive man and the oversensitive woman. But Vinnie was like a steamroller, and what does it mean to be oversensitive to that? You have to know how to get people to do what you want to run a successful restaurant like his. When Vinnie wanted things to happen, they happened. When he didn't want things to happen, they didn't happen. Vinnie was like a force of nature.

Rosemary went along with this for a while for the most obvious of reasons. Vinnie was a typical man, she thought, and what can you expect from a man? He had enough money to call the shots. His business was so demanding that he could get whatever he wanted by saying it was "for the restaurant." Vinnie put out a lot of superficial respect for Rosemary as a "lady," smart, educated, refined—respect she felt she'd lose if she got down in the gutter with Vinnie and challenged him. Besides, Rosemary was an accountant, and the restaurant was one of her accounts, which meant that in a sense Vinnie was one of her bosses.

Rosemary's dilemma was this. Was Vinnie just a forceful, on-top-of-things kind of guy who seemed hard to deal with but who was really just trying to do a good job? Or did he have something else going on inside him, some need, some hunger, that made him a kind of Hitler unable to rest in peace as long as one single

Poland remained unoccupied? Was Vinnie the restaurant's servant or Rosemary's dictator? Was there ever a chance he'd let her draw a free breath?

Let's see just how badly Vinnie rode roughshod over Rosemary. One incident stands out for Rosemary as capturing the truth about who Vinnie really was.

At one point we had an extralong session devoted specifically to Rosemary trying to show Vinnie how everything in their relationship was set up for him to get everything he wanted and for her to get nothing of what she wanted. Maybe that wasn't literally true, but it certainly felt like that to Rosemary.

Vinnie tried arguing with her. "Well," he said, "we never have sex unless you want to."

"I'm not accusing you of *rape*," Rosemary said. "I'm just saying you always win. I wasn't talking about sex anyway, but even there the whole thing is governed by your pressure, your moods, your schedule, your ability to make me feel guilty, your deciding when you want to initiate sex, your making me feel creepy whenever I initiate sex. But you're even doing it now. We're talking about sex. I didn't want to talk about sex. How can you be so powerful to get us talking about sex when sex wasn't the issue I wanted to talk about? The issue is that everything is what you want when you want it."

Maybe Vinnie didn't want to look bad in my eyes. So he suddenly became eager to learn all the things he'd been doing "wrong." Rosemary complied. She poured forth a litany of instances when Vinnie had bullied and dominated her. They ran the gamut from how it happened that they still didn't have kids even though Rosemary wanted them to how Vinnie ended up controlling her accounting business.

The scales seemed to fall from Vinnie's eyes. He acted genuinely sorry. "You tell me every time I do something to be too powerful," Vinnie offered, "and I'll try not to do that, okay?"

Rosemary hoped she'd finally gotten through. Still in the safety of therapy she said, "All right—when we leave here I've got to go right home so I have time to change 'cause I've got to get dressed up for a meeting with a new client. Is that going to be a problem for you?" It was fine with Vinnie.

But later I learned that in the car, driving home, Vinnie had started insisting they quickly swing by the restaurant to see how things were going there. "Besides," Vinnie said, "you don't need to change." Rosemary suddenly had this horrible sense that he knew exactly what he was doing, that he didn't really need to go to the restaurant at all, that for him if they drove right home Rosemary would "win" and that Vinnie was an automaton programmed to not let that happen.

Hidden Power

But do you leave a relationship just because your partner "modifies" an agreement? Rosemary had been asking herself questions like that for a very long time. There's something about power—like the wind—that makes it invisible in relationships even when it's blowing us away.

We've got to understand what keeps power so hidden before we can truly see it. There are a couple of reasons why the ebb and flow of power is a dirty little secret in relationships, why we keep it secret from each other and from ourselves.

Power vs. Love. First, power seems completely antithetical to the idea of love. We feel that power no more belongs in the love context than sex belongs in the church context. If two people are getting close and little red hearts are floating up in the air like bubbles from a bubble pipe, how can the thought of power, much less the reality of power, intrude?

No wonder we're blind to power in the realm of love. It's a terrifying thought: "If I even think it's about power, that means love is dead, and I won't face that." Yes, we reserve the right to complain endlessly about our partners, to even call them controlling, but if this relationship is about power, we think, it can't be about love.

But in the world of how things really are, as opposed to the world of how things are supposed to be, there is all too often something going on with power in our relationships that fills them so full of frustration and confusion that all we can think of is getting out.

Power and Shame. The other reason power is rarely talked about is shame. Imagine how a smart, competent, educated woman like Rosemary felt admitting she couldn't hold her own in the face of Vinnie's power. Outside of coping with a newborn baby or a teenager or a boss, we're all embarrassed to admit we feel powerless. Besides, to do so would mean we're saying we want power ourselves, which is embarrassing. But even more, it would mean we're saying we're weak, which is humiliating.

And so men certainly don't talk about how their wives make them feel powerless. And women today are just as reluctant to seem like helpless victims.

Unfortunately, women also get hit from the other side. While we're ashamed of being powerless, we're ashamed of being powerful too, of wanting power, of caring about power. The image of women in our society these days is that women somehow have a special aptitude for cooperation and connection. This translates for the average woman as saying that if she cares about power and uses her personal power, she's not a normal woman. So if there's shame both from being power*less* and from being power*ful*, the only psychological strategy that's possible is to try to put all thought of power out of your mind.

And, when it comes to dealing with a relationship made iffy by power problems, this means a lot of women have trouble figuring out what's really going on and what they really want in the relationship.

But there's good news. When you look power in the eye, you can't lose. Either there's something toxic going on with power in your relationship that makes it a relationship you'll be happy leaving, or the realities of power in your relationship don't make it too bad to stay in, and you'll very likely find that power problems are fixable.

Step #7: Power People

How in the world does power intrude on our love nests? Simple. It's up for grabs. The only way you could have a relationship without power struggles would be like the famous scene in the fifties movie *Marty*, where Marty and his buddy sit around saying:

"What do you want to do?"

"I don't know. What do you want to do?"

"I don't know. What do you want to do?"

"I don't know. What do . . . ?"

You get the picture.

The point is that from the day you and your partner meet, you have to decide to do things and you have to decide to do them in a certain way. Every single decision is fertile soil for a power struggle, because with every single decision there's a question of who's going to make it and whose needs are going to prevail.

So there are power issues involved with deciding where you're going to go on your first date, when you make love, what you do when you make love, who's allowed to shout and under what circumstances, where you're going to go on your vacation, how much money you're going to save, how long the baby's allowed to cry before you're either torturing him or spoiling him, how late you're allowed to come home from work without getting in trouble for not calling. . . . *Everything is a potential source of power struggles.*

No wonder people fight in even the healthiest of relationships: there's a rough balance of power and they're just struggling to have their say. If you watch the average couple deal with this, you see that sometimes they work out who decides what by letting each partner be in charge of certain things: you're in charge of paying the bills, your partner's in charge of initiating lovemaking.

Sometimes couples work this out on the basis of need: whoever cares the most about something makes the decision.

Sometimes couples work this out through some rough sense

of balance: because you decided what to watch on TV Thursday night, your partner gets to decide what to watch on Sunday night.

Sometimes couples work this out on the basis of knowledge or skill: whoever's best at something makes decisions about it.

Most people work out their power issues through a mixture of these and other fair methods, including a fight that's often just a way of bringing out all the issues and showing who cares how much about what.

But some people can't. They're what I call power people, and they consistently make relationships too bad to stay in.

Power people are different from everyone else. If you're in a relationship with the average person, then the two of you struggle as everyone else does over whose needs will get met. But if you're in a relationship with a power person, then any and all of your needs are a threat to his power. You're not two people with ordinary needs; one of you has an inordinate need for power in and of itself.

Here's the question that gets at this:

Diagnostic question #7. **Does your partner bombard you with difficulties when you try to get even the littlest thing you want; and is it your experience that almost any need you have gets obliterated; and if you ever do get what you want, is getting it such an ordeal that you don't feel it was worth all the effort?**

There's a lot to think about here. You've got to be careful with this question. It's so easy for people in iffy relationships to get annoyed with their partners that they might confuse someone who's very strong with a real power person. Let's make the difference clear in the following Perspectives.

PERSPECTIVES: POWER PEOPLE

So who are these power people that question #7 applies to? Where do they come from? What makes them the way they are?

Turning on the Power

There are two main threads that generally run through the growing up years of power people. The first thread is that they have parents or other influential family members who are in one way or another incredibly powerful people. They grow up with the sense that accumulating power of one's own is the only way to survive. They learn the rule: do whatever it takes to win.

Their parents don't necessarily exert power by being straightforwardly domineering. The parents can get their power by being incessantly, intensely emotional. They can get their power by being outrageous. They can get their power by being nutty. They can get their power by making the child feel like an idiot. The point is that the child of parents like this soon realizes that cooperation is impossible. The only alternatives are victory or escape.

The second thread for power people growing up is that their parents inadvertently ran a school that taught them lessons on how to be powerful. They observed their parents and they saw how when you do *this* you win. This learning gives them an advantage. We all emphasize our strengths in life—intelligence, charm, beauty, energy, whatever. This means that as we pass from childhood to adulthood we enhance the strengths we began with. And power people started out by learning how to be powerful, they used their lessons well, and so they developed further power skills.

A Talent for the Game

Power people also bring their own traits and aptitudes to who they are. In the old nature-nurture controversy, the correct answer is always *both*. That applies to power people, too.

Here's what power people have going for them. One thing is

talent. I've spent years working with individuals in a variety of contexts where power was up for grabs, and a talent for power is as palpable in relationships as a talent for music stands out in a high school band. Anyone who works in an organization of any kind knows exactly who has a talent for power in the circle of people he works with.

But there's a further dividing line beyond having and not having a talent for power. There's the line between being able to acquire power in a particular situation and being unable to stop yourself from acquiring power in any particular situation. The mere talent for power doesn't make you the kind of power person that destroys relationships. But when the talent controls you and makes you its servant, then you and everyone around you are in big trouble. Power people are out of control with the need to be in control.

Reality

Then there's reality. There are practical circumstances in people's lives that make them much more powerful than they might otherwise be in a relationship. Most often this comes from their job.

For example, if your partner is involved with any kind of emergency-type work, whether as a fireman or as head of emergency medicine at a big-city hospital trauma center, the demands of the job are so intense that it's easy for your partner to get whatever he wants by standing on the shoulders of the job. But any kind of job with significant pressures or demands or difficulties can give your partner real power in getting what he wants. "You've got to do this or that because I need it for my job." "You've got to stop doing this or that because it prevents me from doing my job." These kinds of things put a strain on any relationship, but if you're involved with a power person they just add to his power.

There's a surprising range of circumstances that give people power. Owning a business does this. Having real power in the corporate world does this. Political power does this. Having star power in the entertainment world does this. Having to hold down two demanding jobs to make ends meet does this. Having a power person for a boss does this. Even if your partner's not a power person, if your partner's boss is a power person it can still be like being married to a power person yourself.

In some circumstances even being pregnant can give you real power, as was the case with a woman I worked with who was the wife of a mob figure. He'd ignored her and run roughshod over her for years, but she was amazed to find that starting with the day he learned she was pregnant she could get him to do whatever she wanted whenever she wanted. Sadly, her new power lasted only until the day she brought a healthy baby home from the hospital.

But it's crucial to distinguish between external circumstances that change the power dynamics all by themselves and a power person using circumstances to gain still more power.

One more thing power people have going for them is caring. That might sound odd until you think about it for a moment.

Suppose the issue is deciding what you're going to have for dinner. One of you doesn't much care what you eat. The other cares passionately. He emphatically requires certain vegetables cooked a certain way, for example, vehemently hating certain dairy products. Guess who makes the menu.

Or one of you doesn't much care how things go when you make love, as long as you make love. The other has a whole list of must do's, must do's in certain ways, and must not do's. Guess who's in charge of lovemaking.

One of you is pretty easygoing when it comes to the kids. The other strongly believes in a whole list of rules and restrictions. Guess who's in charge of childrearing.

Someone who's not a power person can be very powerful in a relationship the more things they care about and the more strongly they care about them. But at least you can talk to someone like that about the impact their caring has on your power dynamics. A power person goes beyond caring about some particular thing and uses his caring about everything to gain power.

This gives you a sense of what you're potentially up against in a relationship with a power person. Someone who was brought up to have a hunger for power. Someone who learned about power at his or her parents' knees. Someone with a talent for power. Someone willing to go much further than you'd ever imagine in an attempt to gain power. Someone whose power is enhanced by the realities of his or her life. Someone who cares overintensely about specific issues.

To someone like this, you may very well be invisible.

Power People in Action

To help you answer question #7, the issue is are you in a relationship with a power person?

It certainly looked as though Rosemary was. That incident in which Vinnie suddenly had to stop by the restaurant even though it was so important to Rosemary to go right home may not have been important in itself, but it clearly showed something that had been true for Rosemary every day of her life with Vinnie: he was interested in getting his needs met, but he was even more interested in maintaining his power.

Going to the restaurant seemed completely unnecessary. But power people fight for a lot of seemingly unnecessary things. They only seem unnecessary, though, when we focus on their need for *that thing*. They're completely necessary from the perspective of their need for power.

The problem is that if you're not a power person it's easy to understand needing specific things but very difficult to understand needing power. So it's hard for you to accept what a power person's really up to. And that means it's hard for you to accept what's happening to you if you're living with a power person.

Now suppose you're in a relationship with a power person like this and you try to take care of yourself. All you want to do is get some need of your own met, like Rosemary's wanting to go right home so she'd have time to change her clothes. But you have to understand how the power person's mind works. If they care about power so deeply, they can't imagine that you're not the same way. If all they want is power, all you must want is power. They interpret your actions with their own meanings.

So if they do things not to get their needs met but to maintain power, anything you do to get any of your needs met must be to assert your own power. At least that's how they see it.

So while Rosemary was working to make her relationship a place where she could take care of herself, Vinnie couldn't help translating this as a power struggle. He was like the scorpion who stings the frog that's ferrying him across the river and then drowns along with the frog because he can't help himself, because that's just who he is. In the same way, a power person is made stupid in the service of his need for power. Instead of trying to make an entire balanced menu of things work as well as possible, he focuses on power so exclusively he'll destroy everything else.

So let's see what your answer to question #7 means. I bet you can predict what this guideline's going to be:

GUIDELINE #7

If your partner bombards you with difficulties when you try to get even the littlest thing you want, and if almost any need you have somehow gets obliterated, and if whenever you do get something you want it's such an ordeal that you don't feel it was worth the effort—then you'll be happy in the long run if you leave and unhappy if you stay. *Quick take:* Power people poison passion.

What if you're still not sure if your partner's a passion-poisoning power person? Maybe you can't get inside his head, but you can see what he does and how it makes you feel.

Power Moves

The things power people do to maintain their power fall into a number of specific categories. Here are the main ones. Watch out for them:

The Best Defense Is a Good Offense. Whatever need you have, power people claim there's something wrong with you for having that need. They'll try to make you feel ashamed or guilty. They'll make you feel sick or weak. They'll sneer and make you feel inferior. They'll provide a variety of labels—"defensive," "neurotic," "codependent," the list is endless—so you feel, well, anyone who has this need is like *that*, and I don't want to be like *that*, so I'd better not have that need. These tactics are often hard to notice at first because you're so busy dealing with your own feelings about there being something wrong with you that it's hard to focus on what the power person's really doing.

Power Judo. Why do things the hard way? A lot of power people discover that they can win if they yes you to death. Vinnie, in our example, used power judo at first, and it so lulled Rosemary into thinking that she was going to get what she wanted that she wasn't prepared when he slipped in his own need by saying he wanted to quickly go and check out the restaurant. The point of these tactics is that instead of opposing you the power person seems to be going along with you by promising you what you're asking for. But he never delivers.

Snow Jobs. I don't mean flattery. I'm talking about an overwhelming, distracting blizzard of complication and confusion that so spins you around and turns you upside down that you're willing to let the power person have everything he wants if only you can find a sliver of peace and clarity. You can be greeted with an emotional uproar, a verbally abusive uproar, a political uproar, an intellectual uproar, even an uproar of busyness and practical details that obliterates your own needs. It doesn't have to seem like an uproar at all, though. You can be snowed under, for example, by a confusing blizzard of polite considerations all seemingly raised for your benefit.

The Endless Campaign. All you wanted was one simple thing. But the power person keeps coming at you, coming at you, coming at you—battling endlessly over every step and at every possible moment and with renewed energy at every setback. The exhausting relentlessness of this—like a little kid you take to the supermarket who wants you to buy him a certain cereal he's seen on TV—makes you so sorry you brought up your need in the first place that you not only give up now but you don't try again for a long time.

Dirty Fighting. Power people scare and intimidate us. They quickly convey a fearless sense that they'll do anything to get what they want or prevent you from getting what you want. They will literally act crazy if necessary, even though they're not. One guy, on the occasions when his wife told him he was driving too fast (and evidently he was), would either say, "You think this is fast—I'll show you fast," and put the pedal to the floor, scaring her witless. Or, as happened in the middle of sixty-mile-an-hour rush-hour traffic, he'd say, "You want me to slow down—why don't I just stop," and he just came to a complete stop in the middle of a four-lane highway. (When this woman first came to see me the first words out of her mouth were "My husband says I need therapy because I'm too emotional.")

Con Jobs. Your needs make them sick. Literally. Or so they'd have you think. That's how power people work. One woman learned this at her mother's knee when as a teenager she told her mother she didn't want to go to church anymore. Her mother fell on the floor, enacting a full-blown heart attack so convincingly that the daughter called the paramedics. Later, in her own relationship and an accomplished power person in her own right, she'd pull everything from hysterical crying jags to gasping attacks to blinding headaches to get her own way.

Power people will do *anything* to win. This is how you end up feeling that your needs are obliterated and that it's not worthwhile to even try to get a need met. Ultimately what this does to you is give you a looking-for-ways-to-do-things-behind-your-partner's-back attitude.

And the reason you'll be happiest leaving isn't only what all this does to you. It's that any attempts to deal with it or fix it will just seem to your partner like an assault on his power and he'll have to come back at you with whatever tactics he's got. You'll never get the sense that other people in other relationships have, that, "Yes, everything isn't perfect but we both want to work things out so we both get our needs met."

You wouldn't mind having a partner who wanted to get his needs met. You wouldn't even mind having a partner with whom you had occasional fights as you both tried to get your needs met. But all the people I've talked to make it clear that what's unbearable is to be stuck with a partner whose main need seems to be that you don't get your needs met.

The Fairness Test

If you're still not sure whether you're dealing with a full-blown power person, try the fairness test.

For a particular need you have, and without blaming or attacking or labeling your partner, explain to your partner how it's simply not fair that things are the way they are now. For example, you might say, "It's not fair, is it, that we always watch what you want to watch on TV and never watch what I want to watch?" Do they respond to your appeal to fairness?

If they just respond with more power tactics, however confusing or misleading (including the tactic of yessing you to death and then going on to do whatever they want), you know you're dealing with an incurable power person. There are a lot of strong personalities and a lot of not tremendously sensitive people who are nevertheless fair and will respond productively to the fairness test. Power people will not and cannot.

Power people do what they do because they feel incredibly unsafe unless they're holding all the reins of power. They feel as unsafe without power as you'd feel vulnerable walking the streets of Manhattan with no clothes on. But your understanding their need for safety doesn't help you. Their safety is your nightmare.

That's why guideline #7 applies.

STEP #8: THE RIGHT NOT TO BE HUMILIATED

The issue of power in relationships is so important that I've got to make sure I help everyone who couldn't bring herself to answer yes to question #7 but who's still stuck in a relationship with an impossible power person. But how could that be? you might wonder. If your partner makes you feel your needs are obliterated, wouldn't you know that?

Not necessarily. Something I've noticed over and over through the years is the all-too-tragic way men and women get swept up in admiration of power people. Yes, they'll say, my partner is domineering and overwhelming, but, gee, he's so wonderful, too, so smart, so capable. Yes, my needs are obliterated, but I'm just a ninny (they say to themselves). Maybe I shouldn't really have those needs.

What makes it all so confusing is that while power people spoil our lives and are certainly controlling, people who are controlling are often people who are in control, and people who are in control are often people we admire most and feel safest with.

So how do you distinguish between (1) your being trapped by a power person who hoodwinks you into believing among other things that he's "in control" and (2) someone else who's not a power person but who's just very strong and competent and whose being in control conveys a sense of power? If you're trying to decide if you'll be happiest staying or leaving, you need help sorting this out.

Another reason you might not see that your needs are being obliterated is that some consummately subtle power people always know when to stop one step short of your consciously feeling your needs are obliterated. If you fall into this category, you'll sincerely answer no to question #7 because of the way now and then one of your needs does get satisfied. And yet you're miserable anyway.

Let me try to help.

Diagnostic question #8. Do you have a basic, recurring, never-completely-going-away feeling of humiliation or invisibility in your relationship?

This is a question about how you *feel* in the relationship with respect to your partner's power. Let's go back to Vinnie and Rosemary. To put it bluntly, Vinnie made Rosemary feel like a nothing, constantly defeated and frustrated.

There's a flush-faced feeling of humiliation, a hollow-chested sense of being invisible, that never goes away when you are in a relationship with a power person. Almost every day he or she makes you feel like nothing, like a nobody. Clearly, having your needs obliterated will do this. But it doesn't have to be so dramatic. You may not have some strong "need" to be listened to when you talk about what your day was like or about some thoughts you've had about the children, but if your partner's power shuts you up, then that's a slap in the face and you burn with humiliation.

There are two main ways people express their feelings of humiliation or invisibility: rage and depression. When the other's power makes you feel like nothing, you want to destroy them or you want to destroy yourself.

Now it may be that you're directly aware of the fact that your partner makes you feel this way. Not just occasionally—that happens to almost everyone—but most of the time on the surface and deep down, always. But if you're not sure, if you can't say you'd label the way you feel "invisible" or "humiliated," then here are some instances of what other people have felt or gone through. Perhaps these will help make your situation clear to you:

- One mild mannered man whose wife's powerful personality dominated him was shocked to realize that during or after almost every prolonged interaction with her he had thoughts of bludgeoning her to death. (A fantasy like this once in a blue moon doesn't necessarily mean you're being humiliated; it probably just means you're angry.)
- One man came home from work most days to find that his wife had a long list of problems for him to take care of and she tried to control not only what he did but how he did it and when he did it and even how he felt about

doing it. Almost every night going to sleep he planned ways to kill himself.

- One woman's partner topped everything she said. If she said she was tired, her partner was completely exhausted. If she talked about applying for a new job in her company, her partner talked about making a major career move. These power moves made the woman feel like a nothing and put her on what she called the "choo-choo of misery": a train of depressing thoughts that began with her feeling she wasn't important and led to feeling that her life was a complete waste.

- One woman found that every time she cooked for her domineering husband she had vivid, persisting fantasies of poisoning his food and his dying in pain.

- One man's partner constantly ordered him about but did so in a polite, even seemingly sweet way so that she made him furious, and yet on the few occasions when he'd expressed his anger she'd made him feel so completely in the wrong that for years he swallowed his anger and yet it stayed with him like a hastily swallowed, undercooked doughnut.

GUIDELINE #8

If your partner gives you a basic, recurring, never-completely-going-away feeling of humiliation or invisibility, then you're in the kind of situation that people report they were happy they left and unhappy they stayed in. *Quick take:* Humiliation is the barometer of hatred.

Humiliation is an important clue to the fact that your partner's ability to dominate you has made the relationship too bad to stay in. And you measure humiliation by the degree to which your thoughts are filled with fantasies of violence toward the other person or toward yourself, the degree to which you go through your days blue or furious. Just as important, these thoughts or feelings seem to be correlated with contact between you and your partner, typically increasing just before, during, or after any humiliating interaction.

The Humiliation Trap

You have to beware of the humiliation that comes from being in a relationship with a power person. If you don't understand the degree to which it's destroying your happiness and peace of mind, it will keep you trapped in that relationship and trapped in ambivalence about that relationship.

Those violent fantasies and angry feelings seduce you into schemes of revenge, like a gambler obsessed with the thought of recouping his losses. Instead of pushing you out of the relationship, they suck you more deeply into it, because you develop the sick sense that recovering your pride and satisfaction lies in dominating or at least undermining the person who's put the whammy on you for so long. That's the humiliation trap.

And it works the same way with feelings of invisibility. Someone who makes you feel as though you don't exist, as though you were nothing, can trap you into endless efforts to get his attention. Unfortunately, you can grab someone's attention most effectively by acting sick or crazy. This is so common that whenever I see someone in therapy who's been acting sick or crazy or self-destructive in any attention-grabbing way I check to see if they're in a relationship with someone who makes them feel like they're nothing.

It's a mistake to think that unhappy, unsatisfying relationships generally end in divorce. Sometimes they dig both partners more deeply into marriage. There are many long-term marriages in which both people are slaves of hatred and misery. And many of them began with the ensnaring drama of power and humiliation.

It's hard for most of us to go through a typical day outside the home without some humiliating incident, however trivial, without some frustrating reminder of how limited our power is, how unimportant we are. The relationships we want to spend our lives in should be a refuge from this. If they are just a source of more humiliation, they're not healthy places to stay in.

Guideline #8 makes clear that you won't be happy if you stay in a relationship where you generally end up feeling like a nothing and a nobody, and you will be happy if you leave. The reason I've talked about the humiliation trap is to warn you about the forces that might keep you stuck in a situation like this even though it hurts you so much. There's no way you can win by staying. In that sense it's not different from physical abuse.

But the sense of release and relief that comes from getting out of a relationship like this is enormous.

7

Talk to Me

Issue: Communication

"We just can't communicate."

"We never have anything to talk about."

"We just don't understand each other."

People have long recognized that something about communication is the lifeblood of a relationship. A breakdown in communication is one of those signs, like a child's fever, that sends people running for help. That much is clear.

But so much else about communication is confusing, particularly when you're trying to figure out if you'll be happier leaving or happier staying. For example, when there's bad communication, is the communication bad because you're not getting along or are you not getting along because the communication's bad?

If your partner can't listen to you, is that because you're not communicating effectively or because of what you're talking about or because of your partner's anger or what?

And when there's bad communication, what part's fixable and what part's fatal? What just looks bad on the outside and what really is bad on the inside?

And there are so many kinds of bad communication. There's the kind that kills relationships. There's bad communication that's a pain in the neck but doesn't really damage relationships. And there's bad communication that's nothing more than the way people interact in normal relationships.

CONFUSED ABOUT COMMUNICATION

No wonder we're all so confused. To make matters worse, part of us really does want to work at communicating as clearly and effectively as possible, but another part of us feels we're entitled to relax, be our sloppily communicating selves, and let the chips fall where they may. Isn't there a part of all of us that's tired of working on our relationships?

All these communication issues are important because just the way someone with a really bad cold can look sicker and feel sicker than someone who has a fatal cancer, someone in a basically healthy relationship can sometimes be a lot more troubled by their communication than someone in a relationship that's truly too bad to stay in. In fact, sometimes when things are at their worst you're so eager to avoid talking about anything difficult that you *don't* talk about anything difficult, and that gives you the illusion that things are better than they really are.

So, since you're trying to figure out what's best for you to do, we'd better get a handle on exactly what it is about your communication that would point to the need for you to leave your relationship. *Everyone* has problems with communication in relationships. But you need to know if your problems are the kind that are both unfixable and relationship destroying.

Let's sort this all out.

THE DIAGNOSTIC NEEDLE IN THE HAYSTACK OF COMMUNICATION

When it comes to communication we're all stark naked. I might have to guess about or probe for everything else, but in all the years I've worked with couples, communication has been the one thing that's always been right out there in the open. And that's great. When couples finally get to the point where they can tell the truth and hear the truth and convey their needs and get close without making a mess and without making each other miserable, I know they're on the road to working things out.

The problem is that there's so much communicating—good and bad—going on every minute that zeroing in on what's absolutely critical is very difficult. So let me tell you how I found the diagnostic needle in the haystack of communication.

Soon after I started researching this issue I was confronted by two separate piles of impressive candidates, from which I was sure I'd find those signs of fatally bad communication that point to the exits. I labeled one pile *alien communication*—problems caused by two people being very different from one another. I labeled the other *crazy communication*—problems caused by confused, vague, misleading, misconceived words and gestures. These piles contain important communication issues that many of us are overwhelmingly aware of.

But the two piles of candidates proved to be far less helpful than I'd thought in diagnosing relationships. We need to take a moment to talk about them because they figure so prominently in our minds as "relationship destroyers." Let's take them one at a time, before we get to the communication issues that really do determine whether it's best to stay or leave.

Alien Communication

There are more gulfs separating people than you can find in an atlas. But the gulfs that have been getting the most attention recently have been gender gulfs. We'll focus on these gender gulfs here but the point I'm making about them applies to all of our differences.

There's a current fad running around this country where we all get excited talking about how utterly, profoundly, interplanetarily different men and women are. One of my daughters called me the other day, excited because she was reading a book all her friends were reading that "explained everything" to her: The book kept revealing the wide chasms between men and women. Certainly every woman who's ever felt her husband's basically a Martian—and what woman hasn't?—has felt validated by these books. He *is* a Martian! There's been a lot of emphasis on communication differences like the following:

- A man's trying to fix a faucet. The woman makes "helpful" suggestions. She's trying to communicate that she cares, but the message he receives is that he's not competent to do the job without her help.
- A woman's trying to fill out a tax form. The man leaves her completely alone. What he's trying to communicate is his sense that she can do it herself and his support for her doing it herself. But the message she receives is that he just doesn't care about her.

Because so many of us are such big fans of linking miscommunication with gender these days, you can probably supply endless examples of your own to illustrate this issue.

Now I have no doubt that differences between people, like this gender difference, can make getting along harder. *But they don't kill relationships nor are they signs of dead relationships.*

Alien communication is something we can live with. We've been living with male/female differences since we evolved from the amoeba stage, and we've gotten along so far. An overemphasis on gender differences obscures how skilled we are at bridging these differences. There are plenty of happy heterosexual couples who have few communication problems and yet are just as definitively masculine and feminine as unhappy heterosexual couples with communication problems. And homosexual couples, with no male/female differences to worry about, fall into the miscommunication soup just as easily as everyone else.

I think the real problem in relationships isn't how untalented we are at bridging our differences; it's how incredibly talented we are at manufacturing differences out of nothing if necessary, just to create a sense of differentiation, uniqueness, specialness. Besides, communication is the one thing in the universe specifically designed to bridge the gap between our differences. If we're having trouble with that bridge, partly it's because we're so interested in magnifying those differences. But communication is the solution, not the problem.

To get right down to brass tacks, I've never seen a couple for whom inability to throw lines of communication across the sexual gulf was so severe and so unfixable that they just had to give up on each other, not without a lot of far more serious, far different problems. On the day that heterosexuality itself makes heterosexual relationships impossible, the human race is in big trouble. I don't think we're there yet.

The same applies for communication across all of our differences. Talking about differences when it comes to communication is like talking about rivers when it comes to bridges. Rivers are what bridges are designed to cross. And differences are the reason we have communication in the first place.

Crazy Communication

At least it's fun to talk about "he said, she said." We get to play "me Tarzan, you Jane," and that's always a turn-on. The other pile of candidates is a lot more serious. It's what I loosely call *crazy communication*, where confused, unclear, misleading, misconceived words and gestures cause the problems.

I'm not talking about communication by crazy people. I'm talking about communication that makes people crazy. Like when someone talks and you can't figure out why they're saying what they're saying. Or they act like they're disclosing something but you feel like they're hiding something. Or they answer something you say but for the life of you you can't figure out what their answer has to do with what you said. Or they're telling you something and yet you're absolutely convinced they're asking you for something and yet they deny they're asking you for something.

This is very different from alien communication. Here's the difference. Alien communication is where one person says there's a tiger in the grass and the other says grab your gun and the first person says I don't need you to tell me what to do, I know to get the gun, I need you to understand what I'm going through. Crazy communication is where someone sees a tiger in the grass and

says, "What do you think about tigers?" Or you say you see a tiger and as if that would reassure you he says, "What tiger?" or
even tries to convince you there is no tiger. Or he sees a tiger and
starts talking about how all these tigers make him really sad. Or
he sees a tiger and asks you where you put the airline tickets.

Mary and James's Story

The essence of crazy communication is that when it's going on
you don't know what the other person is really saying or why
they're saying it. Believe it or not, crazy communication like this
is infinitely more common than alien communication. It's just a
lot less noticeable, except when there are tigers around.

Meet Mary and James. They might give you hope. All they
had to do was open their mouths and there would be instant total
confusion. They always miscommunicated, and yet they never
stopped being amazed by their miscommunications because they
came from the same Irish Catholic background, same neighbor-
hood, same parish, and had the same friends growing up. Pick
either Mary or James, and you'd find someone who made communication messes.

It doesn't matter whom you start with. This particular example just happens to start with Mary . . . or does it?

As a school nurse Mary would be home from work early. As
a truck owner-driver James would show up later. On this particular day, he brought his rig home, turned it off, and just sat in it.
Mary saw this and wondered why he wasn't coming in. Then she
started getting suspicious. Was he hiding? she wondered. Was he
afraid? There was crazy communication already and no one had
said a word.

After a while James finally walked through the front door.
Money'd been tight, he was supposed to have gotten paid, and
his sitting in the truck had made her nervous, so Mary led off
with, "Did you get the check?"

This was crazy. You're supposed to say, "Hi, honey, how was
your day?" aren't you? Why would she have asked about the
check like that if she didn't want to open hostilities, James and

others among us might wonder, even though we understand her anxiety.

"What check?" James said. He's got the check in his pocket! But he already feels third-degreed and mistrusted. He acts like he's got to defend himself even though there's nothing to defend. This, too, was crazy. So what if she threw him with her question? He could've answered it anyway. He could've said it made him mad. But he shouldn't have spun off in his own crazy direction. I can tell you from my own direct clinical experience that those five words—*where's the check? what check?*—started the biggest fight that had absolutely no content or direction that you can imagine.

But as bad a problem as this is, it is fixable. James and Mary eventually learned to communicate beautifully. This kind or any kind of crazy communication is just not necessarily in itself a sign of a relationship that's too bad to stay in. It's not always fixable and it can sometimes destroy a relationship, but if there's crazy communication (and I've seen few relationships without it), you can go on to discover how much amazing progress you can make toward learning to communicate in a healthy way.

So we've found that some of the conventional wisdom about how poor communication destroys relationships is wrong. What then *are* the real culprits?

STEP #9: OFF-THE-TABLE-ITIS

There's a kind of regenerative property in healthy communication, something in it that allows it to function as the interpersonal equivalent of whatever it is that allows a starfish to grow a new point when one breaks off. This regenerative property exists even in the face of obstacles like alien communication and crazy communication.

You can see a really good fictional example of this regenerative property in the movie *Enemy Mine*, directed by Wolfgang Petersen and starring Dennis Quaid and Lou Gossett, Jr. It's about two space travelers from warring planets who get stranded on some asteroid together, just the two of them. Not only can't they speak the other's language, but they're of different species and each has a mandate to kill the other. But because of communication's awesome ability to build bridges across distances and difficulties, they're eventually able to talk to each other and build a good working relationship.

The movie may be science fiction, but the principle it illustrates is pure science. I arrived in this country as a little girl of four speaking no English. I was immediately put in a nursery school with other kids from other countries. Almost none of us spoke each other's language. Yet within weeks, even days, we were all bridging every imaginable gap of background and culture and playing together like kids who'd all been born on the same block.

This brings me back to my search for the diagnostic needle in the haystack of communication. I realized that if there were something about communication that made a relationship too bad to stay in, it would have to be something that damaged its regenerative capacity. It would have to be something that damaged communication's bridge-building function. And in fact my work with men and women who were going through what you're going through has shown me that my hunch was absolutely correct.

Do you want to find a true villain in the drama of communication? Look at what I call *off-the-table-itis*. This comes from an expression people use in talking about negotiation. It refers to someone taking something "off the table" when he doesn't want to talk about an issue. Off-the-table-itis occurs when someone *keeps* taking things off the table, when someone *keeps* not wanting to talk about issues.

Off-the-table-itis kills relationships. Or perhaps I should say partners with off-the-table-itis kill relationships. I'll show you how in a moment. But first here's the question that tests for it:

Diagnostic question #9. **Does it seem to you that your partner generally and consistently blocks your attempts to bring up topics or raise questions, particularly about things you care about?**

He can do this directly and openly: "I don't want to talk about that."

He can do this less directly and openly: "Okay, but what about . . . ," and the next thing you know you're talking about something completely different.

He can do this threateningly: "If you keep pushing me to talk about that, I just don't want to be in this relationship."

He can disguise his off-the-table-itis with emotional abuse, making you seem somehow stupid or weird or in the wrong for even mentioning certain things that are important to you.

He can even take things off the table with such extreme politeness you don't even know it's happening: "That's a wonderful question and I'm so happy you brought it up, but I'm really going to need time to think about it," except that thinking about it takes forever.

I don't want to go overboard with this. It's not off-the-table-itis if it's simply hard for your partner to talk about something you want to talk about. It's not off-the-table-itis if you merely sense his reluctance. And I'm certainly *not* saying that if he refuses to talk about something once or twice or occasionally because he's in a bad mood or because your timing is bad that you've got a problem with off-the-table-itis.

It's off-the-table-itis only when your attempts to communicate are rejected over and over, so that you feel genuinely discouraged from ever bringing it up again.

And it's *not* off-the-table-itis if your partner simply doesn't know that he's doing it and stops when you point it out to him. If you say something like, "You know, you never want to talk about sex," and your partner says, "Gee, you're right, I'm sorry. Let's talk about sex," it's not off-the-table-itis. But if he consistently denies taking something off the table or makes you feel in the wrong for wanting to put it on the table, that *is* off-the-table-itis.

Diagnosing Off-the-table-itis

You might find yourself saying yes! right away to question #9. But I'm concerned about the cases of off-the-table-itis that people don't realize are happening. When someone tells you consistently to shut up, it makes you mad in the short run but over time you get numb to it.

But off-the-table-itis is often done in extremely hard-to-detect ways. It's not really surprising, when you think about it, that one of the hallmarks of people who take topics off the table is that they take off the table the possibility of talking about how they take things off the table. The subtleties are infinite. But off-the-table-itis destroys relationships anyway. To help you see it in action, here are some snapshots of off-the-table-itis:

- Suppose there are sexual difficulties between you and your partner that you'd like to start talking about. But when you say, "I'd like to talk about how we don't make love so much anymore," your partner gets upset and literally says, "Oh, I hate talking about that. I just don't want to talk about it." And he says it so vehemently and firmly that you just feel squashed. That's off-the-table-itis.

- Every time you talk about how you feel about something, he sighs or he changes the subject or he reads the newspaper or turns to the TV or pets the dog or is busy lighting a cigarette or gets something to eat or does anything else to move away or shut you up. That's off-the-table-itis.

- You're both working far too hard and have no time for each other, and yet you're not bringing in enough money to cover your overhead. The only way you can solve this is changing your lives in some important way. But whenever you bring this up your partner constantly throws the conversation into one distracting sidetrack after another, so that you keep skirting around talking about what you're

supposed to be talking about while these distractions mean
you never actually do talk about it. That's off-the-table-itis.

- You agreed that giving each other feedback is a good idea,
  but whenever you give your partner feedback, although
  she says she wants to hear it, she criticizes so many things
  about the way you do it and when you do it that you
  feel forced to drop your efforts. That's off-the-table-itis.

- The man you've been seeing for the last year seems
  interested in having a relationship with you, but he never
  says I love you and in fact is never really affectionate in
  any way outside of sex. You try to bring this up and he
  listens politely and then tells you how interesting,
  fascinating, intriguing everything you're saying is, how
  much you're giving him to think about, and he promises
  to think about it but he never gets back to you, and when
  you ask him about it he always says politely that he needs
  more time to think about it. That's off-the-table-itis.

- Your partner's in charge of paying bills and as far as you
  can tell she's been doing a poor job. And that makes
  you angry and nervous. You say, "We really need to talk
  about the way you pay bills." She doesn't refuse to talk
  about it, but she acts so miserable that the experience is
  an ordeal and you're sorry you ever brought it up. That's
  off-the-table-itis.

- Whenever you talk about anything important to you,
  your partner sits there and says little, but there's an
  impenetrable, stony quality to his "listening" that
  overwhelms you with the sense that your words are
  reaching his ears and yet he's never allowing them to get
  inside his head. That's off-the-table-itis.

- You talk about some need or problem you have. Your
  partner responds by telling you what's wrong with you for
  having that need or problem. He can do it in a gross way
  with some general putdown. Or he can do it subtlely
  by suggesting that whatever it is you're expressing is a sign

of some kind of psychopathology or childhood trauma or being "just like your mother" or some other problem you have that has nothing to do with what you're wanting to talk about. That's off-the-table-itis.

* You come home from work and want to talk about your job because there's so much going on you just can't sort it out by yourself. But your partner gets restless and impatient after five minutes. She tells you point-blank that she's just not interested in all the office politics and career issues that so preoccupy you. She points out that her father did extremely well in his career without any help from her mother. That's off-the-table-itis.

I could go on and on with examples like these. But it's important for you to develop a sense of all the not-easily-detectable ways people we're in a relationship with can shut down communication. You don't always know it when it happens. But you do feel something. You have to play back in your own mind what whizzed by you to see clearly how what you just felt was connected to your partner's taking off the table what you cared about. In fact, the more successful your partner is at taking things off the table, the better he is at making sure you don't know that he's doing it.

Going Too Far

It's time for the guideline, but we've got to be careful. Off-the-table-itis in its milder, more occasional forms is like the common cold: a huge pain in the neck but not necessarily fatal. So if your partner's taking things off the table weakens in response to your efforts to put them back on the table, that's a good sign. And if the more important something is to you, the less likely your partner is to take it off the table, that's a good sign. And if there's only one or two hot-button issues that your partner takes off the table, that's a good sign. But here's where you have to draw the line:

GUIDELINE #9

If your partner constantly and unyieldingly prevents you from talking about things that are important to you, so that you have a sense of being shut down and shut up, then you're faced with a destructive problem that will not get better by itself. I feel comfortable saying you'll be happiest if you leave. *Quick take:* You'll suffocate if the dirt hits the fan whenever you try to shoot the breeze.

If you feel this guideline applies to you, don't do anything yet. Sometimes it's hard to tell the difference between a real monster and someone who's basically fair but has little self-awareness. So you've got to make a test. When you see a way your partner takes things off the table, point it out.

Say for example, "Whenever I want to talk about visiting my family [or whatever the issue is], you get so upset that I feel I'm not even permitted to bring it up." Maybe you'll make progress letting your partner know what he's doing. Then guideline #9 doesn't apply to you. But maybe your partner will just find another way to make it impossible for you to talk about what's important to you. If holding up a mirror to your partner does nothing to diminish his tendency to shut down communication, then you're confirmed in your sense that you'll be happier leaving.

There's one exception to this guideline. You just might be doing something that fosters your partner's off-the-table-itis. You might be one of those people who absolutely refuse to take no for an answer. No matter how clearly an issue's been discussed and decided, for these people the issue remains open forever and they keep bringing it up.

For example, one woman had a full, frank, and open discussion with her husband about her wanting to spend money to remodel the house. He was very open to talking about it with her and showed her how they simply couldn't afford it at that time. She understood what he was talking about and even agreed with him. But then she wouldn't let it drop. She kept bringing up an already-decided issue over and over. Naturally he didn't want to keep talking about it. That's not off-the-table-itis.

The Problem That Makes Problems

Why am I making such a big deal about off-the-table-itis? Every relationship has disagreements, but when disagreements are ruled out of order and not allowed to get aired, there's an even more basic problem that can't be fixed. How can you fix something you can't even talk about because your partner takes things off the table by getting mad or miserable when you bring them up, or only listens to you with an unyielding refusal to let anything in?

A pattern like this is highly resistant to change because it rules *itself* off the table. It's the communication problem that prevents the solving of every other problem.

Your partner's off-the-table-itis is particularly destructive because of the way it so often focuses on your attempts to give feedback. Feedback is the simple ability to say, "I like this," "I don't like that," "This hurts me," "That doesn't hurt me." This airing of feelings is the oxygen that relationships need to be able to breathe. Without it they suffocate, because without it things go from good to bad to worse without anyone being able to do anything to turn the situation around.

When someone blocks your attempt to give feedback—by getting hurt, by getting angry, by turning the tables and launching into a tirade about what's wrong with you, by simply refusing to listen—it's as if he were putting up a huge sign that said, "I just don't care if this is a relationship that feels good to you."

I see how utterly devastating off-the-table-itis is every day. It's like the difference between a dog and a wolf. Some relationships are like a dog: even a really dumb dog can learn some tricks. But a wolf, however bright and beautiful, refuses to be tamed. He might be magnificent in nature but you can't have him in your house: his wildness precludes any attempt to train him. He won't allow himself to be influenced.

In a nutshell, it's not the things that make communication

difficult that make a relationship too bad to stay in. Even if it's an uphill battle, you can still win it. It's the things that make communication *impossible* that make a relationship too bad to stay in. Off-the-table-itis is one of them.

Now imagine if there were something that went even further, that not only prevented communication but actually subtracted from it. That's our next question, and we'll get to it after we put off-the-table-itis in perspective as part of the central drama in relationships.

PERSPECTIVES: SAFETY FIRST

Some people are surprised that something like off-the-table-itis is so important in pointing to a relationship that's too bad to stay in. It's bad, they say, but it doesn't sound totally horrible. Why are you emphasizing it?

Let me put it in context. Here's something that I believe is at the heart of what goes on in relationships and at the heart of what's necessary to fix relationships:

Telling someone something means revealing something. So in a sense, communication is a process of getting naked. Not physically, but interpersonally. The closer you are to someone, the closer communication brings you to this interpersonal nakedness. And love is the place where it's safe to be naked. Everywhere else in our lives we have to put on half-masks of politeness, regardless of how we really feel. But part of the experience of falling in love and being in love is taking off these masks.

Of course we take off our clothes as part of physical intimacy, but we let our hair down in other ways as well, confessing secrets and showing parts of ourselves no one else in the world sees. So we're not just naked physically but also naked emotionally and naked as who we really are as people. And not only does love mean feeling safe as you get naked, it means relaxing into feeling more safe the more naked you get.

But this doesn't mean you have to get totally naked in every possible way. People also need boundaries, and some people need more boundaries than others. For example, many people will never feel comfortable with their partner's being in the same room while they go to the bathroom. And there's nothing wrong with that. But if there are so many boundaries and they're so high that your relationship is more about hiding and distance than openness and closeness, then your relationship is a place where it's not safe to be naked.

The problem is that when you're naked you're also vulnerable. People can get hurt when they reveal themselves. The things people say and do to reveal themselves can create problems, fear, and pain instead of safety. So I've learned that no matter what problems people bring into therapy and no matter what other issues I work on with them, I've also got to make their relationship a place where each person learns how to *find* safety being himself (for example, "I can reveal my goofy sense of humor without getting mocked") while *providing* safety for the other person to be herself (for example, "I learned how to stop making you feel it's not okay for you to be in a bad mood once in a while").

Shut Up and Put Your Clothes On

Balancing nakedness and safety can be difficult for some people to handle. If it's too difficult, then that's a relationship that's too bad to stay in. And understanding *why* it can be too difficult can help you understand *why* a relationship can be too bad to stay in.

If love is the place where it's safe to be naked, then every relationship is an attempt to answer these questions:

- Can I be safe when you're naked? Will I still feel comfortable when you let your hair down and show yourself for who you really are and say what you feel and do what you really want?
- Can I be naked and yet you still feel safe? Can I reveal through word and deed who I really am and how I really feel without making you feel uncomfortable?

Let's take just one issue: expressing anger. Kiesha, a twenty-eight-year-old police officer, felt that her anger was something very deep and personal, something to share only with someone she was very intimate with. So for her feeling safe enough to feel emotionally naked meant getting to the point of feeling free to show her anger. But for her partner Dennis, a fireman, feeling safe meant feeling protected from her anger.

What made this so hard for them to deal with was the fact that Dennis's being emotionally naked in the relationship meant feeling free to say how really uncomfortable he felt with Kiesha's expressions of anger. But for Kiesha to feel safe, she needed to feel protected from Dennis's saying things that made her feel bad about having her feelings.

You can see how your needs for nakedness and safety and your partner's different needs for nakedness and safety can get so tangled up, regardless of the issues you're trying to deal with. The things that you long to feel safe enough *to* reveal might be the very things your partner wants to feel safe *from* having revealed to him.

Balancing Act

All couples try to balance safety and nakedness. Usually they find a way to work it out. They do so because each person recognizes that they both have to feel safe while they're both being naked. That's the kind of place love is.

But sometimes people come into a relationship with a need for safety that overwhelms their partner's ability to provide safety. This extra need for safety can come from needing to feel safe *from* the other person (from insults, rejections, attempts at control) and in needing to feel safe *in* themselves to do what they want. If one person's extra need for safety is so great that he can't allow the other person to both feel safe and do what she wants, that's a relationship that's too bad to stay in.

Off-the-table-itis fits right into this. The person who takes things off the table is basically saying that your getting naked—by showing the issues that are important to you and showing your need to resolve them—makes him unsafe. So he tries, consciously or unconsciously, to make you unsafe by not letting you talk about it.

Question #1 asked if things were good when they were at their best and question #5 asked if there was one thing you and your partner did together that felt good and that you looked forward to. That is the issue of *pleasure*.

Now I've just talked about the issue of *safety*. This, too, came up before, for example in question #2 when you were asked if you'd been physically abused and in the previous chapter when we talked about power people and your being in a relationship where it's not safe to have any needs.

These twin issues of pleasure and safety will keep coming up over and over as the underpinnings of what makes a relationship too good to leave or too bad to stay in.

STEP #10: TO TELL THE TRUTH

Off-the-table-itis is bad because it prevents communication. Lying is bad because it subtracts from communication. If someone lies to you, then you're worse off than you were before. Before, you just didn't know. After the lie, you think you know but you're wrong. Lying is to communication what murder is to life. Both are a taking away of what's real and precious. Murder is worse, of course, because you can always bring the truth back to life, and yet we feel almost the same loathing for real liars as we do for murderers.

But there's a paradox. Almost all of us lie, from little white lies to spur-of-the-moment lies to protecting-the-innocent lies to just-not-telling-everything lies to it's-all-for-the-best lies to saving-your-butt lies. Some of us lie more than others, but Diogenes attests to how difficult it is to find someone who never lies. So if the fact that you've caught your partner in a lie were grounds for ending a relationship, we'd all be alone.

And that's the problem we have to sort out here: how to find our way between the fact that lying is the norm and the fact that

lying is the worst possible thing that can happen in communication, even worse than off-the-table-itis.

The key here is safety. The fact that most people lie a little
makes most of us feel okay with the idea that our partner might
lie from time to time, especially if they're just little white lies. As
long as we can say, "Well, he'd never lie to me about anything really important," most of us aren't too upset.

But when you lose your basic trust that the other generally
tells the truth, there's a fundamental obstacle to your relationship
ever being satisfying. And so the next question is:

**Diagnostic question #10. Have you gotten to the
point, when your partner says something, that you
usually feel it's more likely that he's lying than that
he's telling the truth?**

Some people get to this point if they catch their partner in even
one big lie. Others can tolerate a lot of little white lies and even
a few big lies. But wherever you draw the line, the question is
whether you've gotten to the point where, if you had to bet,
you'd bet that what your partner says is a lie.

Ronnie's Story

Crabs don't lie. That may be their only virtue, but for Ronnie it
was the kind of virtue she'd been looking for for a long time.

Hal, Ronnie's husband, was her pride and joy as well as her
biggest disappointment. He'd grown up in what he called the
town of Nowheresville, Rural State, USA. But he had the look
and the voice and the ambition for doing TV news, as well as the
luck of there being a small TV station nearby. While he was still
in high school he got a job reporting the news on weekends. The
day he graduated he became one of their regular reporters.
There was little money and not much prestige in that job, but
Hal felt he was on his way to bigger and better things.

After a couple of years of sending tapes around Hal landed

a job with a major market TV station. That's when Ronnie met him. She was an image consultant for a local department store, and Hal needed her badly because he was still the boy from Nowheresville and he had none of the polish and manner he needed in the big city. Ronnie taught him everything, from how to dress to how to comb his hair to how to behave in a restaurant. They soon got more and more involved with each other and fell in love.

Was their relationship doomed from the start? I don't know, but by the time I saw them a lot of damage had been done. Ronnie had been blinded for a long time by Hal's charm. She was also profoundly misled by how well he took to her coaching. Most of her friends could barely change anything about the men they were involved with. It seemed to Ronnie she could change everything about Hal. Except, she found out, his propensity for lying.

It was his talent for lying that prevented her from seeing, for many years, how often he did exactly what he wanted to do whenever he wanted to do it no matter how it affected anyone else. He saw himself as a future TV news star and thought he was entitled to get now as a young man what he might have to wait many more years to get.

At first Ronnie was aware of only a couple of lies, like his saying he was on assignments when he was out with the guys. Then there were a series of misdeeds, nothing really terrible but all reasons to be angry and disappointed, such as large, selfish expenditures of money, all protected by a cocoon of lies.

And as the cycle of screwing up and lying about it worked its way forward, there were repeated breakups and reunitings and a baby and another breakup and another baby and a coming back together yet again. An all-too-typical tale of relationship ambivalence enacted not in the seesaw motions of the heart but on the canvas of life.

The last time they came back together, Hal made promises that Ronnie wanted to believe because Hal always seemed like such a nice guy. She couldn't believe what he said, and yet she couldn't admit that she couldn't believe him.

That's when the crabs entered the picture. How could she

have possibly gotten pubic lice? She knew she hadn't been with anyone else. She asked Hal and he said he had crabs, too. Where did you get them from, she asked. A public toilet, he said.

But Ronnie knew this was impossible. The crabs were telling a truth that Hal was unable to tell. Ronnie could no longer lie to herself about the fact that she knew that Hal was a liar. And that she'd have to assume that anything he said would be a lie.

What devastated Ronnie was the terrible waste of years. It's not just that the relationship hadn't worked out but that she'd stayed in it years after she realized that if Hal said something it was probably a lie, years before the day of the crabs.

Here's the guideline for question #10:

GUIDELINE #10

If you find yourself thinking, "He's probably lying," whenever your partner says anything, or even if you just find there's a tightening in your gut that indicates you're expecting a lie, nothing good is going to happen for you in that relationship. Everyone else in this situation is happier leaving and you'll be happier, too. *Quick take:* When you're married to a liar, your marriage is a lie.

Let me make something clear about this guideline. In a troubled relationship, one person often catches the other in a big lie, such as when one of them has been having an affair. But being found guilty of a big lie is not a relationship-ending offense, not necessarily anyway. Relationships can recover from someone telling a big lie. Yes, trust can be easily damaged, but unless it's completely destroyed it can still be rebuilt.

Guideline #10 doesn't refer to the person who's told one big lie; it refers to the person you believe may be lying almost whenever he talks to you. It's not about how "bad" what he did was; it's about how bad an impact what he's done has had on you, and not just one lie but the pattern of lying.

So you have to be careful with this guideline. The fact that someone's lied to you can make you feel very angry and very mistrustful and very unsafe. It's natural after being told a big lie to go through a period of being convinced that everything else your partner says is a lie, and maybe everything he's ever said to you has been a lie.

But you've got to distinguish between your emotional reactions, which may or may not be warranted and from which you may or may not recover, and an abiding gut sense that if you had to make a bet, you'd say your partner was lying when he opened his mouth.

A Life of Lies

Why are most people happier when they leave if they answer yes to question #10? It's because of what it does to you to live with someone you're convinced is more likely lying than telling the truth. You're headed for a state of bitterness, paranoia, and despair. Your world will turn nightmarish. The only way you'll manage to feel safe if you stay is to disconnect so profoundly from your partner that it'll be as if you've ended your relationship anyway. You might as well in fact do now, cleanly, what you'll do in spirit later, painfully.

And the lying won't get better. As things between you become more difficult, your partner will have just that much more incentive to lie.

As one woman who'd left a man she'd come to see as a liar said, "Every day in my new life on my own is a treat because, no matter what, I know the person I am living with—me—will always tell the truth."

8

What Is This Thing Called Love?

Issue: Is There Real Love Left?

LOOKING FOR LOVE IN ALL THE RIGHT PLACES

Sometimes when a relationship is hanging by a thread, it's a thread of love. Much in the relationship is bad, only a little is good, but the one thing that keeps you hanging in there is that love connection, that thing you say to yourself: "But I love him [or her]."

This is one of the reasons the balance-scale approach to deciding whether to stay or leave drives people crazy. For more than twenty years, people have come into my consulting room carrying their relationship cupped in their hands like a sick puppy, telling me incredible stories of misery, disappointment, and disaster, giving me every reason to believe the relationship could not survive without life support, that they didn't even want it to survive.

"It sounds like you know what's best for you," I say. The balance scale seems totally tilted toward leaving.

And then they reach into their hearts and take out the love that's left and place it on the other side of the balance scale, and that hunk of love has for them a weight as heavy as gold on Jupiter and tilts everything the other way. For people in this situation, love indeed seems to conquer all, even in some cases the putrefying realities of a dead relationship.

But is it dead? Doesn't any amount of love heavy enough to register in our hearts have the power to keep a relationship alive? Aren't you obligated to stay in any relationship where you feel you love the other person?

Or can our feelings sometimes be illusions? Is the love that feels so real and hefty sometimes merely the ghost of dead hopes and dreams?

Yet we feel our love. And haven't therapists like me spent our professional lives helping people learn to trust their feelings? Can I ever say don't trust your feelings to anyone?

So let's talk about those relationships where it feels as though only your saying "But I love him [or her]" prevents the relationship from clearly being too bad to stay in. Let's see if we can find a way to decide how real and strong that love is, to determine how much of a difference it really makes.

Too Jung to Be in Love

You're not alone in being confused by love. Most therapists are so confused by it they just throw up their hands. In one of the most influential textbooks on marital therapy—*Helping Couples Change*—the author's bibliography refers to almost 100,000 pages of material that went into his book, and yet the word *love* barely appears in the text or in any of the references. In the invaluable *Handbook of Family Therapy*, love is mentioned once and then as only one of *forty-two* components of marriage. Love is one forty-secondth of marriage!

Other therapists take a stab at it and then throw up their hands. In his autobiography, *Memories, Dreams, Reflections*, Carl Jung says, quoting the New Testament, that, "Love 'bears all things' and 'endures all things.'" Jung feels these words "say all there is to be said" about love. But then he has the honesty to admit, "In my medical experience as well as in my own life I have again and again been faced with the mystery of love, and have never been able to explain what it is."

Jung and other therapists are responsible enough to admit that they're thrown by the word *love*. Other people just throw the word around. All I know is that whatever this thing called love is, it can be terribly confusing, particularly for people on whom it weighs most heavily.

Nothing More Than Feelings

Let's sort this all out, so you can see what to do with the love you feel, so you can decide if your relationship is too good to leave or too bad to stay in.

Earlier we talked about the preconditions for love, because most people are not happy staying in a relationship with someone they couldn't possibly fall in love with now. What we'll do now is test for whether your feelings have a foundation of personal truth. You can always trust *that* you feel what you feel, but you have to be extremely careful to check out what's really *making* you feel the way you do.

To understand what it really means to trust your feelings, you have to understand how feelings work. Here's a quick way of understanding this that I've found most helpful, not just professionally but personally as well.

Let's go back about ten thousand years to visit our primitive ancestors. Here's the sequence that will show the context in which feelings have their special place. It's just one example, but the stages themselves are eternal:

Stage 1: Reality. A tiger is creeping toward you through the grass.
Stage 2: Perception. "A tiger is creeping toward me through the grass!"
Stage 3: A feeling. "Yikes!" Fear of tiger.
Stage 4: Action. You get your butt in gear and get the hell out of there.

Every feeling anyone's ever had fits into this sequence. It makes clear how we get into trouble with our feelings. Notice that before we have the feeling "Fear of tiger" there should be a real tiger out there in the grass that we should be accurately perceiving.

There's a lot of talk about respecting all feelings, but, let's face it, you're going to feel pretty stupid feeling "fear of tiger" when you are correctly perceiving something but it's only, let's say, some joker in a fiendishly well-made tiger suit. And you're going to feel pretty stupid feeling "fear of tiger" when, like the proverbial hunter in deer season, you're misperceiving what's actually a zebra or a pussycat or a mother-in-law. No one can tell you what to feel, but for feelings to make sense they've got to be based on correctly perceiving something that's real.

Love, like any other feeling, fits into this sequence:

Stage 1: Reality. There's a person you meet and get to know. This person has real qualities.

Stage 2: Perception. "What a wonderful person with perfect qualities for me."

Stage 3: A feeling. "I'm in love!"

Stage 4: Action. You get more and more involved.

Your saying "But I love him [her]" is *only* a description of your feelings. It's not about what's really out there or your perceptions of what's out there. Love of John [or Jane] is a good thing, but only if you would actually feel love if you correctly perceived the real John [or Jane].

Feeling love doesn't mean that your perceptions are accurate or that the realities warrant your feelings. In other words, feelings are not necessarily appropriate just because you have them. Ask any scam victim who was tricked into misperceiving realities that didn't even exist in the first place.

STEP #11: YOU LIKE ME, YOU REALLY LIKE ME

If you're one of those people being kept in relationship ambivalence by love, let me help you make sure your feelings of love make sense given your realities.

Of course this whole book is designed to help you with this, but what we can focus on here is not the other person but love itself, whether you're really being stalked by the tiger of love or a paper tiger or a ghost tiger or no tiger at all.

Here's one of the best ways I know to get at whether love is dead. This question may be as familiar as a thermometer, but like a thermometer it has amazingly powerful diagnostic properties:

Diagnostic question #11. **In spite of admirable qualities, and stepping back from any temporary anger or disappointment, do you genuinely** *like* **your partner, and does your partner seem to like you?**

Just so we're clear, there are really two parts to question #11:

1. We've already established you don't find your partner nasty or stupid or crazy or ugly or stinky. But do you genuinely like your partner? I'm not asking if you'd be friends with your partner exactly the way you're friends with other people in your life. I'm not asking if you get along doing things like making meals or going shopping. I'm not asking if you like the same things. I'm not asking if this is always true every minute of every day. I'm just asking if, when it counts for you, you really like your partner the way you like a friend or someone else you feel comfortable and happy being with.

2. Does your partner seem to like you? I'm not asking you to get inside your partner's head or heart. Instead I'm asking how your partner makes you feel about how he feels about you. Does your partner act as though he likes you? Does your partner make you feel he likes you? I know there are periods of anger and hurt and distance between you, but does your partner convey to you the sense that he likes you outside of these periods?

These aren't always easy questions to answer. Let's see what we can learn from some people I call the Couple Who Tried Too Hard.

Ann's Story

Ann and Dave fell in love and married because they shared the same values. They met at a Quaker Meeting. They'd both been brought up as Quakers but had drifted away from it when they hit adolescence. They'd each been married briefly before to other people and they were trying to get back to their spiritual roots.

What initially drew them to each other was their discomfort with the political activism of some people at their Meetings. Ann and Dave were hungry for more spiritual experiences. When they first found each other, that hunger combined with the background they shared made it seem as though they were a perfect match: two good, kind, gentle, loving people hungry to connect with God, each comfortable knowing the other was right in his or her judgments.

In fact, they agreed so much and supported each other so strongly that, echoing Quaker ways of putting things, they got into the habit of constantly referring to each other as "my best friend."

I'll never forget the downright shame that burned in Ann's face when she came to me wondering how she could be so unhappy in a "perfect marriage" to someone who was her "best friend" that she "loved with all her heart." She didn't make sense to herself. How could all this be true and yet all she thought about was wanting to leave Dave? Surely something would have to be terribly wrong somewhere, probably with her, she thought, probably with some emptiness or coldness or deadness or rage in her soul that was shutting her down to love.

This Can't Be Love. Ann was perfectly willing to blame herself for anything and everything, but when I asked her to talk about her "best friend" the complaints poured out. Although she was careful to remember to point out the high values Dave had that she shared, she had nothing else good to say about him. Sure, he was eager to get close to God and heal the world, but to actually spend her days with, he was mean, complaining, cold, boring, disconnected from his feelings, uninterested in talking about their relationship. He couldn't talk about anyone without putting them down. And if you asked him what time it was, he'd build you a watch.

"But I love him," Ann said to me. "He's not a bad person. Is there something wrong with me that I can't stop wanting to leave him?"

This is actually a very common way people express their ambivalence. For them it's not the person's good qualities in one pile and bad qualities in the other. Instead it's all their qualities, all bad, in one pile, and in the other just a general sense that they're a good person and worthy of being loved.

The End of the Journey. I never know where these journeys are going to take me when I start, but the journey I went on with Ann kept leading me away from something being wrong with her. It led to Ann's need to give herself permission to get clear about this relationship and act on that clarity.

Eventually we got to the question I just asked you "Ann," I said, "I know you're a spiritual person and your values are very important to you, but speak from your gut feelings for a moment and tell me the truth. Do you like Dave? Do you have the sense that he likes you? I know you like the things he believes in that you agree with. But I'm remembering all the things you told me about him that aren't the things you say about someone you like [and I gave her some examples]. So when you really search your heart for how you feel about Dave minute by minute as you go through your days, do you actually like him?"

There was one of those long, long, long silences I've learned not to interrupt. Finally Ann said in a dry, quiet voice, "I don't think I've ever really liked him. I like what he likes. But I don't like him."

It was sad. It's always sad for me to see a relationship breathe its last breath. But it was particularly sad here because I'd seen how hard Ann had tried to like Dave over the years. She'd done so many things with him. The Couple Who Tried Too Hard had gone on pilgrimages and retreats together. They'd taken up joint hobbies. They'd gone to every couples workshop that hit town. In a way, all that trying had worked to Ann's disadvantage. The more she tried to like Dave, the harder it was for her to admit that she didn't like him.

What's the guideline for Ann and for you and for everyone in this situation?

GUIDELINE #11

If it's clear to you that basically and overall you just don't like your partner, then your love is a ghost, no matter what else you have going for you and no matter how loudly your heart cries out that you love him, and you'll be happiest if you leave. And if your partner makes it clear to you that he just doesn't like you, then in this case, too, you'll be happiest if you leave. *Quick take:* In the long run—no like, no love.

Virtually everyone I've encountered who was in a relationship where one person didn't like the other was happy they left or unhappy they stayed. If you're wondering whether you still love your partner or whether there's enough love left in your relationship, the quick take makes the answer clear.

The "Critical Incident"

How does it get clear to people that they don't like their partner? Sometimes you just know it. Sometimes, though, you need what I call a "critical incident" to make it clear. Before this you felt uncomfortable and maybe there were things about your partner you didn't like, but then that one incident comes along and highlights who he really is and how you really feel about him.

For example, one woman had been on the fence for a long time about whether she liked her husband, and her dislike centered around a crass, selfish quality of his that made her think of him as a guy who was all take, no give. But she made excuses about him or pointed to other more positive qualities of his that made it hard for her to admit she didn't like him.

Then they were at a country food fair where locals displayed free samples of homemade products they could ill-afford to give away. Her husband went up to one table and proceeded to gobble up all the pieces of cookies and cakes that had been put out as samples. The sheer, blind, gluttonous greed of this served as a critical incident that gave this woman permission to finally acknowledge that she truly did not like her husband.

If you really don't like your partner on balance and overall, either you'll just know it or a critical incident like this will suddenly make it clear.

A Time Trap

There's a time trap some people fall into with this issue. They get stuck waiting for not liking to turn into liking. On one level this makes some sense. We've all had the experience of meeting someone, not liking them at first, getting to know them better, and then finding we like them a lot. That's what happened to me with my husband. The first hour or so after we met, he seemed so opinionated that I didn't like him. But then the more I learned about him, the more I liked him. There are studies to show that some of the people we like best in our lives are the people we started out not liking so much.

No wonder people who end up not liking their partners can fall into a time trap: if not liking could turn into liking before, then it can do so again, they think, and so they wait. But this is really a completely different situation. Not liking can turn into liking, but liking that turns into not liking can rarely turn back into liking. Particularly not after the kind of time and commitment you've given to each other.

Feeling Liked

It's time to talk about the second part of the guideline, where it's clear to you that your partner doesn't like you. This is *not* about how your partner really feels. It's *not* about whether your partner says he likes you or thinks he likes you. It is about how much liking *gets through* to you.

I know there's no one in the world in a relationship who isn't aware that there are things *about* them that their partner doesn't like. But I'm talking about your having a sense that *on balance and overall* your partner just doesn't like you. Day after day, waking up and going to sleep, eating or talking about the kids or watching television together, you actually feel as if with the heft of a paperweight in your hand that he doesn't like you.

If that's true for you, then you'll be happiest if you leave. The bad feelings just get worse. A relationship like this is too bad to stay in.

If you're genuinely stumped about whether you really like your partner, keep a daily record on a piece of paper. Every day jot down a *D* (for dislike) if basically and overall you didn't like your partner that day. And jot down an *L* (for like) if something happened to make you like your partner that day.

Keep this daily record for about six weeks. Then look at what you've recorded. Look at the pattern of *D*'s and *L*'s. I can't tell you what adds up for you to "basically and overall not liking your partner," but you've got to let the real pattern show you the truth of your life. The truth will be there. You can do the same thing to determine whether you feel your partner likes you.

PERSPECTIVES: MUTUAL SHUTDOWN

There are many ways for a relationship to die. We've just talked about one: there's no liking. But the different ways a relationship can die have something in common—what I call mutual shutdown. Let me tell you about it. You'll find it important for understanding every guideline here and throughout the book.

Like being infected with the deadliest virus, mutual shut-down usually starts small, slow, unnoticed. It can start the day you meet, the day you marry, or not start until you've been to-gether for twenty years. All it needs to get going, though, is a small hurt or disappointment. A slight coldness in bed or a sexual rebuff. The attempted hug that's pushed away. A putdown when you're vulnerable. Something big can start it, like discovering your partner's had an affair. But something incredibly small can start it, too, like feeling that the present you've gotten for your birthday isn't as nice as the present you gave your partner on his birthday six months earlier.

Here's how it kills relationships. Before mutual shutdown starts, when two people come together there's the sense that "I'll make a hundred percent effort to contribute my full fifty percent to the relationship and you'll make a hundred percent effort to contribute your full fifty percent. We each do our best to give our all."

But if you do something to hurt someone or disappoint him, even if it's unconscious and inadvertent, if you do anything to make it seem as though you're not trying a hundred percent and not contributing fifty percent, then it's natural that he'll pull back, too. Maybe not right away. Maybe he'll put up a fight. But even-tually it's going to be impossible for him to feel he wants to keep giving to you as much as he's been giving when he sees you giv-ing less.

What Keeps It Going?

If this were a world of saints, you'd see your partner pull back, you'd see his complaints and coldness, and immediately realize what you'd done to make that happen. You'd immediately start giving back to make him willing to give to you again. But we don't live in that world of saints. Instead what we do is all too of-ten respond to hurt and anger with hurt and anger of our own. If he's going to give less, you'll give even less than that, is in ef-fect what we say. This mutual shutdown is a pure psychological reflex.

Think of it like the two of you forming a relationship and

having a bank account with a fixed amount of money in it that can never grow. As long as you leave that money alone everything is fine. But if you find that he's taken five dollars out, it doesn't feel fair and you feel deprived and you'll not only take a similar five dollars out, but an additional five dollars. Why should he be five bucks ahead of the game when you can be five bucks ahead? But when he realizes you've taken out ten bucks, he takes out fifteen; and then you take out twenty. It doesn't matter how much you started with. Eventually there will be nothing left.

Mutual shutdown works just like this except with an emotional, not financial, bank account.

I've never encountered a relationship in trouble where mutual shutdown wasn't working its evil magic. But like most of the viruses that are in our bodies right now, mutual shutdown is not inevitably fatal. It won't stop all by itself, but it can stop if you do something to stop it. What that "something" is and whether it's enough is the issue I address next.

STEP #12: FREE GIFTS OF LOVE

Let's talk about love some more. What I'm trying to do in this chapter is offer some specific help to people who want to get a handle on what it means that they say "But I love him [or her]." "Do you like each other?" is one way of getting a handle on this, on what's real about your love. Another way is to see if mutual shutdown is more powerful than you are, or you're more powerful than mutual shutdown.

The best way I know to determine this is by asking the next question:

Diagnostic question #12. **Do you feel willing to give your partner more than you're giving already, and are you willing to do this the way things are between you now, without any expectation of being paid back?**

It's so hard to know what's real about love. We talk about love that doesn't exist. We forget where we've hidden treasures of love that do exist and that could change everything. But if I know anything about love, it's that *love delivers.*

Remember our four stages of reality, perception, feeling, and action? There's a tiger. You see the tiger. You're struck with fear. You run or panic or do whatever people do when they see a tiger. But if you don't do anything and you don't even have a real response inside, not even the flush of adrenaline on your face, you have to wonder if you really are afraid. In the same way, if a supposed feeling of love isn't leading you to do things that are the kinds of things love leads people to do, then you've got to wonder if you really are feeling love.

One of my favorite therapists and someone I've learned a lot from was Harry Stack Sullivan. He probably worked as hard as any of us to make sense of love, but at least he wasn't trying to shove any hobbyhorse down our throats. And in a book that was the last place on earth you'd think of finding someone saying anything wise about love, *Conceptions of Modern Psychiatry,* Sullivan said, "When the satisfaction or the security of another person becomes as significant to one as is one's own satisfaction or security, then the state of love exists."

What does it mean to say that someone else's satisfaction or security is as significant as your own? To me it means that love is not the package you carry around, it's the package you deliver. It's not what you feel inside and certainly not what you say you feel inside, it's what you can *give* based on what you feel inside.

Here's how this works in the context of mutual shutdown. If your partner doesn't give to you, it'll be harder for you to feel you have something to give your partner. You still have something left to give though. But at some point during this process of mutual hurt and withdrawal, you and your partner have shut down so much that you simply have nothing left to give, regardless of what you say you feel. That's the death of love.

And the simplest test of this is question #12: Are you still willing to give something unconditionally to your partner?

Some people have trouble answering this question. They

have such a strong sense of how much they've given to the other person and to the relationship in the past, and how much they're giving in the present, that they get indignant. Why should they be willing to give more, they wonder, when they're giving so much now? What can this question possibly prove except masochism?

Let's find the answer.

Barbara's Story

Barbara got married very young. She was twenty, the same age I was when I got married. When you're kids starting out like that, you're full of romantic hopes for the future. You're so young that you have a strong sense of the specialness that brings you together. You have this idea that your destinies are uniting.

For Barbara, the sense of special destiny got all tied up with her husband Sam's business, a costume jewelry manufacturing company. It was a small, downtown sweatshop that from the beginning teetered on the edge of bankruptcy. They weren't wealthy the way we imagine manufacturers to be—they were often broke.

Except for a brief period when her kids were little, Barbara worked in the business for a small salary that was more often than not never paid her. She did it to keep their livelihood, their dream, their marriage alive. Working twelve-hour days, she gave a hell of a lot.

But adversity corrodes. Barbara and Sam fought constantly. Frustration and disappointment kept bringing them to flash points of anger. By the time Barbara came to see me there was a huge pile of twenty years of grievances counterbalanced only by her saying that she loved Sam.

Was This Love Enough? What that boiled down to, eventually, was whether I'd have the guts to ask Barbara, who was in a total mutual shutdown with Sam, if she'd be willing to give him more than she was giving already, even though from one point of view she was already giving a lot.

How bad was the mutual shutdown? No sex, for one thing. She felt used and abused every day at work, so she had no interest in making love at night in bed. For another thing, she just couldn't say anything nice to him. Sure, if he had a meeting with a potential customer she'd say optimistic-sounding things, but it was just to help the deal go through. But she had nothing nice personally to say to him about him. She couldn't say "I think you're terrific." This woman, who was hanging on in the relationship because she loved him, couldn't say "I love you."

I'll tell you what gave me the guts to ask Barbara if she could give more to Sam. I know the terrible power of mutual shutdown to make relationships sick and kill them. But doctors ask sick people to do things all the time that are hard to do but make you better. How can a doctor ask someone suffering from cancer to go through the pain of chemotherapy? But how can she not ask him if it's the best way to cure him? So how could I *not* ask Barbara to give more?

Running on Empty. "Look, I know you've given your life to Sam and your relationship and the business and everything," I said. "But what you're saying to me is that the whole thing is dying. You and Sam are moving away from each other with a terrible speed and something's got to stop that. I need to know if, in spite of everything, you have anything left to give him. I'm not talking about work. I'm talking about an unconditional gift of love, something warm and loving, like what you gave each other when you were kids starting out. I'm not going to judge you if you can't. But we've both got to know if you can give something to him without any expectation of getting anything back. Or are you running on empty?"

Barbara was silent for a minute and then said, "What difference does it make? Suppose I can. What does that prove? Suppose I can't? Does that mean it's over?" Here's the guideline:

GUIDELINE #12

In spite of how hurt and deprived you feel, if you *are* still willing to deliver a concrete expression of love, without expecting anything back in the near future, there's a real chance there's a solid core of aliveness in your relationship. If you *won't* give unless there's a clear expectation of getting something in return, that's evidence you won't be happy if you stay. *Quick take:* When there's nothing left to give, there's nothing left at all.

The yes answer is the really important one here. If, even though your partner's been stingy and miserable and angry and critical, even though you keep taking care of your partner and it doesn't seem as though he takes care of you, you're still willing to give without expecting to get anything back, that means that when you say "I still love him" you're not full of bull. Your feelings are about something real.

What do I mean when I talk about "delivering a concrete expression of love," about "giving" when you don't feel like giving? I'm not talking about anything dramatic or costly. I'm just talking about small, concrete things that may not be so hard to do but that make a difference to the other person. This kind of concrete expression of love could include things like the following:

- Smiling at your partner when he comes home
- Complimenting your partner on the excellent job she's done on a pet project
- Stopping to rub your partner's shoulders when you walk past him
- Picking up something you know your partner will like when you're at the store
- Conceding some point that's been a bone of contention between you
- Offering to help your partner when she's working on something

I can't tell you what to give or what would work in your relationship if you gave it. But if you are still willing to give something like the things I've just mentioned, then that's a sign that your love is real.

It may still turn out that love is not enough. And in the long run, we've all got to feel that we're getting back from our relationships roughly as much as we're putting into them. But for right now, you've got to know whether the "I love you" you claim is keeping you in the relationship is more than just words

Keeping Hope Alive

What does a no answer mean? That's the problem. If someone says to me that they're just not prepared to give unless they're going to get something back in return, then I have to ask where change and hope and healing are going to come from. What's going to make things get better? What's going to reverse the inexorable process of mutual shutdown? Because if you feel that way, your partner probably feels that way, and the two of you are standing there with your arms folded basically saying that even if you have to wait until the day you die, you'll wait for the other to make the first move.

But it may only *seem* that way. Saying you're unwilling to give unless you get something back sometimes means it really is all over, but it *sometimes* means you're just in terrible pain right now. When I gave birth to my babies I used natural childbirth, and that meant I was in the kind of pain I hope never to experience again. If I hadn't been giving birth I would've wanted to die with pain like that. But it *wasn't* the pain of death. It was the pain of life, and that made all the difference. In the same way, if you're in pain in your relationship and the only ray of light is that you love your partner, that pain might just be the kind of pain that goes away.

That's what happened with Barbara. At first she said, "No. I'm sorry, but I feel wiped out. I have nothing left to give." But Barbara and I both needed to understand what her no meant. With question #12, only time makes that clear.

I asked Barbara to do what I'm going to ask you to do if your answer is no. On a piece of paper write these words:

> As of [today's date] I just don't feel willing to give unconditionally to my partner anything more than I'm giving right now.

Then go through the rest of this book. Another question later on might make it clear that you'll be happier leaving. But if by the time you finish this book the signs are that you'll be happier staying, do this. Put that piece of paper in your wallet. Look at that piece of paper six months or so from today's date. If nothing's changed and you still feel the same way, I feel comfortable saying that you'll be happiest if you leave.

Here's what happened with Barbara. She must've had a sense that her running on empty had to do with more than just the relationship. So she took a vacation from Sam and the business. If he couldn't handle that, she thought, that's all she needed to know. But it was fine with him. So Barbara went to stay for two weeks with her mother in Florida. She got physically rested and emotionally left alone.

What surprised her was that when she got back to her life with Sam she *was* nice to him again. The pressures and difficulties were still there as they'd been before, and Sam was the same demanding guy he'd been, but it must be true that she loved him because it seemed as though she had some love to give him again.

It wasn't that alone that made the relationship too good to leave. But when she saw what she was giving to him, she asked herself, "Is there a reason I can't keep this up forever? Does this cost me anything?" Her answer was no to both questions. And that was a reason to stay.

You'll be happy to know that in this case the power of giving unconditionally to the relationship turned things around. It didn't make their relationship at work less stressful, but Barbara gave Sam a present of herself by being nice to him the way he'd remembered before all the difficulties. And Sam responded. He wasn't a completely new man, but he showed Barbara that he had love to give her that he delivered by being nice back to her.

With no other negatives in their relationship making it too bad to stay in, these little but real gifts of love turned mutual shutdown into mutual turn-on.

Every once in a while someone's afraid to give unconditionally. They feel they do have something left to give but they're afraid if they actually give it they'll get screwed, used, suckered into doing all the work in the relationship.

But I want to say that these fears are generally unwarranted. You already know the relationship's iffy. You're already thinking of leaving. If you give and nothing happens and you get nothing back, the forces of mutual shutdown are powerful enough to make it likely that you won't have anything left to give the next time, and you'll have found the clarity you're looking for. At least you'll have tested the reality of your love.

9

It Don't Mean a Thing If It Ain't Got That Swing

Issue: Sex and Physical Affection

Here it is. Sex. But I've got a surprise for you. In a way this whole book is about sex. Let me explain.

There are all kinds of sexual problems we deal with in our relationships that can drive us nuts, make us miserable, and make us wonder if there's something wrong with the relationship, something so wrong that maybe we'd be happiest leaving. I'm talking about the whole gamut of sexual problems, such as one of you just not wanting sex, fights over how often you make love and who initiates lovemaking, sex without passion, the desire for more foreplay, sexual needs that one of you has that the other doesn't want to satisfy, sexual boredom, premature ejaculation, difficulty reaching orgasm, or 101 other sexual problems.

The issue we've got to face here is where to draw the line between (1) sexual problems that frustrate and disappoint us and (2) sexual problems that make a relationship too bad to stay in. This chapter focuses on what it is about the physical part of your relationship that indicates a basic discord in the entire relationship, meaning you'll be happy if you leave, as well as what provides evidence for the possibility that you'll be happy if you stay.

The guidelines here are so specific that you might think I'd

somehow left out all the other sexual problems I've just mentioned. Isn't there some minimum frequency of lovemaking that
means you'll be happiest leaving? Isn't there some level of sexual
pleasure that's so low that you'll be happiest leaving? Isn't there
some degree of difference between you when it comes to sex that
means you'll be happiest leaving?

Sexual Guidelines

I didn't leave *any* of this out. It's just that the sexual part of your
relationship doesn't exist in isolation from the rest of your relationship. Every chapter of this book provides guidelines that
point to issues that are all-important in determining what it
is about sexual problems that makes a relationship too bad to
stay in.

Take this sexual problem for example: a woman has trouble
reaching orgasm with her partner. There's nothing about this particular sexual problem that tells you that you should leave. The
real issue is whether she can talk about it with her partner. It's
not trouble reaching orgasm but off-the-table-itis that determines
whether she'd be happier staying or leaving.

People whose partners take off the table discussions about
sexual matters are the ones who end up being miserable if they
stay. People whose partners do *not* take sexual discussions off the
table are much more likely to feel their relationship is too good
to leave. Here's why. Because their partners are open to talking
about a problem like having trouble reaching orgasm, they'll either make progress resolving their sexual problems or at least
feel close to their partners and feel they're working together to
build a solid relationship.

The Bottom Line

Let me put it like this. Think about some couples who've grown
old together. Being able to say "We could always talk about anything" buys you a lot of happiness, regardless of how many orgasms you've had. But if you have to say "We could never really

talk about anything important," then that buys a lot of disappointment and unhappiness, regardless of how many orgasms you've had.

Besides, being able to put things on the table can solve sexual problems. But good sex can never solve the problem of not being able to talk to each other.

And it's like this for almost every issue in every chapter of this book.

Take the very first guideline in the book: that you'll be happy leaving if things were never good when they were at their best. If things were good in general, then even if sex hasn't been particularly good there's a basis for hoping and connecting. If they were never any good anywhere, where's there going to be a basis for their being good in sex?

Later on we'll get into other issues, like mutual respect, the ways you and your partner are different, your partner's having particular problems, intimacy, and many other issues. All of these have some bearing on whatever might not be working for you in your sexual relationship right now. *The point is that sexual problems are not separate from relationship problems.* It's the same problems that make a relationship too bad to stay in that turn sexual difficulties into relationship-ending problems.

If there's no reason why you'll be happy leaving your relationship based on these problems, there's certainly no reason to leave because of any specific sexual difficulty, other than what I deal with in this chapter.

A RED HERRING

Let's get past an important source of confusion when it comes to bad sex and troubled relationships. There's a high correlation between deteriorating relationships and a drop in the frequency of lovemaking. When people start fighting they stop making love.

But what causes what? *Deteriorating relationships cause people to stop making love.* This means that if you know things are going bad in a relationship you can predict that that couple isn't sleeping together as much as they used to, and you'll have a good chance of being right.

But you can't flip this around. You can't say that just because a couple isn't making love all that much that things are going bad in the relationship. Here's an analogy. If you know someone's sick you can predict that there's a good chance they'll be in bed. But if you know someone's in bed, you can't predict they're sick. Most people in bed are just sleeping.

And getting clear about what predicts what is important, because problems with lovemaking are a major reason people start wondering if their relationship is too bad to stay in. The bottom line is that if you and your partner have stopped making love as often as you used to or as you'd like to, it doesn't necessarily mean there's anything seriously wrong between you. It's not a reason *by itself* for you to conclude you've got to leave or even that there's anything necessarily wrong with your relationship.

It could be that the two of you are content not making love as much anymore. It could be that the two of you are mad at each other and that when your anger cools off your bed will get hot. It could be that the two of you need to talk but you haven't for all kinds of reasons, including the fact that you're so busy. It could be, believe it or not, that having kids in the house spooks you, and once they become horny teenagers who are out of the house a lot, the two of you will get horny again, too.

The point is that sex is like those canaries miners carry into a mine to see if the air is safe: it's a highly sensitive responder to what's happening in the atmosphere. Whatever's going on with sex is far more likely to be a symptom than a disease. So if none of the guidelines in this book that say *leave* apply to you, then the odds are overwhelming that you'll either be able to work out your sexual issues or you'll be happy enough with things the way they are.

Now let's get down to business. When *does* it mean a thing if it ain't got that swing?

STEP #13: REACH OUT AND TOUCH SOMEONE

The physical side of a relationship is a huge area. There are whole libraries about what goes into good sex and how to get it. Couples argue constantly about when to make love and how to make love and what to do when making love. But where do you find, in the midst of the stormy and confusing sea of lovemaking, that one clear beacon that tells you there's something so wrong between the two of you physically that your doubts are at an end and it really is best for you to leave?

This question is very basic.

Diagnostic question #13. **Do both you and your partner want to touch each other and look forward to touching each other and make efforts to touch each other?**

I'm talking about things as elemental as kissing, hugging, stroking, holding hands, rubbing a neck, putting a hand on a leg, and any other form of touching that goes on in committed relationships. And in any of these ways, do you feel that you want your partner to touch you, even if it's just holding hands? Do you wish your partner touched you more often? Are you happy when your partner touches you now? Or do you feel that your partner gives you the creeps physically and that you actively and affirmatively do not want him to touch you?

And, since it's so closely related to this, do you want to touch your partner in any way too, even just to give her a kiss on the cheek?

And, even though you might have to guess about this, based on your experience, would you say that your partner wants to touch you in any way, and does your partner want you to touch him? I realize that some people are naturally very physically affectionate and others are naturally more "hands off," but given your partner's basic personality, has he moved to a zero point where he wants no physical affection?

Where does lovemaking fit into this? For now, just think of

it as another form of touching, like any other. Don't give it a higher status than other forms of touching. But since lovemaking is a form of touching, you could ask yourself if you want to make love to your partner. If you're not making love, do you wish that this period of coldness and distance were at an end and lovemaking started happening again? I'm not asking about how often you want to make love to your partner. I'm just asking if in general you want to make love to your partner at all.

When you look at him does it ever occur to you to make love to him? When he touches you do you ever feel you want to make love with him? When you're by yourself do you ever have the feeling that you want to make love with him?

And do you guess that even though your partner's acting mad at you he really wants to make love with you, too?

All these questions point to the basic issue of whether you and your partner are physically attracted to each other. Wanting to touch and wanting to be touched are the bedrock of the part of your physical relationship on which your emotional relationship builds.

Most other sexual problems people can and do cope with or live with. But if you're agonizing over whether to stay or leave, here's the guideline:

GUIDELINE #13

If either you or your partner has stopped wanting to touch the other or be touched by the other, and this goes on for several months without any sign of abating, then you're making a profound statement about how alienated you are from each other, and based on the experience of other people in this situation you won't be happy if you stay and you will be happy if you leave. *Quick take:* If someone makes your flesh crawl, it's time to crawl out of the relationship.

There's one thing you have to be careful about with this guideline. It's why I talked about this going on for several months without signs of abating. You have to be careful about the fact that people get into weird places when they're mad at each other or when they feel hurt by the other. So there are very commonly periods in troubled relationships where there isn't any touching going on, much less sex. And there are periods where emotions are running so high that you don't want to be touching each other. But I'm not talking about situations like these, and you've got to make sure that you don't apply this guideline to what's essentially a temporary situation.

Guideline #13 applies only when it sinks in that literally not wanting touching has become permanent for you or your partner.

The Bridge Back

Why is not wanting touching the touchstone? Why is this the place I go to in the sexual realm to diagnose a relationship that's too bad to stay in, other than the fact that this is where most people feel comfortable having drawn the line?

It has to do with the way people in a troubled relationship that's basically too good to leave find their way back to each other. One way they do so is by building on some kind of physical bond or connection. As bad as things are, they hold hands or kiss each other good-bye, or their bodies make contact when they lie in bed at night, or suddenly out of nowhere they find themselves hugging, or in the midst of their distance from each other they find themselves wanting to touch.

You remember that I talked about mutual shutdown, the way two people pull back from each other, and keep pulling back, each waiting for the other to make the first move, emotionally, conversationally, on every level. Well, wanting touching is one of the most important ways two people find a way to stop this mutual shutdown. Some "accidental" or spontaneous touching happens that both people want, and the touching escalates, and shutdown becomes turn-on. And that's how millions and millions of couples find their way out of a nightmare of hurt and anger.

You could think of wanting touching as the brakes on a car. Of course brakes can't steer you out of danger but they do stop you from reaching it. A car without brakes is undrivable. A relationship without the braking mechanism of both people wanting to touch and be touched on some level and in some way is a relationship without this protection against a crash.

The good news is how seldom guideline #13 applies. But when guideline #13 does apply and there's no one there to want to touch the other, then they're just trapped in a nightmare of hurt and anger and there's no way to get out.

Step #14: Getting Physical

A question people often ask me is how good sex has to be before it makes a relationship too good to leave. And where this question comes up most often is with people who're feeling very ambivalent about their relationship because there are a lot of things going on they don't like, and yet sex itself is still really good. And so they wonder if they're being too finicky, if great sex doesn't in fact cancel out a whole bunch of bad stuff, the way you might stay in a crappy house that happened to be right on the ocean.

Let me tell you where I've learned to draw the line. It's between two parts of your own sexuality. There's the part you carry around with you wherever you go. Let's call this your general sexuality. I'm talking about sexual responses and feelings that you've generally had in most of your sexual relationships. For example, the physical process you actually go through to reach orgasm in most of your relationships is part of your general sexuality.

And there's the part that responds to the person you're with. Let's call this your person-specific sexuality. This refers to parts of your sexuality that are different with your current partner than with other partners.

Your general sexuality shouldn't have anything to do with whether you stay or leave a particular relationship. So even though it might feel wonderful to be touched and your orgasms are satisfying now, if this is something you've experienced in other relationships or think you'd probably experience in other relationships, that's great but it's no reason in and of itself to stay in your current relationship. It might seem as though there is great physical chemistry, but that's only because of what you are carrying around with you wherever you go. It's because of who you are, not because of what there is in the relationship.

But your person-specific sexuality, the part that responds to the person you're with, is the part that's absolutely critical for ending your relationship ambivalence. If you want to see what it is about the physical side of your relationship that makes it too good to leave, just ask yourself:

Diagnostic question #14. Do you feel a unique sexual attraction to your partner?

I'm not asking how great sex is with your partner now. That wouldn't be fair to this relationship, because great sex can so often have to do with your general sexuality that you carry around with you wherever you go. And when I've worked with people in iffy relationships and it became clear that for whatever reason the relationship was too bad to stay in and yet they stayed anyway because of great sex, they didn't end up happy with that decision.

But more often than you might think I run into people who somehow feel uniquely physically attracted to their partner. It's not that they can't imagine having sex with anyone else or that sex wouldn't be good with anyone else or that sex is even so unbelievably great with their partner. But for whatever reason there's something sweet or safe or special or comfortable about their sexual relationship with that person that simply puts other people in a different category. Other people just don't feel right to them. But this person does.

One man I interviewed had had a lot of sexual experience before his current relationship and was still one of those guys who liked looking at attractive women. But here's the thing. He might flirt with other women at parties, but if he danced with them or sat close to them he felt, as he put it, "distinctly not turned on." On the other hand, there was something about his partner's skin—the way it felt, the way it looked, the way it smelled—that was unusually appetizing for him.

That's the kind of thing that makes the difference. Here's the guideline:

GUIDELINE #14

If you feel a physical, sexual attraction to your partner that puts him or her in a special category for you, where you're drawn to him or her strongly and in a way you're not drawn to anyone else, then I feel comfortable saying you'll be happy if you stay because most people in this situation are happy they stay, as long as there are no powerful reasons to leave. *Quick take:* If you're especially attracted to your partner, there's something special about your relationship.

If this guideline doesn't apply to you, don't worry. People can be perfectly happy in relationships with someone they're no more physically attracted to than they are to anyone else. All you absolutely need is what the previous guideline pointed to, that you want to touch each other. So what if you're physically attracted to other people, too?

It's just that in those cases where someone's partner feels special to them physically not because of any unique beauty but because of some chemistry that makes them feel different from others, then as long as there are no other problems, people in this situation are usually happy they stayed and unhappy they left.

10
All the Things You Are

Issue: Your Partner's Problems

BEFORE IT'S TOO LATE

Here's what can happen if you don't deal with things in a timely way. Sally was married to an alcoholic for thirty-two years. For the last twenty of those years he made her life miserable, coming home high during the week and getting loaded every weekend. He never abused her, not physically anyway, but his drinking made him angry and unavailable. Sally spent most of her marriage pretty sure it was too bad to stay in. Only her blind hope that he might change one day made her think it was too good to leave. But her hope turned out to be pointless. Finally, all their money gone, and far later than she should have, she ended the relationship.

Within six months she was absolutely stunned by how good she felt about herself and her life on her own in her new apartment.

She was truly at peace for the first time in decades. But she was bitter, too. She'd never really grappled with the issue of her husband's changing and dealt with it one way or another. Not until it was very, very late in the game.

But it doesn't have to be that way for you. Let's talk about the problems our partners have that contribute to our relationship ambivalence. Of course every problem we have in a relationship feels as though it's connected to there being something wrong with our partners. But for now let's talk about those situations where your partner has some kind of problem and yet it seems as though everything would be different if only he could change.

What problems am I talking about? Any of the things that destroy lives and relationships. Alcoholism, of course, and any other form of substance abuse like cocaine addiction or being hooked on painkillers. It could be being a pothead, a hothead, or a fathead. It could also be depression. It could be resentment of authority. It could be unwillingness to settle down and have a career. It could be carelessness with money. And it doesn't have to be a psychological problem. It could be lack of education. It could be premature ejaculation. It could be anything that drives you crazy and makes you think if only he didn't have "that one thing" everything would be great, except he does have "that one thing" and your life is hell.

How do you sort all this out? You want to be fair. You want to be patient. But you also want to be happy.

The Ideology of Like-It-or-Lump-It

Few things keep more people more stuck in relationship ambivalence than confusion about whether we have a right to ask for change at all. Aren't we supposed to accept our partners for who they are? Aren't we supposed to think only about changing ourselves and not the other person? Let's see.

Going back to one of the very earliest historical marriages we have any knowledge of, the one between Socrates and Xanthippe, people have understood that it's their right to do everything possible to change their partners and to demand that their partners solve their problems.

But there's also been a very strong like-it-or-lump-it attitude throughout history, one generally associated with people (usually men) who could afford to say "like it or lump it." Unfortunately for people in relationships today, the like-it-or-lump-it attitude got a strong boost in the sixties and has gone on to affect the twentysomething offspring of people who grew up in the sixties. It's also an attitude that a lot of baby boomer therapists promulgate.

You can see this attitude illustrated by something called the Gestalt Prayer. It says in part:

> I do my thing, and you do your thing.
> I am not in this world to live up to your expectations
> And you are not in this world to live up to mine.

There is some value in these lines, but the throw-away-relationship attitude exemplified by the Gestalt Prayer went way too far. I'm not a politician or a theoretician or any other kind of *-ician*. I'm just a therapist on the front lines of men and women trying to keep their love alive and balance being happy together with being happy in themselves. And I know that the lifeblood of a relationship is people feeling they can influence each other, particularly about really important things.

It's Okay to Ask for Change

Nothing works more powerfully to make people feel rage and create distance than the sense that they can't influence their partner. And to influence someone is to get them to change, whether it's getting them to go from being someone who never picks up his socks to being someone who almost always picks up his socks, or getting them to go from being someone who always picks on you to being someone who never picks on you.

If I wanted to write a prescription for how to have a doomed relationship that was overwhelmingly too bad to stay in, I'd have both people say I can't change, I won't change, I don't want to change, and I don't see a reason to change, but if we find each other, it's beautiful. The point is that *you're entitled to feel you want your partner to change things about himself.*

But then what? How do you then decide when your partner has problems that they're too serious or too difficult for you to deal with for you to be happy staying with him? The solution we'll work with here is to separate out four different issues:

- Can he acknowledge his problem?
- Is he willing to change?
- Can you let go of being bothered by the problem?
- Is he able to change?

Let's deal with these one at a time.

STEP #15: BEYOND DENIAL

The word *denial* is tossed around so often and so glibly these days that I'm afraid it's lost its usefulness. So I'm going to use that word as little as possible here. Instead I'm going to talk about things like blindness and ignorance about who you are and what you're doing and what its effects are on the people around you and what the long-term consequences are.

Blindness and ignorance about what problems? We can begin with alcoholism and other forms of substance abuse: "I'm not a problem drinker, I just like to have a couple of drinks in the evening to unwind." But he always has these drinks, and there are more than just a couple, and he unwinds himself into a stupor.

I'm also talking about a range of psychiatric problems, such as paranoia and a number of personality disorders that involve a refusal to acknowledge that there's anything wrong as part of the symptomatology.

And I'm also talking about all the other things we're blind to that we do to spoil relationships, from constantly maneuvering for control to not answering questions to issuing an endless stream of putdowns disguised as humor to nagging to having no energy to not being informed about what you're talking about to being essentially uninterested in the people close to you. I'm talking about things like people not knowing they're boring lovers or domineering parents or neglectful housekeepers or overbearing personalities who can't stand to lose an argument or hotheads who blow up into wild rages.

I'm talking about someone like King Lear, whose daughter said about him, "He hath ever but slenderly known himself," and whose whole tragedy grew out of that.

Mandy's Story

People can close their minds and eyes to any possible aspect of who they are. Let me tell you about Mandy's husband Bob, aka Mr. Selfish. While Bob might seem superficially like a lot of men and women you've known, he takes selfishness much further.

Bob is a professor of philosophy. If Bob were merely self-absorbed in a charming absentminded-professor way, or if you could somehow wake him up from his deep sleep of self-absorption, it might be easier to tolerate him. But no matter how blatant an act of selfishness you catch Bob in, he will either not admit he did it or not admit it was selfish. He might even rigorously defend it.

There are two ingredients here:

1. *Selfishness*. It's not that Bob has any interest in dominating his wife, Mandy. He's happy for her to do what she wants and be what she wants to be. It's just that he simply cannot see outside of his own needs any more than someone on television can see you watching him.

So, for example, with very few demands on his time and a sense of himself as a free spirit, Bob hates plans, schedules, and appointments. If they have to do anything together, Bob simply can't "get" a conversation about making appointments and is unable to participate in it. If Mandy says it's important to her to schedule things because of her many commitments as an acupuncturist, Bob cannot see why it would be important. If they somehow do manage to schedule things, he can't see why his adhering to the schedule is important.

2. The other ingredient is Bob's utter *cluelessness*, his inability to perceive his own selfishness. What an enormous difference it would make if Bob could say yes, I know, I am selfish. But instead he's got a million reasons and explanations

and justifications for what he does, thereby annihilating everyone else's needs. You've seen talk shows on which some selfish guy is paraded for all to see, but most of them don't have a philosophy professor's ability to come up with passionately reasoned justifications.

For example, when it comes to his refusal to cooperate with Mandy in any scheduling of an event Bob needs to be part of, he chides her for being uptight, petty, rigid, controlled by time instead of controlling time. He essentially has a philosophy for why her need to plan events is wrong. That philosophy is what keeps him blind.

I asked Mandy the question I'll ask you:

Diagnostic question #15. Does your partner neither see nor admit things you've tried to get him to acknowledge that make your relationship too bad to stay in?

Of course this kind of blind ignorance is annoying no matter what it's about, but what I'm talking about here is your partner's closing his eyes and mind to one of his problems that bores right through you like a bad headache when you think about the things that make your relationship too bad to stay in.

The Quicksand of Denial

If these things don't matter to you, there's no problem. But if they really do matter, you're in for sheer hell. It's not only that the problem won't change—that's obvious. But there's something about this kind of blindness and ignorance that endlessly tantalizes you. People whose partners deny something important like this don't usually come right out and say their partners cannot and will not see the problem. They say instead, "I am really trying to get him to see the problem and even though I was discouraged about it yesterday, today I really feel I've come up with a way to make him see it."

After all, what's easier than seeing? It's something we do ten thousand times a day on the other side of every blink. It's that seeming ease of seeing that's so tantalizing. Any day now, we think, they'll get it. Dawn will come. Light will shine. As if poked by an electric prod, our partners will leap into sudden realization of whatever it was they hadn't seen before. It all seems so tantalizingly easy that we don't acknowledge what should have been so easy for us to see: *that if our partner can't see something that's so easy to see, there's something wrong there and that means there's a good chance they'll never see it.*

So what do you do if you answered yes to question #15? Here's the guideline:

GUIDELINE #15

If there's something your partner does that makes your relationship too bad to stay in, and if you've tried to get him to acknowledge it and he simply cannot and does not, then that problem will just get worse over time. If the thought of a lifetime with it getting worse is not acceptable, you'll be happiest if you leave. *Quick take:* If your partner can't even see what it is about him that makes you want to get out, it's time to get out.

Let me be blunt: People are rarely happy they hung in there with someone who refuses to acknowledge an issue of critical importance to them. But what does it mean exactly for your partner to "acknowledge doing something that makes the relationship too bad for you to stay in"?

One thing is for sure: *it's got to be more than just words.* Your partner's got to have a shock of recognition about what he's doing. Of course acknowledging means saying "yes, I do that" or "yes, I am that way." But he's also got to convey the sense that he sees how what he's doing is a problem for you; and that there is nothing wrong with you because it's a problem for you.

In the story I just recounted, Bob would have to smack himself on the forehead and say something like, "My God, I finally realize what it must be like for you to live with me, how I insist on always doing things my way, and I never compromise toward doing things your way. I might have all kinds of justifications for being the way I am, but I can see how from your point of view it looks like pure selfishness. I'm sorry for how hard I've been for you to deal with."

You've got to watch out for one of the slipperiest ways people refuse to acknowledge their problems: they get hurt. Your asking for acknowledgment makes them sad, discouraged, desperate. It seems to make them feel so bad about themselves, it's such a blow to their ego, that you start getting the sense that even mentioning the problem makes things worse, not better. But what these people are really doing, consciously or unconsciously, is using emotional blackmail to convince you that night is day and that not dealing with a problem is a more effective way of handling it than dealing with it. Actually, they're using a form of off-the-table-itis to prevent you from asking them to acknowledge their own problem.

Regardless of how he does it, if your partner can't even recognize what he's doing and the impact it has on you and the fact that it makes the relationship too bad to stay in, how can things possibly improve? One person out of touch with reality is bad enough; two people like this are an insane asylum.

STEP #16: WILL HE BE WILLING TO CHANGE?

Okay, there you are in a terrible state of relationship ambivalence. And let's say that the problem your partner has that makes you think about leaving is something he acknowledges. That's good. Acknowledgment delivers real hope.

But now let's take the next step. Yes, he acknowledges the problem, but is he willing to do something about it? Is he at least willing to try? Let's say (because the story coming up is about this) that the problem is that your partner is too fat. This is a politically incorrect issue, but inside our relationships political correctness flies out the window. And my job is to talk about the real things people deal with on the level they deal with them.

And a huge problem for people in relationship ambivalence is what happens after their partners admit they have a problem. They may admit it but they're too often not willing to change. Here's the question that's helped a lot of people get out of their ambivalence:

Diagnostic question #16. Is there something your partner does that makes your relationship too bad to stay in and that he acknowledges but that, for all intents and purposes, he's unwilling to do anything about?

The key is that word "unwilling." It might sound simple, but like the iceberg that sank the Titanic it's ten times bigger than it seems and most of it is submerged. For every person who comes right out and admits they're unwilling to change, there are ten people who won't say they're unwilling to change and yet they'll fight you every step of the way to prevent change.

Jim's Story

Let me go back to the case of the man whose partner was too fat for him. I know you probably hate him already, but let's look at his side of things for a bit.

Jim was a fitness coach for a professional sports team. Being in shape and looking in shape was his life and livelihood. When he'd first married Peggy she'd been a dancer and was in terrific shape. They'd shared a focus on the body. Just the way two really smart people might come together with the understanding that they'll spend their lives enjoying each other's intelligence and that if one of them should start acting stupid it's all over, it was like that for Jim and Peggy with respect to having beautiful bodies, at least from Jim's point of view.

By the time I saw them together, Peggy weighed 290

pounds. Here's the impact this had on Jim. Sex was physically uncomfortable and unsatisfying, but even more than that he simply
didn't desire Peggy any more. He was ashamed of being embarrassed by her, but he was embarrassed nonetheless. Most of all,
perhaps, Jim went around in a constant state of rage inside for
what Peggy had done to herself and to him.

I checked carefully and as far as I could see Jim had done everything possible to convey to Peggy the full import of how he
felt and what things meant to him. Peggy knew that for Jim her
living fat was a violation of the unwritten spiritual contract that
had brought them together. Peggy knew that as Jim weighed the
pros and cons of staying and leaving there was a 290 pound
weight in the balance on the side of the relationship's being too
bad for Jim to stay in.

Jim's ambivalence came from all the things on the other side
of the balance, like the fact that he still loved Peggy and the part
of him that felt guilty about making appearance such an important issue.

Let's check in with Peggy. Acknowledgment wasn't a problem: she knew she was fat, she knew it was unhealthy, she knew
it was unattractive, she even knew it depressed her, and, most
important for our purposes, she knew it was driving Jim away.

But this is where we have to face the issue of what real willingness to change means. It would have been clearer if Peggy
had simply said, "Yeah, I'm fat, and I know you find it obnoxious,
but I like myself this way and I don't want to do anything about
it." But Peggy was a textbook illustration of how people who state
a superficial willingness to change actually convey a real *un*willingness to change, regardless of what the particular problem happens to be. Here are some of the things she said:

- "Of course I want to lose weight but I don't make it
  the be-all and end-all the way you do. It's more important
  that I eat healthy food and concentrate on my work and
  most of all eliminate stress from my life."
- "It's not for you to tell me what to do. In fact, your telling
  me what to do makes me not want to do it."

- "It's wrong of you to want me to change. You're supposed to accept me the way I am."
- "Every time you complain about this it makes me depressed and I just put on more weight." (People who aren't willing to change always say that expressing your need makes them dig themselves deeper into the problem.)

Then there's the ultimate expression of unwillingness-hiding-in-seeming-willingness:

- "I want to lose weight, too, but I've got to do it for myself, not for you, and I've got to do it in my own time and in my own way."

You might be wondering what's wrong with this last statement. Aren't we supposed to believe this? Well, it's certainly the kind of thing therapists like me have tried to get people to believe, because it's important that we own our own lives and do things for ourselves. But there are two completely different possible translations of Peggy's last statement:

- The first translation is "I want to do it and I will do it, but it'll only work if I do it my way." And that's good if it's sincere.
- The second translation is "I'm *un*willing to do it, and you can hang around and watch if you want but I'll never do it, and when I say 'my way' I mean if it happens without my making an effort, fine, otherwise too bad." And that's not good.

The second translation is what Peggy really meant. She was saying she was willing when she was really unwilling. Here are the facts. Jim had made his feelings clear to Peggy for many years. Peggy had said she'd lose weight "in her own time and in her own way" for just as many years. But her body exhibited her unwillingess to change.

So let's see if we can be a little more sympathetic to Jim. Sure, he should have been a more noble, more spiritual person. But he never pretended to be a different kind of guy than he was. And he'd made it very clear to Peggy what was at stake. By her saying in a dozen ways both directly and indirectly that she was unwilling to change, *she was in effect giving Jim permission to end the relationship.* The gap between them was just too big.

If your answer to question #16 is yes, here's the guideline:

GUIDELINE #16

If there's something your partner does that makes your relationship too bad to stay in, and he acknowledges it, but he's in fact unwilling to do anything about it, and if his unwillingness has been clear for at least six months, you'll be happier if you leave. *Quick take:* If you're waiting for your partner to want to change, you're waiting for Godot.

This guideline is clear. When people are miserable in a relationship because of something the other person does and the other person is not willing to change, they're usually satisfied with their decision if they decide to leave the relationship.

Sometimes you know your partner's unwilling to change because he says so. Or because he shows you in a dozen different ways, like Peggy. But sometimes he says he's willing but he's not. If your partner is willing to change, he's willing to *do* something to change. But do what? How does this work in practice if you're in this situation?

Demonstrating Willingness

It really works when people come up with some specific idea of what it means for them for their partner to be willing to change and then they tell their partner what this is. They say something like, "This problem of yours makes me want to leave our relationship. You've said that you acknowledge that you have this problem. I'll know that you're willing to do something about it if you . . . ," and then they say what that something is. Clearly there's got to be room for negotiation. You can't just arbitrarily lay down the law. But your partner can't just say he's willing to change and then not do anything that demonstrates real willingness to you.

So how do you come up with this thing that demonstrates real willingness to you that you'll tell your partner about? Since there are a million different problems and a million different reactions to each of these problems, all I can say is that whatever you come up with has to be real and specific and meaningful and observable. It's got to be something that'll actually make you firmly believe your partner is genuinely trying to change. It's got to be some action about which you can say, "I know he's willing to change because when he does *that*, I know he's really trying."

What kind of actions am I talking about? Here are some examples:

- For one person, a partner's being willing to change with respect to substance abuse might mean going to some kind of AA-type meeting. For another person whose partner has the same problem, being willing to change might mean stopping hanging out with the same old crowd. Either way either person can say, "He's really trying to change."

- For one person, a partner's being willing to change a pattern of earning little money and having long stretches between jobs—for whatever reason—might mean going back to school and getting some kind of skill or credential that will create good options. For another person whose partner has the same problem, being willing to change might mean taking that kind of serious real-world job

they'd said in the past they'd never take and sticking
with it for a year without getting fired. Either way either
person can say, "He's really trying to change."

* For one person, a partner's being willing to change being
depressed, tired, and miserable much of the time might
mean going into therapy and sticking with it. For another
person whose partner has the same problem, being willing
to change might mean going to a doctor and trying to get
a prescription for an anti-depressant. Either way either
person can say, "He's really trying to change."

Then you make an agreement about the specific change, which
includes some kind of time frame. I'm talking about something
like, "I'd like you to start doing this within a month and keep it
up for a year. Not because I'm trying to boss you around or lay
down the law but because it's a simple fact that your not showing
me you're willing to change just makes the relationship too bad
for me to stay in. That's not a threat, it's just my reality."

The Waiting Trap

If you make an agreement you can save yourself from one of the
many ways people fall into what I call the Waiting Trap.

We're all susceptible to falling into the Waiting Trap all the
time in our lives. Here's an illustration of how it works.

Say you're waiting for a bus. If you wait for ten minutes, you
immediately convert that waiting time into a kind of investment.
Because you've invested ten minutes in waiting for the bus, it
feels stupid not to invest another ten minutes. Before you know
it you've invested twenty minutes, and with an investment like
that, how could you not keep waiting more and more. This is
how you end up waiting forty-five minutes for a bus to take you
somewhere you could walk to in fifteen minutes.

People do the same thing with problem partners. If you've
waited a year for your partner to change, you're almost magically
drawn into waiting another year. And then how can you not wait

two more years after waiting the first two years? Do you remember Sally from the beginning of this chapter? She was married to her alcoholic husband for thirty-two years because she was a victim of the Waiting Trap, wherein the more she waited, the more she felt she had to keep waiting to recoup her initial investment.

It's to avoid the Waiting Trap that you specify a time frame when you talk about the specific thing you want your partner to do to show that he's really willing to change. Some people hate the suggestion I'm about to make, but it's really helpful to actually write down what your partner's willing to do and the time frame on a dated piece of paper. Then you both sign it. (If he won't even sign it, how can he be showing his willingness to change?) Then check in with this piece of paper a year (or however long you agree on) later. If he hasn't done what the two of you have agreed, then he's shown that in fact, regardless of his words, he's *un*willing to change and guideline #16 kicks in.

STEP #17: LETTING GO

Okay, so your partner isn't willing to change and this problem is making you miserable. Here's an option that never occurs to some people: it's your just letting go of being bothered by the problem. Here's the question for you:

Diagnostic question #17. This problem your partner has that makes you want to leave: have you tried to let it go, ignore it, stop letting it bother you? And were you successful?

I'm not talking about enduring the unendurable. I'm not talking about learning to live with suffering. I'm talking instead about something I've seen people do in the face of real problems, even in the face of problems that have bothered them for a long time. This problem that was attached to them like a ball and chain— they suddenly treat it like a helium-filled balloon they're holding

in their hand; they just let go and it flies away. They're not enduring anything, because there's nothing there anymore to endure.
Here's an example.

John's Story

Shortly after John moved to Boston from Texas for business, he
met and married a woman who was a food writer and locally
based editor of a women's magazine. Because of what Beth's
work was about, John assumed that she'd be as traditionally ori-
ented as he was. He understood that she'd continue to work professionally, but he took it for granted that she'd do most of the
cooking and housework as well. He figured she'd want to.

Imagine John's shock when he found that Beth was a slob,
never did housework, and never did any cooking except for assignments. As his situation dawned on him he got more and more
angry and disappointed, and they had bitter fights about "her"
problem. She acknowledged that she didn't do anything around
the house and she expressed a kind of willingness to do more
only in the sense that she said that if her schedule ever lightened
up she'd do her fair share. Other than that she didn't want to
change.

There was a period when this issue really felt like a deal
breaker to this Texan. He'd spent his whole life anticipating being married to a woman who would be a wonderful homemaker.
I asked John if he could let go of his expectations. That possibility had actually never occurred to him before. He said he'd need
a week to think about it.

When he came back, he said, "You know, I thought to myself
if this works, it'll be the easiest thing I've ever done. Let me see
if I can just take a big breath and let go of the stuff I had in my
head about Beth doing all the work around the house. I couldn't
believe it but it worked."

It's not always so easy to let go, and the odds are that you've
already tried it and it hasn't worked for you, but if you haven't
tried to let go of either paying attention to or being bothered by
this thing that's making your relationship too bad to stay in, then

it's worth trying now. Give it a week or two and see what happens. Then what's your answer to question #17? Can you let go? Here's the guideline:

GUIDELINE #17

If you can really let go of the problem that's most making you feel you want to leave your partner, if you can stop paying attention to it or stop letting it bother you, there's a real chance this relationship is too good to leave. *Quick take:* In a relationship with a future, people can let go of the problems they can't solve.

People often talk about how you can't change someone else, you can only change yourself. That's what this guideline refers to. But the reality is that this kind of letting go is a lot harder to come by than we'd like. Most of the time, after we've tried to let go and failed, we're forced to confront our need for the other person to change. As long as your partner's willing to acknowledge that the problem exists, as long as he proclaims a willingness to change, there's hope. But *can* he change?

STEP #18: CHANGE AND THE WORLD CHANGES WITH YOU

The answer to the question "who are you?" is that we are all the things we are now and all the things we can be in the future. This is what I often say to patients when I ask them to make a change and they say, "I can't because it's not who I am." But you don't know who your partner is to the extent that you don't know who he can be in the future. And the only way you can find that out is to try and see how much he can change.

Julia's Story

It was one of those tragic cases I've seen where someone is painfully stuck in relationship ambivalence for fifteen years. That's how long Julia had spent feeling horribly dissatisfied with her husband, Oscar. She'd done things to half leave the relationship, things like renting a studio of her own to work in or talking to lawyers. But she'd stayed and stayed, making plans for their future together, plans she looked forward to and dreaded at the same time.

They were a cultured, intellectual couple. She was a classical musician, not tremendously talented by her own admission, which was part of the problem, because if she'd felt more talented she'd have felt more entitled to have her own life as a musician. But that was hard because Oscar was a genius. He was a prize-winning world-class scientist and businessman.

You'll have to believe me when I tell you that Oscar was both one of the most frustrating, infuriating, exasperating people around and at the same time rather sweet and charming. I know this doesn't sound like it makes sense, but here's an example.

He'd come home from work, interrupt Julia in the middle of whatever she was doing, turn off her music, because he'd forgotten for the millionth time her million requests to not intrude on her when he came home. And yet, his intrusions were always for the sake of telling her an amusing story or about some small triumph that had occurred during the day.

The tragedy was that Oscar desperately wanted to connect and yet was unable to connect. His slightest utterance had the quality of a formal lecture by an Old World professor. He was boring, incredibly long winded, and insensitive to the point where he never looked at anyone he was talking to.

Was this relationship too good to leave for Julia, or too bad to stay in?

In His Own Sweet Way. It might sound amazing, given Oscar's air of imperviousness, but he knew there was something wrong with how he acted, and the sweet part of him was sincerely willing to change. But his ability to change was limited and frankly weird. He was to personal growth what an extremely brilliant parrot would be to learning English. He could change very fast, but only when I presented his task in almost mathematical form, and then he'd change completely but only in that one narrow respect.

For example, everyone in his family complained passionately about the way he monopolized the conversation no matter how many people were in the room. Nothing could get him to change this until I presented him with the following little formula: Divide the amount of time available by the number of people in the room—that's the percent of time you can talk and the rest of the time you have to listen. If there are two people in the room, you can talk half the time; if there are four people you can only talk a quarter of the time; and so on. He got it and he did it. But not one single other thing would change until I'd come up with another mathematical formula.

What should I do, Julia asked, stay or leave?

Here's the question I asked Julia:

Diagnostic question #18. As you think about your partner's problem that makes your relationship too bad to stay in, does he acknowledge it and is he willing to do something about it *and is he able to change*?

How can you tell if your partner is able to change? There are many ways, and it's important to understand them. Oscar had his own unique style of changing. It was weird, but it *was* change.

You see, asking if an individual *can* change means asking what an individual *needs* to change. One person might simply need to be asked. Oscar needed extremely precise, concrete instructions, the kinds of things he used every day as a scientist. Other people need other things. Some examples follow.

Knowing You Care. A lot of people need the sense that you really care about what you're asking for. You're probably surprised at this. How can she not know you care if the two of you have done nothing but fight about this for years? Well, it's a mystery to me, too. And I've resigned myself to knowing that I'll probably grow old and die without ever solving this mystery.

But from the perspective of my years of clinical experience, although I don't know why this is true, I know it's a fact that people can spend decades yelling and crying and fighting over an issue and their partner will still say in all honesty, "I never really knew how much it mattered to you."

So before you can say your partner can't change, you've got to make sure your partner knows how much the issue matters to you—not based on your thinking he should know, but based on his *proving* he does know. Ask him: on a scale of 1 to 10 how important do you think this is to me? If he doesn't say "10," you know he doesn't know how important it really is to you.

Motivation. Other people need adequate motivation. But isn't knowing you care enough? It should be, in a perfect world, but in this imperfect world of ours change is painful and scary. And sometimes it's hard for people to change even with all the motivation in the world. At least with adequate motivation the likelihood of change increases.

If you've been suffering in an iffy relationship because of something your partner does, you need to ask yourself, "Have I made it clear to him how his life will be better if he changes?" If his life won't be better, why should he change? If you haven't made it clear to him how his life will be better, why should you expect he'll want to change?

Therapy. Some people need therapy to change. The statistics are that about two-thirds of the time a good therapist can succeed in producing change where the people themselves have tried and failed. The question is what constitutes a good therapist, because your partner should certainly go to one before you give up on his changing.

Here's what you should look for. Some good signs are

- Someone you know says this therapist has helped her with a similar problem in concrete ways.
- The therapist offers a plan that focuses on helping you reach the goals you've set, and it's clear to you how what the therapist does will help you reach your goals.
- This therapist uses a variety of methods depending on your problem and who you are.
- You have an ongoing sense that this therapist is more often than not helping you feel better in your life and helping your life work better.

Some bad signs are

- There's no change in your life or how you feel or what you do after four sessions, or things actually get worse.
- The therapist seems uninterested in the concrete realities of your current life.
- The therapist is focused exclusively on ways you've been damaged, instead of on your needs or strengths.
- The therapist seems to have one all-purpose theory or "answer" that explains everything.

So before you say your partner can't change in the specific way that makes your relationship too bad to stay in, my personal rule of thumb is that a good therapist has had a crack at it and it still hasn't changed. Good therapists always make some real difference but they can't fix all things.

So what do you do about question #18, which asks if your partner can change? This guideline emphasizes the positive:

GUIDELINE #18

If your partner shows a real sign of being able to change with respect to a problem that makes your relationship too bad to stay in, there's a good chance there's something healthy and alive at the core of your relationship and you won't be happy if you give up on it at this point. *Quick take:* It's the ability to change that turns frogs into princes.

The point of this guideline is that the ability to change is very, very good news.

But what if your answer to question #18 is no? That's not necessarily bad news. Remember, we're talking about someone who has acknowledged there's a problem and demonstrated a solid willingness to deal with it. With someone like this you don't give up hope, not until you learn a lot more about the situation. A therapist is a doctor of the mind, and doctors are virtually commanded to look for the possibility of someone becoming healthy no matter how sick they happen to be at the moment.

So even if your partner hasn't yet shown signs that he can change, as long as he's passed the acknowledgment and willingness to change tests, there's always the possibility of change in the future. Whether that change will actually come and whether it's enough for you are important questions, but I think they can be put off until later. Right now, because your partner's passed the acknowledgment and willingness to change tests, people in your situation make it clear that you can afford to wait and see what happens.

By the time you get to the end of this book you'll have explored all the possible areas that clearly point to reasons you'll be happiest if you leave. If none of them apply, including the deal breakers we'll get into next, then your relationship is most likely too good to leave.

11

Let's Call the Whole Thing Off

Issue: Personal Bottom Lines

At the very beginning of this book I said that the truth about your relationship you'll discover here is a truth you'll know when you see it. Up until now, I've helped you probe for this truth by bringing to your attention issues I've learned are important in deciding whether to stay in or leave an iffy relationship. Now it's time for a brief change of pace for this chapter only: instead of my bringing an issue to your attention, here you'll have the opportunity to bring a custom-tailored issue to your own attention.

STEP #19: DRAWING THE BOTTOM LINE

If you're trying to decide what to do with an iffy relationship, you want to avoid two mistakes. You want to avoid leaving when you'd really be happiest staying. And you want to avoid staying when you'd really be happiest leaving. Right now, let's focus on avoiding the second mistake.

Guess what one of the biggest differences is between people who stayed when they should have left and people who avoided this mistake.

People who were happy with what they did had said to themselves, in effect, "What's a personal bottom line for me? Has my partner gone over the line?" And they knew what their personal bottom lines were, they saw that their partners had gone over the line, and they were willing to act on that knowledge.

People who were unhappy, by and large, had done none of this. They couldn't or wouldn't say what their bottom lines were, they couldn't or wouldn't acknowledge that their partners had gone over the line, and in any case they weren't willing to act on any transgression.

A Backdoor Accomplice

What happened next to people who ignored their bottom line was tragic. If there's something that's really a bottom line for you and your partner crosses it and you don't act on it, then you're performing an act of psychological self-mutilation. It's as if you'd say, "I felt that *that* was completely unacceptable and part of me still feels that way, but then he did *that* and yet I couldn't or wouldn't do anything about it. So what right do I have anymore to say that *that* was my bottom line?"

And then in a weird, sad way you become a backdoor accomplice to whatever it is your partner does. It's as if you were saying, "*That* ruins the relationship for me but I give you permission to do it anyway and I give myself permission to do nothing about your doing it." You might as well just say, "Let's set things up so we can hate each other."

Your complicity traps you in the relationship and makes you feel you've betrayed yourself. It's psychologically devastating. Children who've been sexually abused often have this kind of experience. They too had a "personal bottom line," a boundary that they knew should never be violated, but their powerlessness as children made it impossible for them to protect themselves. And so they often develop a sense of themselves as having complicity in their own violation.

I realize this is an extreme example, but not acknowledging your bottom lines and not acting when they're violated has permanently damaging psychological consequences.

What's My Line?

You must know what your personal limits are, and if your partner's crossed the line you must act on them.

What is a personal bottom line actually? We're so used to "stating" our bottom lines that many people make a crucial mistake here. They think of a bottom line as something you assert, as if it's about somehow generally standing up for yourself, as if you could stand up for yourself by "issuing" a series of bottom lines.

But this is premature. Before you "state" your bottom line, you have to discover it. It's not like you wake up one morning and "decide" that if your partner does *that* then it's all over between you. Instead, *that* being your bottom line is something you learn about yourself. Experience with the things that happen to you and the ways you react to them teach you that when someone does *that*, things are in fact all over for you.

Here are just some of the things people have said they learned were bottom lines for them:

- "If he goes for six months again without wanting to have sex, then I'm out of here and he knows it."
- "If she ever humiliates me in front of the children again, then I'm ending the relationship."
- "I know it's sometimes hard to coordinate two people's lives, but if I thought he was trying to prevent me from having my own career then it would be all over."
- "We live like paupers even though we're not. If he doesn't give me an adequate budget, I just won't take it anymore."
- "This sounds awful but if you knew her record and the damage it's done me, you'd understand: If she spends more than five hundred bucks again without discussing it with me first, then that's it."
- "If he ever goes into the hospital again for depression, even though I'll feel guilty I'm going to leave."

- "If his mother comes to live here, that's his choice, but then I'm moving out. It's me or her."

Only you know what your personal bottom lines actually are. Whatever they are, you've got to acknowledge them and be prepared to act on them.

Checking for What's Real

Some people think they don't have any bottom lines. They see themselves as being very flexible and open-minded. One woman I interviewed said, "Well, I love my husband so there's nothing he could do that would make it clear to me I had to get out of the relationship. I mean, even if I came home early from work one day and caught him in bed with two high-school girls, well, I'd be hurt and angry and everything but we'd try to work it out."

This is self-deception. I don't know what your personal bottom lines are and I would never tell you what they should be, but I know that they exist. If you're having trouble coming up with yours, say this to yourself: "Even though I love my partner and even though I'd rather be in a relationship than be alone, there are some things that if they were going on would mean I just could no longer be happy or at peace in this relationship." Then let yourself imagine what those things are for you and put them on the list.

Only you know what your bottom lines are. What I know is that you *have* them. All the other questions and guidelines in this book are based on things I've learned are true for *most* people, even though they may not realize it at first. Your personal bottom lines are the things you know are true for you even though they may *not* be true for others. They are the lactose or strawberries or cat hair that's not a problem for some people but that you can't tolerate.

It's up to You

So here's your chance to say what your bottom lines are. Search your heart, then fill in the blanks. The three spaces I've left for each statement are just a suggestion. You might have one bottom line or you might have many.

- "If my partner did

    (a) _____

    (b) _____

    (c) _____

    then I'd feel I'd have to leave the relationship."

- "If my partner didn't do

    (a) _____

    (b) _____

    (c) _____

    then I'd feel I'd have to leave the relationship."

- "If these things were true about my partner—

    (a) _____

    (b) _____

    (c) _____

    —then I'd feel I'd have to leave the relationship."

This is where you can give yourself the opportunity to write down any of your partner's problems that came up in the previous chapter. If there was something about your partner that he knew was a problem and was willing to change but you don't know he can change, then you've got to decide if the possibility of that problem staying the way it is is a deal breaker for you or not. The possibility of change is very hopeful. But you can't live on possibilities when realities that might not change go below your bottom line.

In a sense this is a book about happiness. And for you taking care of your happiness means envisioning a lifetime with your partner not changing or changing only slightly. Then be honest with yourself about whether what you see is just an annoyance or disappointment or if it's something you simply don't want to spend the rest of your life living with.

The question here is obvious:

Diagnostic question #19. **Has your partner violated what for you is a bottom line?**

Let's go right to the guideline.

GUIDELINE #19

If you've made it clear what your real bottom lines are and your partner's violated them anyway, then *by definition* you will not be happy if you stay and you will only be happy if you leave. *Quick take:* The bottom line is the end of the line.

You have to be fair, though, in implementing this guideline. You can't just walk around knowing what your limits are in your own mind, while your partner simply doesn't have a clue, and then if he crosses the line that was invisible to him, you end the relationship. If you know what your bottom lines are, you must tell your partner. This is particularly important in an iffy relationship in which things are so volatile and up in the air.

For example, for you it might be the end of the line if your partner has an affair. Now, your partner probably knows that if you discovered he was having an affair you would be hurt and angry, but he might be surprised to learn that for you it would mean that your relationship was actually over, if that in fact is the case for you. You'd have to let him know this in advance, because I've seen too many relationships blown apart when one person crossed a boundary he didn't know was there, like those two American oil workers in Kuwait wandering across the desert and accidently walking into Iraq. And this is preventable if you make clear what your boundaries are in advance.

Charlotte's Story

A problem occurs when you can't make clear what your boundaries are because you don't know what they are. And it's a lot easier not to know what they are than you might think.

Just remember what it was like when you were in love for the first time back when you were a teenager. Back then, nothing was impossible as long as you loved each other. You couldn't even imagine something spoiling your love feast except your falling out of love. Then one boyfriend or girlfriend did something really lousy and you realized that for you the relationship was over. You didn't invent your bottom line, you discovered it.

You're probably not such a kid anymore, so you know yourself a lot better. That means you know some things your partner could do that would mean things were all over between you. But a lot of personal bottom lines can still come as a complete surprise to both of you.

Here's an unusual example. Charlotte, a self-aware, experienced woman came home early from work one day to find her husband all dressed up in her clothes and wearing her makeup. She was horrified. Even though somewhere inside she felt she should be more broadminded or accepting, she knew immediately that her husband had crossed a bottom line for her. A husband wearing her clothes completely weirded her out.

The problem was that *neither* of them had known before that moment that it was a bottom line. It had never occurred to Charlotte that her husband would wear her clothes and makeup. And her husband would have guessed that she'd be upset if she found out about it, but it didn't occur to him that it would in fact mean the end of their relationship.

If This Ever Happens Again

What do you do if your partner crosses some boundary and it's only then that you discover that it's a bottom line for you, that a line like that even existed? The rule of thumb that I've found works best is that you've got to allow yourself the opportunity to establish a bottom line *and* you've got to allow your partner the opportunity to know what your line is.

So when someone crosses a line neither of you knew existed, it's time for the "If this ever happens again . . ." speech.

But a lot of people don't deliver the speech correctly. The typical mistake you should avoid is "If you ever do this again, it's all over." It's not that this isn't true for you, but it sounds like a threat or a power move, and that's apt to prevent your partner from seeing the truth about how you really feel.

What works is to say, "I really need to let you know that such and such is my absolute bottom line. That's simply a fact for me, so if you ever do it again I'll know you want to end our relationship." That's the point about bottom lines: you're dealing with facts, not threats.

How to Be for Real

Some people who are badly caught in relationship ambivalence are terrified of bottom lines. I remember one man who'd spent over a decade telling everyone he knew about wanting to leave his relationship because his wife was "cold" and "mean." But when he came to see me and I asked him if there was anything his wife could do that would signal that she'd gone too far and broken the bond between them—a bottom line—he said he wouldn't want to specify anything like that because he didn't want to be "too businesslike about love."

When I pushed him a little and said that surely there had to be something that his wife could do or be that would signal to him that the relationship was over, he mentioned the very coldness and meanness he'd first complained about! She'd broken the deal, but it wasn't a deal breaker! That leads to a riddle: When is a bottom line not a bottom line? Answer: When you're married not to your partner but to your ambivalence.

That's what this guy really wanted: to stay stuck in ambivalence. You remember I talked about mutual shutdown: where no one will give anything until the other gives something. The "benefit" of that is that you don't have to do anything. Perfect for people who want to hold their ambivalence over their partner's head and get things from their partner without giving anything back.

This guy wasn't coming to me to get clarity. He was coming so that he could tell his wife he was dealing with his ambivalence so that she'd be scared into doing whatever he wanted because in fact she wanted to stay in the relationship.

Being married to your ambivalence is a lonely place to be, so I can't believe you'd want to stay stuck in this place. That's why you have to allow yourself to see your personal bottom lines when and where they exist and allow them to clarify the boundaries of what's acceptable and unacceptable to you.

The Bottom Line About Bottom Lines. Let me sum up what's important for you to know about bottom lines:

> **1.** You've got to give yourself permission to have them, because otherwise you're damaging and betraying yourself by going along with things that violate a bottom line that really exists.
>
> **2.** You've got to discover what they actually are for you. You learn what your bottom lines really are through experience with what you feel about what happens to you in your life.
>
> **3.** You've got to tell your partner what they are. But in doing so you can't seem as though you're threatening. It's got to come across as a factual statement about what's real for you.

4. You've got to follow through. A bottom line is a deal breaker, not an annoyance. You and your partner can struggle over something you find annoying until the day you die. That's normal even in satisfying relationships. But since a bottom line means the end of the line, you've got to let your partner know that when he gets close to it. And you've got to act on it when he goes over it.

You don't have to make anything a bottom line that really isn't a bottom line for you. But if it is a bottom line and you don't act on it when it's crossed, you're writing a prescription for misery. And that's too bad because a bottom line is a prescription for happiness: it's your way of saying, "I know what I need to be happy."

Ultimately, having a bottom line is all about safety and freedom. Knowing how much is too much means you can always feel safe. Knowing where to draw the line means you're always free to have the kind of life that meets your needs.

12

You Say "Tomayto," I Say "Tomahto"

Issue: Differences Between You

Here's a four-line history of many relationships:

- "I can't believe how many things we have in common."
- "Actually, in some ways we're very different."
- "We are really so different."
- "We were just too different."

If you talk to a lot of people after their divorce and ask them what happened, they'll so often focus on differences that were too large or too difficult to live with. It's even a point of divorce law: irreconcilable differences. Few people get to the point of wondering whether they should leave their relationship or not without having thought long and hard about ways they're different from their partners.

DIFFERENCES THAT MAKE A DIFFERENCE

The issue of differences between two partners is unusually compelling as a way for people to understand what goes wrong in relationships. Whenever we meet anyone for the very first time, the first thing we're aware of is the degree to which they're similar to us or different from us. And if someone seems very different, that fact feels both striking and uncomfortable.

Whatever combination of similarities and differences brings two people together, once we're in a relationship some differences have a way of magnifying themselves, the way a pebble in your shoe has a way of calling attention to itself all out of proportion to its size. And we've all had the experience of gaps or discordancies in relationships that are just too enormous for love to bridge.

Here are some differences people have brought to me as reasons their relationship *might* be too bad to stay in:

- *Active/lazy*. One can't stand not getting things done; the other can't stand doing things.
- *Hot/cold*. One partner is warmer, more passionate, more emotional; the other is cooler, more reserved, more intellectual-seeming.
- *Optimist/pessimist*. One is happier, more hopeful; the other is negative, gloomy, depressed.
- *Fast/slow*. One does things quickly; the other goes as slow as possible.
- *Extrovert/introvert*. One of you likes people, parties, popularity; the other likes staying home alone.
- *Male/female*. This separates people in most relationships but some people are exaggeratedly masculine or feminine or exaggeratedly aware of gender differences.
- *Black/white*. Actually, it doesn't have to just be the black/white difference; any profound racial or ethnic difference can separate two people.
- *Physical/sedentary*. One likes to get a lot of exercise and do sports; the other just likes to sit around.
- *Ambitious/pleasure bent*. One wants to accomplish things; the other just wants to enjoy life.
- *Thrifty/spendthrifty*. One of you hates spending money; money seems to burn a hole in the other's pocket.

- *Smart/stupid.* One partner is faster, brighter than the other and prefers using her head to solve problems. The other thinks his partner is arrogant and arbitrary.
- *Left/right.* One is a dedicated Democrat; the other is a rabid Republican.
- *Aggressive/passive.* One likes to make things happen; the other likes to wait for things to happen.
- *Rich/poor.* One either earns a lot or comes into the relationship with a lot of money; the other neither earns a lot nor has a lot.
- *Practical/dreamy.* One always operates on a down-to-earth level; the other is driven by more idealistic or whimsical considerations.

This is, of course, just a partial list. I've heard it all, from the couple who was different because one liked to talk when they came home from work and the other liked to be left alone, to the couple who was different because one heard God talking to him and the other didn't.

Where all this gets confusing, and where I know you're looking for help, is figuring out where to draw the line when it comes to the issue of difference. Exactly what kinds of differences really do make a difference? How big does the difference have to be to make a real difference? How uncomfortable does it have to make you feel? By the end of this chapter you'll be able to distinguish between differences that might be merely annoying but don't really make things bad in themselves and differences that stick a knife right into the heart of a relationship and make it too bad to stay in.

Surprises

When it comes to the impact of differences on relationships, a lot of the things we think are true aren't.

For one thing, there's what I call the Darrin/Samantha factor (from the old TV show *Bewitched*): some huge differences don't truly make much of a difference after all (except perhaps to a neighbor like Mrs. Kravitz). In the first episode, Darrin discovers that he's married a *real* witch. She's not even a human being! But other than her turning his life upside down every week, they get along fine.

An example of this factor from the real world is relationships between a black person and a white person. While statistically black/white marriages have a higher than average divorce rate, when you exclude people who enter these relationships for the wrong reasons (such as getting back at parents or looking cool to friends), there's actually a better than average chance of success. So this is truly a difference that doesn't make much of a difference when it comes to love. And there are many other differences that exemplify the Darrin/Samantha factor.

On the other hand, there's what I call the city mouse/country mouse factor in which, sometimes, a seemingly small difference of a certain kind ruins everything. After all, the city mouse and the country mouse were both mice—they just liked living in different places, but that made things impossible.

I worked with a couple like this. They were as perfectly matched as, well, two mice. The only difference was that one really wanted to live in the country and the other really wanted to live in the city. We all kept thinking that this simple difference could easily be worked out, but it proved to be utterly unbridgeable and eventually broke them up.

A Therapist's Perspective

What is it about some differences that makes people happy they left the relationship and unhappy they stayed? What is it about other differences that makes people say, "I'm so happy I stayed and worked through this difference" or "What an idiot I was to leave when this tiny difference was the only problem between us"?

It's important that you understand the issue of difference from a therapist's perspective. It's a very different perspective than even the one I have in my own relationship when I'm experiencing the differences between my partner and me. It's like the difference between a doctor's perspective and someone who's sick. When you're sick you think about the germs or viruses that are attacking you. From the doctor's perspective, as important if not more so is the immune system—the entire set of forces and processes through which your body fights a specific germ or virus—and how she can support or utilize your immune system to fight whatever's attacking you.

So from my perspective when people come to me with a relationship in trouble, they typically complain about difference, difference, difference, but I see something else: the forces and factors that prevent them from resolving their differences and the ones that could help them resolve their differences.

A Sexual Difference

Here's an example of a common perspective: A couple comes in complaining about a "huge" difference when it comes to lovemaking. He "never" wants sex. She "always" wants sex. They're furious, hurt, and in despair. A difference like that can cripple a relationship.

But look at this from my point of view as a therapist. There are a lot of ways this can play out.

Perhaps what seems like a "difference" problem is really a *communication* problem. You'd be surprised how many times I've asked polarized couples like this to give a range of how often they'd like to make love in a typical week or month, and the "never wants sex" guy says he'd like to make love once or twice a week and the "always wants sex" gal says she'd like to make love "ideally every day, but I'd be happy if we made love a couple of times a week." They overlap! They just had never been able to talk in a practical, down-to-earth way about what they were really talking about.

Or perhaps what seems like a "difference" problem is really a *negotiation* problem. Let's say the couple had not only been torn apart by how often or not they made love but by who initiated lovemaking. Here's how one couple worked things out: the

person who wanted to make love more often got more lovemaking in exchange for letting go of her desire that her partner initiate lovemaking. This meant that she'd get to make love more
often but she'd have to initiate more often. And for many differences there are many possible negotiated settlements that are out
of people's reach only when they have poor negotiating skills.

Or perhaps what seems like a "difference" problem is really
a *power* problem. Let's say there've been power struggles over
many things in the relationship for a particular couple, and now
there's a power struggle over "who says" how often they make
love. They each want to be the one "who says." It's not so much
that one wants to win as that he wants the other not to win. All
that needs to happen is that the therapist or any other respected
figure comes in and establishes a fair, objective rule for how
they'll split the difference. For example, a rule I've often established is that they rotate weeks or months, doing it the way one
person wants during one time period, the way the other wants
during the next time period.

Unbridgeable Differences. We've already talked about power
and communication in earlier chapters and before long we'll talk
about negotiation. Then we'll have covered everything that could
prevent people from dealing with the differences that inevitably
come up whenever two people try to make a life together. These
are not the differences that in themselves make a relationship too
bad to stay in.

This chapter focuses on what's left. You'll find the answer to
the question: What makes differences in and of themselves toxic
and unbridgeable?

STEP #20: WHO YOU LOVE AND HOW YOU LIVE

To get at just where a difference makes a real difference you've
got to focus on what's really most important to people, to all of
us: how we live. If you want to zero in on a difference between
you and your partner that all by itself will *really* make you miserable if you stay in the relationship, answer this question.

Diagnostic question #20. Is there a clearly formulated, passionately held difference between you that has to do with the shape and texture and quality of your life as you actually experience it?

This question gets at the issue of lifestyle. Let's say one of us likes leading a physically active life and the other does not. That's a difference. Still, if it's okay with both of us that I stay home on weekends while you spend those days bicycling out to the country and back, then we actually *agree* about our lifestyle.

But if your vision of a relationship is two people spending weekends cycling out to the country together and mine isn't, then we *disagree* about our lifestyle. And if we not only disagree but do so passionately, and if this vision of a relationship is of the essence of what you want to get out of life, and mine is for me, too, then this disagreement gets at the heart of how we each want to live and attacks the heart of our relationship.

I'm not talking about details or fragments of a lifestyle. I'm talking about what I call the armature of a lifestyle, the inner framework that gives a life shape and substance. It's about what you care about in how you actually live.

The difference could be about something as basic as having children. It's not an issue of one person wanting children more than the other—that difference is very often the case. But when one person in a relationship sees having children as a central feature of her vision of what her life will be like and the other person, for whatever reason, has counted on and is committed to a life free of the obligations children entail, then this is a difference about the essence of what you care about most in how you actually live.

TV or Not TV, That Is the Question

To show you how lifestyle is the one place where a difference makes a difference, just perform this little experiment in your mind: Imagine what would happen if, in every one of the 70 million marriages in America today, one of the partners suddenly insisted that all TVs in the house must go, that their marriage must be a totally TV-free marriage for both people. Assume they really meant it and would stick by it no matter what.

How many marriages do you think would be left a year later? How many people would stay together if they realized that a lifetime with their partner meant a lifetime without television?

I think most of us, no matter how much we believe in love, would guess that out of 70 million relationships *a lot* of people would choose to leave rather than actually spend every day of the rest of their lives without the possibility of watching their favorite shows or vegging out in front of the tube.

Now let's look at this idea of lifestyle differences as we actually experience them. Here's an example. I've rarely seen couples, either those seeking help or those who didn't feel they needed help, either heterosexual or homosexual, where there weren't all kinds of differences between the partners about what they liked in lovemaking. But even huge differences here were not necessarily relationship-undermining lifestyle issues in themselves.

On the other hand, there have been some couples where for one or both people something about sex *was* a lifestyle issue. Then their difference made all the difference. For one woman, making love for hours was the centerpiece of what she looked forward to every day she didn't have to go to the office. This wasn't the all-too-common issue of a woman complaining that her partner didn't like to spend enough time in foreplay. It was an issue for her of who she was as a person and virtually the meaning of her life. But her partner felt bored, trapped, humiliated, and deprived by this lovemaking that went on for hours and hours and used up every bit of spare time.

The Quality of Our Lives

The quality of our free time is the centerpiece of the quality of our lives for most people. The difference between these two people wasn't about one little thing in their free time but about the entire nature and structure of their free time.

You can see why, in the country mouse/city mouse factor I mentioned earlier, the couples I referred to had an unbridgeable difference. When one of you passionately wants an urban lifestyle and the other passionately wants a rural lifestyle, then the thing you want affects every part of your life.

It's clear why the lifestyle difference is so critical. It's the reason people end up choosing a lifestyle over their partner: it's what you want from a relationship in the first place. Think back to the relationship choices you've made. It's never just a person you wanted to be with. *You wanted that person combined with the lifestyle you'd have (or you thought you'd have) with that person.*

I'm not saying every possible aspect of lifestyle is what you wanted. It may be that whether you had money or not wasn't important to you. Or whether you lived in the city or the country wasn't important to you. But your vision of happiness with that person included a vision of how you'd live with that person, what your life with that person would be like.

So when two lovers look into each other's eyes, they're saying, "You are my lifestyle." Well, they don't actually say this, but in effect that's what they're choosing when they stay, and it's also what they're rejecting when they leave. When the overall, basic quality of your life is at stake, you need to feel you can give yourself permission to choose the life that feels good to you over the life that doesn't.

Robert's Story

What happened to Robert and Agnes is sadly all too common. They'd had a relatively successful marriage for many years. It was a traditional marriage, in which Robert had worked hard to become a rich and prominent attorney, while Agnes stayed home to bring up three children and do the endless entertaining and civic duties that were so important for his career. They both felt it was a worthwhile partnership. It was the lifestyle they'd both married.

But things don't stay the same, whether you've been together many years or just a couple of years. When their oldest child went off to college, Robert and Agnes started moving rapidly in opposite, incompatible directions. Robert had grown weary of the legal grind. He found work boring, depressing, and empty, and he'd talked about retiring early and moving to a modest villa in the countryside of Northern Italy. Besides, he had his "go to hell" money: the dough he needed to walk away from work and never come back. He wanted to spend the rest of his days enjoying himself.

Agnes was the opposite. All those years she'd spent taking care of home and family had turned her into a coiled spring of ambition, more and more compressed, ready to explode when the pressure was taken off. With the children starting to leave home, she wanted a life of her own, a career out in the world, accomplishment, success.

Devastating differences over lifestyle were starting to take hold of Robert and Agnes. Before, whatever their differences, their visions of their lifestyle were complementary. Now their differences were about their lifestyle and were incompatible.

Robert didn't want to retire to an empty house; he wanted Agnes to share a hobby-filled, trip-taking retirement with him based on a completely new life in someplace like Northern Italy. But Agnes wanted freedom. She'd felt tied down by Robert and his life and now she wanted a life of her own. But it would be hard enough for a woman in her early fifties to build a career; she'd have to stay where she was with all of her friends and connections to have any chance.

Two people who'd lived in harmony for years ended up in bitter opposition. They still liked each other well enough and still had similar tastes and values. But now Robert was horribly torn. There was the life he wanted: somewhere far away where all thought of responsibility was gone and with a companion by his side. There was the life Agnes was willing to offer: staying put, facing an empty house every day. For Robert the lifestyle Agnes offered didn't feel like the retirement he'd dreamt of; it felt like premature death.

I'll tell you what happened to Robert and Agnes in a moment. But first here's the guideline:

GUIDELINE #20

If you and your partner have passionately felt but profoundly divergent preferences about how to live, and if
the lifestyle you prefer is impossible with your partner,
and if it's clear that you'll be happier living that lifestyle
without your partner than living with your partner without that lifestyle, then you'll be happy if you leave and
unhappy if you stay. *Quick take:* You live a life, you don't
live a relationship.

This guideline is about where happiness and contentment and
satisfaction come from in life. They come from the way you live,
from the things that are important to you about the way you
live. Of course someone you love is extremely important to the
way you live, but don't put the cart before the horse. Your life is
your life, and the person you love is a part of your life.

You *can* allow yourself to choose the life you need to be
happy. If your lifestyle difference is not such a big deal or you
can accommodate your differences within your lifestyle, then you
don't have a problem. People who break up an otherwise decent
relationship for a minor improvement in their lifestyle usually
live to regret it. But all by himself your partner cannot make you
happy if on the other side of the fence there's a different way of
living that makes all the difference for you.

Robert *didn't* give himself the permission this guideline offers you. He felt guilty at the thought of leaving Agnes, even
though she clearly indicated she would choose to be alone rather
than go with him to Italy. And, he later realized, he was scared
and habit-ridden. So he stayed in his old house in his old city sur-
rounded by all the old reminders of a life he wanted to get as far
away from as possible. His early retirement, instead of feeling
like a release from imprisonment, felt like a twilight zone, where
he was stranded in the middle of nowhere between the life he'd
left and the life he wanted.

Agnes blossomed. Her new life was more and more what she
wanted it to be. But her happiness didn't really touch Robert because it wasn't about them or any life they were having together.

It was in a way like the happiness of a child going off on some trip by itself for the first time. Robert saw her happiness like someone looking through the wrong end of a telescope. For all his success and plans Robert ended up feeling marooned, a stranger stranded in someone else's life. They've stayed together, but to Robert it feels like a mistake.

Yes, life with another person can press our noses against all kinds of irritating differences. But the difference we can't live with is the difference that's about how to live.

STEP #21: "I MARRIED A MARTIAN"

Any difference can be annoying, but most differences are either resolvable or ignorable. You can resolve a difference by working out some kind of compromise. You can ignore a difference by just being who you are and doing what you want and paying no attention to the gap between you. Most of the time some combination of love and skill enables you to resolve or ignore your differences. One exception to this is the difference I've just talked about, where you differ about the fundamental way you want to live.

Are there any other differences, though, that are so important they transcend your ability to resolve or ignore them?

The Sense of Connection

Yes, there *are* differences that transcend your ability to resolve or ignore them. These differences have to do with utter, deep-down alienness. If you've ever had a cat or a dog, you know how on some level, in spite of your knowing that the two of you are from different species, you have a sense of some shared bond. You both like a good meal. You both like a comfortable place to curl up. You both like physical affection. You both like to play. You both have the capacity to care about each other. This sense of similarity or connection deep down is part of what creates a real bond between you.

But when you start moving away from the dog/cat level toward the chicken/rhinoceros/snake level of existence and then toward the clam/worm/beetle level of existence, at some point the sense of any connection disappears. With the sense of connection, you can share your life with the creature. Without the sense of connection, you eat it or call the exterminator.

The same thing is true with the people we find ourselves falling in love with. Sometimes there's that deep basic sense of connection, but, surprisingly, sometimes there isn't. Sometimes we fall in love with someone who's terribly, horribly, profoundly, unbridgeably different. Yet it's very hard to see or admit this, because, after all, this is someone you've fallen in love with. You could understand falling in love with a dog or cat, but how could you fall in love with a clam or a worm?

It's easier than you might think. We deceive ourselves, among other things, because we all belong to the same species. You're physically attracted to each other. You both like the Grateful Dead and both hate Country music. Or you both agree that Dostoyevsky is a terrible bore and a dreadful writer and you both admit to being Nick at Nite fans. Or you both like to sleep with the windows open and hate making love in the morning. All you need, then, is to go shopping for furniture together and have a couple of kids and the fact that you're actually as alien as two people from different planets who have no interest in each other completely eludes you.

So ask yourself this:

Diagnostic question #21. In spite of all the ways you're different, would you say that deep down or in some respect that's important to you your partner is someone just like you in a way you feel good about?

Searching for this deep-down, basic similarity often forces people to look at their relationship with their partner in a completely different way. For example, one woman had been complaining about being a golf and TV-sports widow, about how her husband was a "typical insensitive man." She was really starting to get carried away with the sense that the two of them were too different to stay together.

Question #21 shed a different light on things. What was undeniable to her was the fact that he believed as strongly as she did that being a good parent was the most meaningful experience they'd ever have. Even though he played golf and watched sports on TV he always made time for the kids—he *sought out* ways of being with the kids. She knew, beyond question and in spite of all the things about him that annoyed her, that what was most important to her was most important to him.

Proving There's No Connection. The issue of finding a deep, basic similarity must be handled carefully when you're afraid there is no similarity between you and your partner. It's a question of evidence. You can prove a similarity *does* exist because you see it and feel it. But you can't prove it *doesn't* exist just because you don't see it and feel it. You can't prove a negative. To use a common example, we may be sure that unicorns are purely mythical creatures, but who knows?—maybe there are a whole bunch of them somewhere and no one's found them yet. In the same way, just because on one of your bad days when you're bummed out about your relationship it feels as though there's not one single way your partner's like you—well, maybe there's a profound similarity somewhere you've just overlooked or forgotten.

Trusting Your Feelings

Your feelings have to be your standard here. Do you *feel* you and your partner are truly similar deep down and in a way that's important to you? It can't just be a superficial similarity. There's got to be something deep down, where your similarity is actually meaningful to you.

For example, the fact that you both think screwball comedies from the thirties are wonderfully funny may be a way that you're the same, but there's got to be something deep down this similarity is *about*. If it's about sharing a deeply nostalgic view of life or sharing a madcap, devil-may-care attitude, then your similarity is about something. But if your having some preference in common doesn't go any deeper, you're really just two strangers who by the luck of the draw happen to like the same movies.

I knew a couple who answered question #21 by saying they both loved to go for walks in the woods. This is certainly a real if small lifestyle similarity. And they're certainly similar with respect to liking the same thing. But here's why they ended up being happy they broke up. They realized that their both liking to walk in the woods wasn't about anything that made them similar to each other in any deep-down way. It wasn't about a deep and special kind of love of nature that made them feel they specially fit together. Instead they both liked walking in the woods the way two people chosen at random might both like pepperoni pizza or might both think that yellow is the perfect color for a taxicab. It's a kind of superficial similarity that doesn't go anywhere or add up to anything.

I keep thinking about Gertrude Stein's comment about Oakland, California: "There's no there there." What she meant was that there was no downtown where everyone comes together. And for this couple, just because they liked walking in the woods didn't mean there was any deep-down similarity where they could both come together. This is a ticklish, subjective issue but the guideline is real and true.

GUIDELINE #21

If you truly feel that your partner is like you in some way that's meaningful and that you feel good about, there's a real chance your relationship is too good to leave. But if there's no similarity at all in any way that's important to you—so that you feel as if your partner is alien—most people in similiar situations ended up being happy if they left. *Quick take:* Somehow, somewhere, when you look deep in your partner's eyes you've got to be able to see yourself.

I sometimes call this the I-married-a-Martian factor. It's what leads people after decades of marriage to say, "We just have nothing in common." It's not about the width or number of your differences. It's about finding an utter gap, however narrow, in that one place where you were counting on there being no differences.

The Mystery of Difference

Now, I hope, you see more clearly through the mystery of difference in relationships, of how some differences mean everything and other differences mean nothing. There's always the possibility that you can ignore or resolve your differences, most of them anyway, even seemingly huge and annoying ones.

But not when the very way you live that you care most about is at stake. And not when there's no deep and meaningful bridge of similarity to connect you. You need to feel you can give yourself permission to not be with someone who in every way feels like a Martian to you.

What I've seen in relationships is that just the way a picture's worth a thousand words, a deep and basic similarity that's meaningful to both people can overcome a thousand differences in creating a satisfying relationship. But without that similarity, even one difference can be unbearable agony.

13
If Ever I Should Leave You

Issue: Post-relationship Options

TUNNEL VISION

While I was leading one couples group a while back, a woman started complaining that her husband was "no Mel Gibson."

Another woman leaned forward and said, "Honey, you couldn't get Mel Gibson. So let go of it."

The second woman not only made an important point, she opened the door to a whole set of considerations that are often neglected by people trying to figure out what to do with an iffy relationship:

> If you're trying to decide if you'll be happiest if you stay or leave, you can't look only at what's going on *in* your relationship. You have to look at what your options are *outside* of it and at how clearly and realistically you've been thinking about them.

And that's what I'll help you do here. You might be thinking your relationship is too bad to stay in because you're looking forward to something after you leave that just isn't going to happen. You might be thinking your relationship is too good to leave because you're afraid of something out there that just isn't out there. The questions here will help you peek over the rim of your relationship and see what's on the other side. If you don't look at the big picture, you're headed for big trouble.

That probably sounds like the last thing you want to hear. If you've been wrestling with whether it's best for you to stay or leave, it probably feels as though you've been thinking too much about what's waiting for you on the other side. How will you be able to afford a new apartment? How big a burden will childcare or child support be? What new relationships will you find?

I'm sure you've been thinking about all kinds of practical details. But my job is to share with you the experiences of people who've gone through what you're going through now. And they tell me that while you probably have thought about all kinds of things, you've also quite possibly *not* thought about something really important.

Ask the Experts

If you could boil down what people who've been there learned, it would be this: "I had plenty of worries, but looking back I can see that I spent too little time checking into what my alternatives were outside the relationship. I was way too passive about discovering what it really would be like to leave and whether it would be better or worse than what I had. I kept looking at the little picture of this or that about my partner or this or that hope or fear about what it would be like if I left, when I should've been looking at the big picture."

Inside the tunnel of relationship ambivalence, what you see is how stuck you feel and the endless realities of your current life and a few scary or enticing slivers of what awaits you on the other side. You've got to get outside that tunnel if you want to clearly see what your options are.

Let me illustrate how examining your options more fully makes all the difference.

Outside the Tunnel

Suppose you were deciding whether to spend a few thousand dollars going away for your summer vacation or just staying home. If you've fallen victim to tunnel vision, all you'll be able to think about is whether to go and spend the money or not go and not spend the money.

But that's a big mistake. Outside the tunnel, looking at the big picture, what you really have is a choice between what you get spending the money on a vacation and what you get spending the money on whatever else it is you'd spend it on if you didn't go on vacation. The vacation that sounded so great might not sound so great if you thought you could get a remodeled bathroom or a down payment on a nice new car instead.

But the vacation might sound better than you first thought if you knew yourself well enough to know that if you didn't go you'd just spend the money on side trips and eating out that wouldn't add up to the pleasure a real vacation would give you.

I know it sounds awfully crass to compare the most heartfelt decision imaginable with spending money. But the point is that figuring out the choice that's best for you requires that you look at the whole picture. Here's what happens if you don't.

Matt's Story

It was a classic tale of two people meeting in college, falling in love, and getting married after graduation. Wendy and Matt originally got involved with each other because they were part of the same group of friends and because they liked, and more important, disliked, the same kinds of music. They felt comfortable with each other, and once they started saying they loved each other they felt it and it seemed impossible not to get married.

Things were great for a while, particularly with Matt earning a good salary as an electronics technician for a local defense contractor and with Wendy working as a middle-school teacher. Then they turned a corner.

It's a mystery, I think, exactly when and how things go wrong in a relationship like theirs that starts out with a lot going for it.

This mystery's maintained by the fact that people like this rarely seek help when things start going wrong, so that by the time hurts and resentments have grown, the seed that began it all has been deeply buried.

By the time they went to someone for help, Matt in particular was convinced that he and Wendy had grown in very different directions and he just didn't feel there was much connection between them.

He saw himself as a guy who was interested in the larger world of politics and social trends. From his point of view, after the kids came and Wendy stopped teaching, she seemed almost completely absorbed in the minutiae of family life. Besides, Matt had noticed a trend in the first couple of years they were married: the madcap college kid Wendy had started out as was getting tough and serious and all-too grown-up. Having kids didn't soften this; it speeded it up. Wendy just didn't seem to him the sweetheart she used to be.

What it all added up to for Matt was that *compared to what he'd been looking forward to* his marriage had turned into a very iffy relationship. He kept staying, but he kept thinking about leaving.

Then his best friend got divorced. It seemed miraculous to Matt the ease with which his friend "won his freedom." Why stay bound to a nagging sourpuss, Matt wondered, when the freedom he'd missed out on could still be his? There was a simple equation in his mind: leaving equals freedom. Oh, boy! Staggering toward that oasis, or mirage, of freedom, Matt got divorced himself.

What did he find "out there" that he might have seen before he got divorced if he'd looked more carefully?

Do you remember the very last shot in the Truffaut movie *The Four Hundred Blows*? The kid who'd spent the movie running away from home and reform school finally got to the ocean he'd been seeking. And when he saw it for the first time he froze with a sad, blank expression on his face because where he'd been expecting everything he found nothing.

That's what happened to Matt. Being single just wasn't so great. The amusement park of single life turned out to be a barren strip of loneliness, a lifestyle filled with incredible difficulty at meeting new people, awkward dates with women he couldn't connect to, and the cruel realization that the young women he'd been fantasizing about getting together with considered him too old.

And he missed his kids. He'd thought he'd have these wonderful weekend experiences of pure parenting pleasure, divorced from the hassles of getting kids off to school on time and making sure they do their homework. Instead, the weekends were nightmares of boredom and disconnection, filled with the frustration of trying to amuse kids whose friends and lives were elsewhere.

To cap it all off, when he finally did get into some kind of semicommitted, semi-long-term relationship, he found that that woman, once she felt she could take Matt a little for granted, ended up being just as demanding and businesslike as Wendy had been.

Here's Matt's judgment on himself. "You just can't compare a reality to a dream, and that's what I'd tried to do. Of course my reality couldn't compete with my dream. But if instead I'd compared my reality to the real alternative that was waiting for me, I wouldn't have left. My life with Wendy was far from perfect, but there was nothing about it that meant I couldn't stay or that I wouldn't have been happy staying and working things out."

Matt's case is a perfect example of the enormous difference it makes when you move from tunnel vision to a broader, more realistic perspective in trying to sort out whether it's best to leave or stay.

For Matt, tunnel vision led to a mistaken decision to leave. It can just as easily lead to a mistaken decision to stay.

Donna's Story

For many years Donna's life with Margot was a gilded cage of her own making. Donna supplied the cage, Margot supplied the gilding. When they'd first started out they'd both lived the life of counter-culture-type people without much money. But very soon Margot started getting into computers and with the help of what

Donna eventually realized were extremely rich relatives, Margot started building what turned into a highly successful company manufacturing specialized computer devices for the financial world.

While all of this splendor was in the making, Donna chugged along, dilettantishly dabbling in one nonremunerative area after another, from making harpsichords to counseling inner-city youth. Meanwhile her relationship with Margot was getting more and more iffy. There was a loosely connected spectrum of problems starting with their having less and less in common at one end of the spectrum, through Donna's having problems feeling intimate with Margot (particularly with Margot's being increasingly preoccupied with business and money), down to their lovemaking being rare and cold at the other end of the spectrum.

Besides the fact that she still had some feelings of love for Margot, money made the whole situation confusing for Donna. To put it bluntly, here were her alternatives, as she saw them at the time through the tunnel vision of relationship ambivalence.

On the one hand, there was a life of comfort and prosperity if she stayed with Margot. Not only would there be more than enough money for Donna to do pretty much whatever she wanted, but Donna felt she'd indirectly helped Margot get the business going and so felt an emotional stake in it. Tantalizingly, there was a strong possibility that with a combination of Margot's wealthy relatives dying and/or some giant corporation buying out her business she (and by extension Donna) would end up not only prosperous but seriously rich.

On the other hand, Donna was convinced that leaving Margot meant a life of desperate poverty. With no money of her own she'd soon be as poor as the young women she'd been counseling. At least that was her fear.

So she was miserable, but she stayed for years, blinded by the gilding on her cage. Then by chance she had an experience that opened her eyes. She got involved with trying to find a place to live for an eighteen-year-old woman she'd been working with. Talking to friends and acquaintances she discovered opportunities for sharing houses and apartments that were cheap, safe, and comfortable. It suddenly dawned on her that if she switched to working full time as she'd frequently been invited to do, she'd be able to afford a perfectly decent life on her own, supporting herself.

She was filled with regret at the thought of how she could have changed her life years and years earlier if only she'd seen past her fears to her real possibilities.

Look Both Ways

Matt's story and Donna's story illustrate the opposite ways tunnel vision can lead to disaster. If Matt had opened his eyes more widely, he would have seen that his iffy relationship was really too good to leave. If Donna had opened her eyes more widely, she would have seen that her iffy relationship was really too bad to stay in. It's not that opening their eyes changed any of the realities they'd already been aware of. But they would have put them in a completely fresh perspective.

Let me help you avoid either kind of disaster.

STEP #22: NEW REASONS TO STAY

The questions in this chapter are a little different from the ones in other chapters. The others are each essentially self-contained. The two here are based on your first taking a fresh look at your situation before you answer them.

Do this. At the top of one sheet of paper write the words: "Things I look forward to in my new life when I think about leaving." At the top of another sheet of paper write the words: "Things I'm afraid of in a new life that make me think about staying."

Then write down whatever has been most important to you as you've struggled with whether you should stay or leave. Based on the examples you've just read, Matt would have written something like "Dating nice sexy women" and "Having a better relationship with my kids" as things he was looking forward to. Donna would have written something like "Not having money" and "Having nowhere to live" as things she was afraid of.

In particular, when you're writing down the things you're looking forward to, include the specific offers of support you're counting on from friends and family.

When you look at what you've written down, you'll have the opportunity to see the picture that tunnel vision might have created for you.

Now you have the opportunity to correct that tunnel vision. For each item on your list ask yourself,

- "Is this true?"
- "Is this likely?"

Then ask yourself,

- "What else is possible?"
- "What's most likely?"

For Matt, it was true that he could date other women once he was on his own, but what else was possible was that dates would be hard to come by and not very satisfactory, and this was more likely, too. And it wasn't true that things would be as great with his kids as he'd imagined. Matt could have learned all this if he'd talked to other divorced men.

For Donna, it simply wasn't true that she couldn't support herself. The possibility that she hadn't considered was that being on her own would force her to earn a decent living and that she could live comfortably on what she earned.

I can't do this part for you. The specific circumstances of everyone's life are so different. Only you know your hopes and fears and the realities that generate them. Only you have access to developing new information that will completely change your understanding of the realities you face. But you've got to develop this new information.

If nothing else, ask people you know whether they think your hopes and fears are realistic. What hopes and fears do they think are more realistic? You're not asking these people about the realities inside your relationship, but about realities outside your relationship that they're a lot more qualified to comment on.

Then ask yourself this question:

Diagnostic question #22. With your new, more complete, more realistic set of information about what it would be like for you if you left, have you discovered new, more probable realities that now make leaving seem impossibly difficult or unpleasant?

To help you develop this information, think about what awaits you by going through this checklist of issues:

- Where will you live? How will you be able to afford it? Will you be able to commute to your job from there?
- How much savings will you have available to you after you leave? How much of your income will you have available? Will that be enough?
- What are your prospects for meeting people? This is a time to be brutally honest: do you have the characteristics that'll make it relatively easy to find dates? Will you want to go through the process of meeting new people?
- Is it realistically likely that you'll be lonely in your new life? How well do you cope with loneliness?
- What's going to happen with the kids? Is joint custody a possibility, and do you want it? Is *not* having custody likely for you; is that acceptable to you? Is *having* custody more likely, and have you thought through what it's like to parent kids on your own?
- What will being on your own do to your ability to work?
- Is it realistic that the friends you're counting on being there for you will end up being there? (The friends you had as individuals usually end up staying friends with the woman, not the man, but married friends of yours often distance themselves from both of you.)

- How do your relatives feel about what you're wanting to do? Will they provide moral support? Perhaps more important, will they actually deliver the practical or financial support they might have been promising?

Feel free to add to this checklist whatever is most important to you in your life. Now here's the guideline:

GUIDELINE #22

At this point in the process, as you look more realistically at what it will be like for you to leave, if this fresh look clearly makes leaving seem too difficult and makes staying seem desirable, then you've gotten the clarity you were looking for and you know you'll be happier staying. *Quick take:* If staying makes sense when you really check into it, it makes sense to stay.

But you want to make sure you don't fall back into ambivalence by using the balance-scale approach. This guideline is not an attempt to get you to weigh more things in the balance. *It's an attempt to help you find that one piece of overlooked reality that suddenly sheds a completely different light on everything.*

If thinking more realistically about what awaits you decisively changes the way you'd been thinking about leaving, fine. If not, some other question coming up will give you clarity.

STEP #23: NEW REASONS TO LEAVE

Now go back to your two pieces of paper: "Things I look forward to in my new life when I think about leaving" and "Things I'm afraid of in a new life that make me think about staying." Ask yourself the following question:

Diagnostic question #23. With your new, more complete, more realistic set of information about what it would be like to leave, have you discovered new, more probable realities that now make leaving seem easier, more attractive, and make staying no longer desirable?

If, for example, you've been convinced you have nowhere to go, is that really true? If you've been convinced you'll be alone and lonely, is that true? If you've been convinced you won't be able to support yourself, is that true? Use the same checklist you just used. And remember to use your friends as a source of information about what it's really like "out there."

Here's the guideline:

GUIDELINE #23

If looking more realistically at what it will actually be like for you to leave your relationship clearly makes leaving seem easier and more attractive to you and makes staying seem like a bad idea, then you've gotten the clarity you were looking for and you'll be happier if you leave. *Quick take:* If leaving makes sense when you really check into it, then it makes sense to leave.

Suppose this guideline does apply. It means that by looking more realistically at your life you've gotten the clarity that eluded you when you focused narrowly on your relationship alone.

No Sister

This might seem like an oddly practical chapter in a book that has focused on the emotional and psychological ins and outs of iffy relationships. But in my experience the issue I've raised here is extremely important. I'll never forget a patient I had many years ago before I developed the understanding I've been sharing with you. She and I spent weeks talking about whether she'd be better off staying or leaving. And every time the topic came up she'd refer to her sister's vague offer to come live with her in San Francisco as a powerful magnet drawing her out of her current relationship, as a major factor pulling the balance scale down toward leaving.

Finally I urged her to check out whether her sister's offer was serious. She came back the following week and said she had a long talk with her sister. After her sister ran through a long list of objections, it got through to her that her sister really didn't want her to come stay with her and wasn't really welcoming her.

She never again said she wanted to end her relationship. It's not that the relationship was any better—it still had its problems. But the precise degree of bearability of those problems could be measured by the fact that it felt worthwhile for this woman to leave when she thought she had someplace great to go to and it didn't feel worthwhile to leave when she had nowhere to go to. Years later she and her husband are still together. Remembering people like this woman and Matt and Donna—that's why it's important to reexamine your options. They don't change the reality of your relationship, but a clear view of your options may very well change how you feel about the reality of your relationship.

PERSPECTIVES: "BUT WHAT ABOUT THE CHILDREN?"

If you have young children living at home, this Perspectives is for you. Certainly thinking about your children is part of your thinking about what awaits you on the other side if you and your partner break up.

My guess is you're torn between two thoughts about this. On the one hand, you know that divorce isn't good for the children psychologically and emotionally, and it's an incredible, stressful, expensive hassle for the parents. On the other hand, you know how bad it is for children to grow up with parents whose bad relationship spoils the family atmosphere.

The two thoughts you're torn between are not only correct, but they actually sum up all the volumes ever written about the impact of divorce on children. Divorce isn't good for children but neither is staying in a relationship that's too bad to stay in.

The problem you face now is how to include children in the stay or leave decision so that you're fair to yourself but you're also fair to them.

Here's what I've found works best for almost everybody. You've got to keep things clear. That means you've got to decide whether this relationship in itself is too bad to stay in or too good to leave. I know your children are extremely important to you, but they're separate from this decision, in the same way that your relationship with your children is separate from your relationship with your partner.

Focus on the relationship itself. If by the end of this book you can see that your relationship is too bad to stay in and that you'll be happiest leaving, then you should leave.

Each diagnostic question focuses on some aspect of the relationship that is so important that it actually made a huge difference to people's happiness. Any guideline that points to leaving points to something that poisons the environment your children are growing up in. If a relationship is too bad to stay in according to the guidelines in this book, then it's too bad to stay in when there are children.

But children do make a difference and the differences are these: First, this chapter focuses on *practicalities* that, when you see them, make you change the way you feel about staying or leaving. These practicalities could certainly include the realities involving children. I'm talking about things like having infants or toddlers that need tremendous amounts of attention. The likelihood or unlikelihood of the noncustodial parent paying childcare. The difficulty of finding someone to look after the kids while you work. The scarcity of time for yourself. You've probably thought about most of these already. If not, just ask some of your friends.

Second, here's the difference having children can make. They can appropriately affect the *timing* of your decision. If one of your children is going through a particularly difficult time right now, waiting a bit might be in order. And children should affect how you go about *implementing* your decision. A good pediatrician or family therapist can make wonderful suggestions on how to help children cope with a divorce. And children should also have some input into the decisions you and your partner make about who will live where. All these issues are really outside the scope of this book, and I'll trust you to look into them if it turns out you need to.

But by themselves children don't determine whether you will be happiest leaving or staying.

Some people hearing this talk about selfish adults and the devastating psychological impact of divorce on children. But as I said at the beginning of this Perspectives, you already know that divorce and staying in a bad family atmosphere both have a negative impact on children.

It's important not to overstate the negative impact of divorce on children. Psychologically speaking, the studies that show the greatest negative impact of divorce on children delve into the psyches of children of divorced parents without delving into the psyches of comparable children *of comparable parents who did not divorce.* So when these studies drew their conclusions they were essentially comparing the real children whose parents had divorced with an ideal image of children whose parents had an ideal relationship.

But you can't compare the ideal to the real. The psychological life your children will lead if you and your partner divorce can *only* be compared to the psychological life they'll lead if the two of you stay together. And imagine what kind of psychological life that will be if you stay in a relationship that in fact is too bad to stay in.

As I've said before, this is a book about happiness. If your relationship is too good to leave in spite of its problems, then you and your children will be happy if you work on the relationship and make it as good as it can be. However, if the conditions in it are so bad that most people in your situation said they were happy they left, then you and your children will be happy moving on to new and better lives.

14
R-E-S-P-E-C-T

Issue: Do You Respect Each Other?

Respect is the soil out of which self-esteem grows. But the fighting and familiarity of relationships is the soil out of which *disrespect* grows. That's the problem and the issue we have to face here.

We all vitally need to feel respected—overall, deep-down, and in the ways that are most important to us. And we need to respect our partners, if for nothing else than as a resource in our lives. But if there's stuff that goes on universally and inevitably in relationships that germinates seeds of disrespect, then disrespect is a problem for *all* of us. That means I can't just say, "What? He doesn't respect you? You've got to leave!" There's so much disrespect in so many relationships that if people acted on this we'd be living in a world of singles.

People are hungry for respect in relationships as they're hungry for nothing else. And they're just as hungry to feel respect for their partners as they are to receive it.

So the challenge here is to understand where to draw the line. It's to understand where problems with respect cross over from being something like rush-hour traffic—an unpleasantness we can live with, maybe even cope with, maybe even overcome—and turn instead into something that damages us psychologically.

STEP #24: WHEN DISRESPECT GOES TOO FAR

Let's put things in perspective. What is *normal* disrespect, the kind of stuff that goes on in most relationships? We've got to know this because the kind of disrespect that turns an iffy relationship into one that's clearly too bad to stay in must be much more extreme and much more damaging than this normal disrespect. We've also got to know this to be able to see the levels of respect that might turn an iffy relationship into one that's clearly too good to leave.

Normal Disrespect

It's certainly normal for there to be disrespect in relationships. You disappoint each other and you yell at each other. You criticize each other and point out every flaw. You remember every failure. In every sense of the word, you see each other naked, and if nakedness is the source of desire it's also the source of much sad, disappointing knowledge.

But you also have a lot of ways of coping with this disrespect. Sure, your wife complains about how you're tired all the time, but for one thing you recognize that she's just telling the truth, and for another thing you know she cares, and for another thing it's not as if being a go-getter were the most important thing in the world to you. So, yes, you feel disrespected, but it doesn't get to you.

Besides, you know that in some important way you've not really fallen in your wife's eyes. The thing that she's criticizing you for actually isn't all that important to her.

Coping with Disrespect

Sometimes the disrespect gets really bad and yet you can survive that, too. Perhaps when you first started out together your partner had been convinced that as a smart, talented, driven person you were going to take the business world by storm. Now years later you've screwed up badly. You've proved yourself to be not only less capable than your partner had thought but in some ways a real screwup, and a lot more lazy than everyone had thought, too. Your partner's disappointment is palpable. You see every day how you don't carry the sense of importance to your partner that you used to.

And yet you can cope with this disrespect, partly because you agree with it (you're disappointed in yourself, too) and partly because on some level it doesn't really touch you. You've developed a sense of who you are and what you care about over the years that's sturdily impervious to your partner's disrespect. Maybe you've fallen in his eyes, but inside yourself you feel you still stand straight. What's more, while you know he doesn't respect you the way he used to you have a sense that he loves you and cares about you anyway.

We're still in the territory of disrespect that's normal in relationships, that most people find they can live with, that doesn't make a relationship, for most people, too bad to stay in. But we're getting close, now, to that line that, when your partner crosses it, does mean that your relationship is clearly too bad to stay in for the vast majority of people.

Ask yourself this:

Diagnostic question #24. Does your partner do such a good job of conveying the idea that you're a nut or a jerk or a loser or an idiot about parts of yourself that are important to you that you've started to really become demonstrably convinced of it yourself?

What is this question getting at really? Let me tell you about one woman's experience.

Leila's Story

Ben, Leila's husband, decided one day that she was an idiotic nut and a nutty idiot. Perhaps in their conversations she'd been over-emotional or not perfectly rational. Perhaps she didn't know about some of the practical or financial realities Ben knew about. Perhaps she didn't have the same values. Perhaps Ben wanted to control her. Or perhaps Ben was just one of those macho guys who believed men were from Mars and women were strictly from hunger. Whichever of the many causes were operating, at some point Ben started administering a daily bath of messages designed to convince Leila that she was too neurotic and too just plain dumb to handle things.

"You're going to screw it up, you always do," he'd say. "You always make bad choices. I've seen the choices you make and I've seen how they're always bad," he'd say. "You don't know how to think. You think with your feelings. Your thoughts are a tangled mess," he'd say.

We think of this kind of stuff as having taken place in the nineteenth century or the 1950s, but I can assure you it's still going on today. Leila's not the only woman today on the receiving end of this kind of brutal disrespect. In fact, while you'd think it would diminish with so many women in the workforce proving they're competent in the larger world, the degree to which some men are threatened actually serves to increase expressions of disrespect like this. But I don't want to make this a gender issue, because it's not. Men are on the receiving end of disrespect at roughly the same rate as women.

Here's what happened with this disrespect Leila was assaulted with. She didn't have much protection. Hers wasn't one of those cases where the disrespect is as annoying as hell, but just doesn't convince you that it's true. For Leila, Ben's disrespect did real damage when he did such a good job of putting her down that she started believing his statements about her, *about things she couldn't change.* And then she started being destroyed from within even as her world of possibilities was destroyed around her. I *am* crazy, she thought, I *am* stupid.

And just the way an anorectic starves herself because the mirror "tells" her she's too fat, Leila did what you do when you believe you're crazy and stupid: she acted crazy and stupid.

Sometimes You Feel Like a Nut

If the words that are used to put you down really do convince you you're a nut or a jerk or an idiot or a loser, you just give up, because these are things you can't do anything about. So if your partner convinces you you're a nut, the same kind of thing might happen to you that happened to one man whose wife disrespected him to the point of convincing him he was a nut.

She said so many times, "You always go to weird places with things. You always make crazy connections," that he felt he was a bad influence on their children. He started having less and less to do with his kids out of fear that he'd somehow contaminate them with his "mental illness." Whenever they'd ask him a question, he'd say ask your mother. I know from working with him that he fell well within the norms of mental health. But his wife's disrespect damaged him by depriving him of his role as a father.

The damage that occurs when your partner's disrespect convinces you you're a jerk or a nut or an idiot or a loser doesn't just have to come from the things you start doing or stop doing. One woman whose husband convinced her she was simply an awful human being got so depressed as a result of this that she ended up being hospitalized.

This process is a lot like what you might have seen in the old Ingrid Bergman movie *Gaslight*, where her husband, played by Charles Boyer, convinces her she's crazy and so she acts crazy and stays locked up. But there's a difference, too. In the movie there was a deliberate plot against her. In the process I'm talking about here with disrespect, the partner isn't necessarily doing anything deliberately. But the effects can be just as devastating.

Here's the guideline for where to draw the line between disrespect that's annoying and disrespect that makes a relationship too bad to stay in:

GUIDELINE #24

If your partner is starting to convince you through disrespectful words and actions that you're a nut or a jerk or a loser or an idiot about parts of yourself that are important to you, then he's starting to damage the way you see yourself and your entire sense of what you're able to do. For almost everyone in a relationship where disrespect reaches this point, they're happy when they leave and unhappy if they stay. *Quick take:* If someone is starting to cut your legs out from under you, you've got to walk out while you still have legs.

Here are the crucial ingredients in this guideline:

1. "Starting to convince you." Your partner is saying things that you're actually coming to believe are true. Notice that if the things your partner says *don't* start to convince you, then this guideline doesn't apply. My husband tells me that he doesn't think I'm a very good driver, but nothing he's ever said or done has convinced me that I'm not a good driver.

2. "Through disrespectful words and actions." Your partner convinces you not only by saying things that put you down but by doing things. For example, he may not say in front of the kids that you don't know what you're talking about, but whenever you finish telling them to do something he goes behind your back and tells the kids they don't have to pay attention to you.

3. "You're a nut or a jerk or a loser or an idiot." Who cares if their partner convinces them that they don't know how to tune up a car's engine or judge modern art? The disrespect I'm talking about here gets at the heart of what we need to function as whole people. You can't function if you think you're crazy or if you think that no one likes you or if you think that you never do anything right or if you think that you're basically stupid. Disrespect that starts to convince you of this is disrespect that undermines what you need to function.

4. "Parts of yourself that are important to you." You not only can't function if you believe there's something wrong with you as a whole. You also can't function if the very things that are most important to you to do in life are made impossible by the impact of your partner's disrespect. If being a parent, for example, or trying to get ahead in business is not only something you do but something that's vitally important to your sense of yourself, then if you're convinced you can't do that your partner's disrespect is crippling.

These are the ingredients to focus on if you're trying to decide whether guideline #24 applies to you.

You Can't Drink the Water

Let me share with you the image I've used to help me draw the line between the kind of disrespect that goes on all the time and the kind of disrespect that means you have to head for the hills. Later you'll see how this image applies not only to this guideline but to the other three guidelines in this chapter. It's the image of pollution.

Imagine a reservoir from which the people in your town get their drinking water. Most tap water, even though it meets health code standards, isn't perfectly pure. But it's pure enough for most of us. The place where you draw the line is the point at which that water becomes toxic. You can quibble over parts per million of this or that chemical or microbe, but when people start becoming sick you shut the thing down. We can live with drinking water that's a tiny bit murkier or smellier than we'd like, but damage must not occur.

And it's the same with disrespect in our relationships. When "putdown pollution" starts to cause real harm because you start believing the bad things your partner's saying about you and when your believing these things changes how you act and live, then you're being maimed or destroyed psychologically just the way any poisoning victim is damaged by a particular toxin.

PERSPECTIVES: LOVE AND RESPECT

To diagnose what to do with an iffy relationship, you've got to draw the line between disrespect you can live with and disrespect you cannot live with. Since I'm trying to help you with this I've got to be concerned with two things: I've got to prevent people from leaving perfectly decent relationships and I've got to prevent people from staying in harmful relationships.

It's important to understand why disrespect is as universal in relationships as low-level pollution is in every part of our daily lives. If you understand where disrespect comes from, then you can see it better and deal with it better in relationships that are otherwise too good to leave without having unrealistically high standards and giving up on those relationships.

Not for Amateurs

One of the most famous things anyone's ever said about love comes, appropriately enough, from Erich Fromm's *The Art of Loving*. That's where he said, essentially, that you have to love yourself before you can love someone else. Few ideas are more widely held than this. I remember my parents telling me this as I was growing up. I remember how my friends and I used to say this to each other as young adults. And I remember how surprised I was to hear my daughters recounting this bit of wisdom to me as they were entering adulthood.

But why was Erich Fromm making a point of this? Why is it important? And why do we believe this?

What I now know, having studied the real workings of love in relationships for a very long time, is that you have to love yourself before you love someone else because once you're in a relationship things will happen that will make it hard for you to sustain your self-love. Fromm understood that, as I said earlier, relationships contain the soil out of which disrespect grows.

After the Campaign

So here's what we're all up against. In the beginning you meet someone and fall in love. As you fly through the air, falling head over heels, you're thinking to yourself, she's wonderful, she's special, she's great. The rocket of love is hard to launch without this fuel of mutual adoration.

But what goes up must come down. Just as there's always a

difference between campaign promises and the real floundering
the candidate actually does once he's in office, once you've
elected yourselves an official couple you arrive at that promised
land of intimacy you've been seeking so avidly. But time turns intimacy into familiarity, and we all know what familiarity breeds.

Disrespect doesn't happen everywhere, because there are always ways in which people surpass our expectations, usually in
areas where we didn't have such high expectations to begin with.
But in the back alleys of intimacy where we see each other physically and emotionally naked, flaws and failings emerge from every crack and crevice. To understand how disrespect grows, let's
look at where respect comes from:

- You get respect from being who you're supposed to be in
  your relationship, such as lover, income earner, parent,
  house maintainer.
- You get respect from how well you deliver on your
  promises, such as your promise to be a successful business
  person or artist or your promise to keep your youthful
  figure or always be supportive.
- You get respect for delivering surprises, for somewhere
  along the line accomplishing something or being
  something beyond your partner's expectations.
- You get respect for having strengths and abilities in areas
  where your partner happens to be weak, such as being a
  whiz at family finances where your partner has trouble
  balancing a checkbook or being really good with the kids
  where your partner gets overwhelmed.

Just think of how easy it is for respect to turn into disrespect in
each of these areas:

You try to be who you're supposed to be, but differences and
disappointments creep in about what it actually means for you to
be a good lover or income earner and about how well you've
done in each of these areas.

You try to deliver on your promises, but half your promises

were unrealistic and the other half, frankly, you don't even remember making.

You'd love to surprise your partner with some accomplishment, but just when he starts getting jaded your ability to produce surprises diminishes.

And you count on being able to do a good job in those areas where your partner has weaknesses, but all too often your partner one day decides to learn what you've been doing and discovers you're not so hot after all.

Please don't get the wrong impression. In spite of all this talk about disrespect, there's also a lot of respect in the average relationship. Maybe no man is a hero to his valet, but in most relationships there are surprisingly strong currents of respect and even admiration. So I don't want to disrespect the average relationship by overemphasizing how much disrespect there is in it. But you have to have respect for all the forces that constantly work to produce disrespect and for our own ability to overcome these forces. Sometimes we do overcome them. But sometimes they overcome us, and that's when we have to worry about relationships getting too bad to stay in.

STEP #25: THE ATMOSPHERE OF RESPECT

The realm of respect is where lots of people need help drawing the line. Let's go back to our pollution example. One reason you might stop drinking the water from your reservoir is that it was toxic, that you were afraid it would actually hurt you. We've dealt with that, when it comes to disrespect, in guideline #24.

But there's another reason why you might stop drinking the water. Maybe you know for sure there's no way it can hurt you, but suppose every time you look at a glass of water it looks so unclear, and every time you smell it there's an odor of something that doesn't appeal to you. When do you sign up for expensive home delivery of spring water? Where do you draw the line?

It's like this for a lot of people in their relationships when it comes to disrespect. There's no danger of their actually being hurt by all the disrespectful things their partner says. But there's

still an endless barrage of putdowns and criticisms and patroniz-
ing questions and demeaning comparisons and seemingly "helpful feedback" that's really just a polite excuse for your partner to
express disappointment, dismissal, and disgust.

Where do you draw the line? This question will help:

**Diagnostic question #25. As you think about your
partner's disrespect, is it clear to you that you do everything possible to limit your contact with your
partner, except for times where you absolutely must
interact?**

This question points to the issue that's proved essential for people trying to determine when their partner's disrespect has
crossed the line from being annoying to being impossible. But
why do we need this question at all? You're not stupid. You'd
know when water was too bad tasting to drink. Why wouldn't you
know when enough is enough when it comes to living in an atmosphere polluted by disrespect? You get sick of it and then you
leave, right? So why is drawing the line like this hard for some
people?

A constant atmosphere of disrespect, in terms of its psychological effects, has some of the same ingredients as childhood
abuse. Some of the same psychological factors that make it hard
for children to see what's happening to them make it hard for
you to see what's happening to you. Let me tell you about Hank.

Hank's Story

It was one of those classic, tragic cases of childhood sexual abuse.
To put a lot of pain in one small nutshell, Hank had an uncle who
forced him to have sex almost monthly for a five-year period between the time when Hank was nine and fourteen.

A question that plagued Hank for years after this whole experience came out in the open was why he'd put up with it. Sure
he was a little boy, but he wasn't *that* little and he wasn't *that*

powerless. Hank was haunted by his inability to have drawn a line in the sand.

Through therapy, Hank learned to be more understanding and forgiving of himself. He got some insight into how these things work psychologically. Why don't children who are subjected to this kind of abuse try to stop it even when they're not terrorized into keeping silent? There are four main reasons:

1.   Children get used to this happening, particularly when it starts at an early enough age. It's bad, but it soon becomes a regular part of their lives. And regularity creates a false sense of normality. This false sense of normality can paradoxically coexist with a sense of horror.

2.   Children mistakenly believe there's some validity to what's happening. Children who are physically abused are led to believe they're bad. Children who are sexually abused are often led to believe they're sexy, seductive tempters.

3.   Children employ the classic psychological technique of dissociation, where they distance themselves from their own emotions as a way of coping with the bad things that are happening to them. They train themselves to stop feeling what they're feeling.

4.   Children find it so impossible to imagine that a parent or grandparent or an aunt or uncle would do something like this to them that, even though they know what's happening when it's happening, they're somehow able to deny that it's been happening the rest of the time.

I'm not saying that all these things happen for all abused kids all the time. But they're extremely common, even normal, responses to this kind of abnormal experience.

During the period Hank came to understand this, he became aware that his partner was continuously and intensively assaulting him with a barrage of disrespect. From some inner resource, Hank was able to avoid coming to believe that the things his partner was saying about him were true. So guideline #24 didn't apply. At the same time, he was shocked that he was putting up with all of this verbal abuse at all. Why would he live with it and not leave?

Then it hit him. The identical four reasons that explained why he'd been unable to try to stop his sexual abuse as a child were operating right now with his partner's verbal abuse.

1.   He'd gotten used to it, so it seemed normal to him.

2.   While Hank didn't believe the details of his partner's putdowns, he did believe in a general way that he needed "improving," and so there seemed to be validity in his being put down.

3.   Hank put up an inner barrier that allowed him to not seem to experience the feelings his partner's putdowns must have been stimulating in him.

4.   And because he couldn't imagine that the person he wanted to love him would feel so little respect toward him, he was able to deny that the disrespect was happening at all.

These are the four things that you have to learn to see past if you're going to be able to draw a line when it comes to disrespect. Have you simply gotten used to it? Do you believe it's justified? Have you prevented yourself from feeling the impact of these putdowns? Do you not believe that your partner could be putting you down this way?

Now you're ready for the guideline:

GUIDELINE #25

If your partner is all too often all too disrespectful to you and you realize that you do everything possible to limit your contact with your partner, except for those times where you absolutely must interact, then the level of disrespect has spoiled the atmosphere of your relationship and you'll be happy if you leave. *Quick take:* The water's too bad to drink when you find you've stopped drinking the water.

Avoidance and distance are the measure of a level of disrespect that, even though it's nontoxic, is too unpleasant for you to have to put up with.

It's important to understand that your doing "everything possible to limit your contact with your partner" goes far beyond physical avoidance:

- Every time you think about something and it occurs to you to share your thought with your partner and you don't, you're limiting your contact with him.
- Every time you want to ask her a question and you don't, you're limiting your contact with her.
- Every time you want to tell him about some small triumph or disaster in your life and you stay silent, you're limiting your contact with him.
- Every time you think of the two of you doing something together and yet don't even bring it up, you're limiting your contact with her.
- Every time there's a real opportunity for some kind of intimacy and you let that opportunity slip past, you're limiting your contact with her.
- Every time there's a decision to be made, instead of discussing it with him you just go ahead and make the decision on your own, you're limiting your contact with him.

We all do these things in our relationships *some* of the time. But if you realize that you do everything possible to do these things *most* of the time, then you've got to see that avoidance like this means you've already said your relationship is too bad to stay in. We talked about safety a while back. If your partner's disrespect makes you feel so unsafe that you stay away from him in ways like these, then it's time you gave yourself permission to physically leave a relationship you've emotionally left already.

STEP #26: RESPECT THAT DELIVERS

What a sad and murky issue this business of disrespect is! On the other hand, if the last two guidelines apply to you, think about how happy you'll feel to get on with your life. And if they don't apply, it's nice to know that in those two aspects things are okay in your relationship.

Still, it's time for a boost, something positive to think about. Fortunately, the area I want to turn to now is also very important. It's the way respect that really comes across can make a relationship too good to leave.

In all the work I've done with couples, both therapy and research, I always ask one person, "Do you respect your partner?" and I always ask the other person, "Do you feel respected?"

I'm long past the stage where I'm surprised by what I hear in response to this but I'm still shocked: the respect that actually gets through to Jane from John is actually small compared to the respect John thinks he has for Jane. It's almost as if respect in our relationships were like some of those awful charities that get exposed from time to time where only a tiny portion of the contributions reaches the people who were supposed to be helped.

But every once in a while I run into a relationship where the respect really does come through. It's not just that your partner says that she respects you—she makes you feel it. And she not only makes you feel it but it actually makes a real difference in your life. Here's the question that gets at this:

Diagnostic question #26. **Do you feel that your partner, overall and more often than not, shows concrete support for and genuine interest in the things you're trying to do that are important to you?**

This goes far beyond and is really very different from your partner's saying you're a "good person." This is really about your partner's delivering support and interest about the things you care about in life that are hard for you that you're trying to do something about.

For example, a person can complain about how his partner criticizes him, but suppose he decides to go on a diet because that's important to him and yet it's hard for him, too.

If his partner is supportive and helpful and interested and concerned, that's respect that delivers. If she does solid, practical things to make him feel she wants what he wants for himself, that's respect that delivers. If she does everything she can to make his losing weight easier and to increase the odds of his being successful, or if she can really tune into what he needs the way he needs it and not her preconceived image of what he should be needing, or if she can listen to him talk about how hard it is to lose weight and convey the sense that she really wants to hear what he has to say, then any of these is respect that delivers.

Sasha's Story

Sasha had complained about her iffy relationship with Willie for a long time to all her friends. She was working as a junior researcher for a large mutual fund company and Willie, an environmental activist, constantly criticized her job, her profession, her company—basically the whole environment she was trying to make a career in. His criticism wasn't toxic for Sasha (it didn't make her feel bad about herself, for example) and because on some level it was just Willie being Willie it wasn't really so obnoxious that she started avoiding him.

Still, it would have been nice to hear words of respect. There was another big negative in the relationship: it bothered Sasha a lot that Willie could barely earn a living as a writer and organizer for one environmental cause after another. Like a lot of women starting out in life she kept wondering if she could do a lot better than the guy she was with.

Coming Through. An opportunity emerged for Sasha to get on track for eventually becoming a portfolio manager and actually being in charge of one of her company's many mutual funds. Instead of being one of the researchers she could be the performer, the director, the star. Her work load suddenly increased enormously. It was no longer a matter of looking up business data for eight hours a day and then going home. Now she had to actively seek out investment opportunities and not just check up on them but point to the ones that would be winners. If she worked hard and did well she could create an entire future for herself.

And Willie amazed her. His opinion of the business world didn't change, of course. But he "got" how much Sasha cared about what she was doing and how difficult it was for her and how hard she was trying to make it happen. Whatever doubts Sasha might have had about Willie's respect ended here.

He treated her like a worthwhile person who was doing a worthwhile thing. For example, instead of his complaining about how hard she worked and how she was never home for dinner, he made dinners that would keep and that they could eat whenever she got home.

Her head was filled now with all the companies she was researching as possible buy recommendations to the portfolio manager she was auditioning for. And anticapitalist Willie listened with interest and patience to all the fretful details Sasha talked about. He asked questions. He even offered up ideas of his own.

All this was a revelation for Sasha. Whatever disrespect Willie'd shown before had been nothing but words, verbal chaff. When it was a question of actually making a delivery of something real, Willie delivered respect that made an actual difference in her life. Her doubts about the relationship ended.

Gold Threads Among the Slivers

It's very easy when you're in an iffy relationship to not see real treasure because it gets lost with all the junk, like a fabulous antique that can't catch your eye because it's in a store filled with second-rate secondhand furniture. But there was real treasure for Sasha and there might be real treasure for you. Here's the guideline:

GUIDELINE #26

If you feel that your partner shows support for and interest in the things you're trying to do that are important to you, and does so in ways that are substantial and concrete and that make a real difference to you, then most people who've been in your situation have said that they're in a relationship that's too good to leave. *Quick take:* Being there when it counts is respect that delivers.

If you said no to question #26 and this guideline doesn't apply, that doesn't mean your relationship is too bad to stay in. As long as the lack of positive respect isn't harmful and doesn't literally drive you away from your partner, there can still be a satisfaction-producing core to a relationship with someone who doesn't provide the kind of support and interest you'd like. It may not be ideal, but you can still live with it.

Besides, if you're not getting respect that delivers, that may be because of energy you've withheld from the relationship because of your ambivalence. If your relationship doesn't turn out to be too bad to stay in, there could end up being changes in it that produce the respect you're looking for once you recommit to it.

How can you be sure guideline #26 applies to you? When you call Domino's Pizza, a half an hour later the guy shows up with a box and in the box is *a real pizza*. He doesn't show up with an empty box. In the same way, guideline #26 applies when the support and interest your partner delivers is real. It's not just words. Who wants to be told they're respected by someone who won't actually listen to what you have to say or who won't do anything that means respect, support, and interest to you?

Going back to our image of the possibly polluted reservoir again—water you got from your tap that had real, certifiable, health-enhancing, life-extending properties could make you overlook a lot of imperfections.

Step #27: Respecting Your Partner

Now for a major shift. I'm still talking about respect, but now I'm going from feeling respected *by* your partner to the issue of the respect you feel *for* your partner. Up until now we've talked about how it affects you when your partner does or does not respect you. But what does it do to you when you don't respect your partner? Where do you draw the line?

You remember the discussion we had about why you have to love yourself before you can love your partner and how easy it is for respect to come under attack in relationships. That means, particularly if you're in an iffy relationship, that the respect you once had or hoped to have for your partner has slipped a bit. When you first met, it was, "He's so great." Now it's, "He is what he is." Sigh.

We've all got to learn to accept our partners for who they are up to a point. But when do you bail out? When does the respect you feel for the person you see sitting across from you fall below the point where your relationship is no longer good enough to stay in?

I can't tell you how many people I've worked with who've agonized over that question. I'm talking about people whose partners had trouble earning a living, whose partners had no ambition, whose partners made stupid and disastrous choices, whose partners revealed stubborn depths of blind stupidity, whose partners did all kinds of things that made it hard for them to say, "I respect you," to their partners and mean it.

When does it make sense to keep on loving someone like this and stick by them? What makes it a mistake to stay?

Good but Not Good for You

Where people need help when it comes to how much respect for their partners is enough is in seeing the difference between who the partner is as a person and who he is *for you*. Here are two alternatives:

1. Sometimes we respect or even admire people who are not good for us or who can do nothing for us.
2. Sometimes someone who has something to offer us personally that's real and important to us isn't someone we otherwise have a lot of respect for.

Which is the sign of a relationship that's too bad to stay in?

Most people who feel iffy about their relationships, I've found, still have some respect for their partners, even though a lot of respect has also been lost. Otherwise they'd have left. But this is respect for their partners as people in their own right. But where relationship ambivalence blurs your vision is in making it hard for you to see whether a partner whom you have some respect for has anything to offer you. In other words, can you respect your partner as a resource for you in your life?

Here's the question:

Diagnostic question #27. **Would you lose anything important in your life if your partner were no longer your partner? Is what you'd lose something that makes you feel good about your partner for being able to provide it?**

Of course you'd lose *something* if your partner weren't your partner. But is it something you couldn't do without? Is it something you'd actually miss? And whatever it is you'd lose that you'd miss or that you couldn't do without, do you feel good about your partner for being able to provide these things?

For example, even in this day and age some women might say that if their partner were out of the picture, they'd miss his ability to open jars and fix toilets and move heavy furniture. But for them to respect their partner he's not only got to be an important resource but they've got to respect him for doing these things. No matter how painfully you'd miss your partner's ability to open jars, if you don't feel good about your partner for being able to do that, if his being able to do that doesn't make him seem like a valuable resource, then that's not a basis for your respecting him. And if that's *all* he had going for him you'd have to answer no to question #27.

Let's take another example. A lot of men say that if their partner were out of the picture they'd miss her ability to make good things happen, like getting together with friends, or having nice meals. But the question is whether they feel good about their partner for doing these things. If they feel that their partners' doing these things is nice, yes, but is essentially a waste of time, then they don't respect their partner as a resource and they'd have to answer no to question #27.

Here's a positive example. One woman's husband turned out to be less ambitious and successful than she'd hoped, and that undermined her respect for him as a person. But he had a wonderful, intelligent, comprehensive perspective on things that made her feel he was someone she could bring any problem to and he'd shed light on it. She had to value what this gave her and respect him for having it to give her. Her answer to question #27 was yes.

It doesn't matter what it is that your partner offers as a resource to you that you respect him for. It can be anything, from being a hard worker to being funny and making you laugh to being unusually patient when things get chaotic. The point is that there's something not about who he is but who he is for you that matters in your life and that you think deserves respect.

Think about what it means to say no to question #27. It means your partner doesn't offer you anything real and significant for your life, whoever he is and whatever he does in himself, at least nothing you value him for, nothing that makes him seem special. It means you lose nothing worthwhile by leaving.

Fran's Story

Let me tell you how this first became clear to me, before I even thought of researching it. I was working with a woman years ago who was struggling to decide whether to stay in her relationship. Fran happened to have two children. She was complaining on and on about all the things that were wrong with her husband in

every way, including as a father. I was looking for hope somewhere and I asked her, "Well, do you think Jerry would at least
make a good *ex*-husband?"

Finally Fran was clear. No. The thought of Jerry being in her
life once he was out of the house was no comfort to her. The fact
is that some people make terrific ex-spouses, especially when it
comes to carrying out their responsibilities as parents. Lots of
people feel good about their ex-spouses as parents of their children and they rely on them. But for Fran, Jerry was a total loss
even as an ex-spouse.

The point was that Fran had no respect for Jerry as someone
who might have something to offer her. The paradox is that in
some ways Fran respected Jerry a lot. Jerry was a sculptor. He
was a fine and dedicated craftsman. His more artistic pieces were
in a number of important collections and he made a decent living
(for an artist) from his more commercial work. Jerry wasn't famous, but Fran cared about art and both Jerry's struggles and his
accomplishments impressed her.

But once Fran saw how little Jerry had to offer her, she was
able to see past her respect for him as a person and face the real
concrete fact that her not wanting him as an ex-husband meant
to her that she didn't want him as a husband.

Here's the guideline. The context is your thinking about what
it would actually be like to live without your partner, on each individual day and for years at a time.

GUIDELINE #27

If it's clear to you that you wouldn't lose anything you
couldn't do without if your relationship were over, then
your partner doesn't have anything real to offer you and
he's not a resource for you. Even if your partner does
provide things, if what he provides are things you don't
particularly respect him for, he's not a respected resource
for you. Most people in this situation were happy when
they left the relationship. *Quick take:* There's no need to

keep something you wouldn't miss if it were gone or that you don't value when you've got it.

This guideline has an importance that's easy to overlook. We all need help. You and I both need as many resources in our lives as possible. If you live with someone who is simply not a resource for you in any important way, then not only are you living with whatever other problems are going on that make this relationship iffy, but you're depriving yourself of the possibility of spending your life with someone different who could really be a resource for you.

There's good news in this guideline. It shows why our partners don't have to be rich and famous and successful for us to love them and have a good relationship with them. It's only who our partners are *to us* that matters.

15

Who's Sorry Now?

Issue: Hurts and Betrayals

LINGERING HURTS

People in relationships do things that hurt their partner all the time. They do them accidentally. They do them deliberately. They do them once. They do them over and over. There's almost no relationship that hasn't had to digest its share of hurts, grievances, and betrayals. The things people do to hurt each other include everything from buying their partner a dorky anniversary gift to sleeping with their wife's sister.

That's the end of the spectrum we'll focus on here: the damaging end, the things people do like having affairs that cause tremendous pain and introduce the risk of lasting damage. We'll focus on the stuff that all too often breaks people up.

This is where we'll deal with affairs and other "crimes" from the past that linger in the present. This chapter is specifically addressed to you if you or your partner has done something really hurtful and damaging and you're wondering whether it should break you up. Perhaps you're wondering if it's broken you up already. Or can you survive this, even though you still feel the pain and experience the damage?

But you need to know that a lot of your questions about past hurts have *already* been answered:

- If the damage was so bad that you've actually already decided to leave, you've learned that in the "It's Too Late, Baby" chapter.
- If your partner makes it impossible for you to talk about what happened by taking things off the table or has destroyed your ability to trust him by lying, you've learned that in the "Talk to Me" chapter.
- If the damage is ongoing as a result of your partner's need for power, you've learned that in the "You've Got a Hold on Me" chapter.
- If the love between you has been destroyed, you've learned that in the "What Is This Thing Called Love?" chapter.
- If the sensual part of your relationship was destroyed, you've learned that in the "It Don't Mean a Thing If It Ain't Got That Swing" chapter.
- If the damage to your relationship comes from a problem your partner has, you've learned if there's a basis for his solving that problem in the "All the Things You Are" chapter.
- If whatever happened simply crossed your bottom line, you've learned that in the "Let's Call the Whole Thing Off" chapter.
- If you've not been able to accept the fact that the damage is unhealable because you've been mistakenly afraid of what awaits you if you leave, you've learned that in the "If Ever I Should Leave You" chapter.
- If the damage actually reflects unbridgeable differences between you, you've learned that in the "You Say 'Tomayto,' I Say 'Tomahto' " chapter.
- And if the damage destroyed your ability to respect each other, you've learned that in the "R-E-S-P-E-C-T" chapter.

So you can see how far you've come! If you've learned that you'll be happiest leaving, you can see how powerful the forces are that have made this relationship too bad to stay in. If you've gotten no indication so far that you should leave, you can feel happy about how strong your relationship must be to have survived the possible disasters I've just listed. So if by this point one of you did something to hurt the other and yet it's still not clear to you that you'll be happiest leaving, then that's a good sign all by itself. But you're still looking for more clarity. You still need to resolve once and for all whether the damage was too great or whether you can get past it.

Not Just Affairs

Affairs are of course the classic form of hurt and betrayal that damages relationships. But there are many other things people do to cause this level of damage.

Here are some examples:

- One woman who'd grown up in a poor, disadvantaged family gave a dinner party for her husband's boss and colleagues. Perhaps because he was embarrassed by her lack of polish, her husband made joking but humiliating references to her cooking, her clothes, and other things he knew that she felt insecure about. Her sense of hurt and betrayal lasted for years.
- An opportunity had come up for both a woman and her husband to go back to school and finish their degrees. This seemed like a perfect time for them to have a baby, but only because the husband promised he would contribute a full fifty percent of the childcare. But, claiming he was too busy, he contributed almost none of the childcare, and her studies suffered.
- One man had been saving money so he could quit the job he hated and go into business for himself. Even

though his wife knew about his plans and how important they were to him, she gave his savings to her father when he had some money troubles. Not only was her husband furious at his future being stolen from him, but his sense of betrayal was deepened by his knowing that his wife's father had abused her when she was a child.

These stories and all the others like them have in common that one person did something in the past to hurt the other and there's still some kind of wound or damage years later.

We're only going to focus on the hurt and betrayal from the *past* that may make this relationship too bad for you to stay in now—the thing that was done a year ago or ten years ago that still carries with it suitcases full of bitterness and anger, where you and your partner are still fighting over how terrible a thing it was and whether forgiveness is possible.

DAMAGE AND HEALING

How do you measure how big and terrible the damage is from something someone did in the past? Here's one reason why it can be so difficult to assess the damage.

Let's say you're in the copy room of your office with a colleague and you accidentally step on your colleague's foot. You jump back in embarrassment and say, "Oh, I'm so sorry." And your colleague quickly says reassuringly, "Oh, it was nothing."

Think about those words, *it was nothing*. They show how forgiveness works by saying that your crime isn't so terrible. It's not one of those unforgivable crimes. It's a smaller, easier-to-forgive one. So if there was some doubt about just how big a crime stepping on your colleague's foot was, or any other crime, the other's ability to forgive you tells you exactly how big it was.

But where we run into huge difficulties in relationships is when someone does something to hurt and betray the other and forgiveness doesn't flow easily and the sense of hurt and betrayal lingers. Anger, fear, and distance fester. That's where you may be now. And what makes it all so confusing is that the two of you can't agree about who's responsible for this impasse.

Let's say you're the one who committed the "crime" against your partner. Is the inability in both of you to let this go a result of the terribleness of your crime? Or is it a result of the other person's inability to forgive and forget?

Is your crime really so objectively terrible that anyone would have difficulty forgiving and forgetting (which may be what your partner's been saying)? Or are you just an ordinary fallible human being who screwed up only to discover that your partner has some sick need to hold on to her grievances (which may be what you've been saying)?

Notice how you circle around each other here. The size of the crime determines the amount of forgiveness that's necessary. But it's circular: the amount of the forgiveness that comes across also measures the size of the crime.

For example, if you had an affair three years ago with someone from work, has your affair made the relationship too bad to stay in because having an affair really is such a terrible thing or is it because your partner's having such a hard time forgiving the affair?

Let's compare this to a physical injury. The size of the crime in your relationship is really the same as how damaging the injury is. The ease with which forgiveness comes is really the same as how much healing is possible.

That's the way it is with any wound: the final effect is built out of some combination of damage and healing. If you're trying to figure out whether you or your partner's crime ultimately makes the relationship too bad to stay in, then you've got to determine the degree of damage and the possibility of healing.

STEP #28: THE WOUNDS THAT TIME CAN'T HEAL

How in the world can we actually determine how damaging is the thing that you or your partner did? It can be hard. A team of therapists would probably have trouble assessing the exact degree of damage. How can *you* do this, particularly from your vantage point inside the relationship where you spend half your time feeling hurt and angry about what happened and the other half trying to forget about it?

I've thought about this issue of damage assessment for a long time. So I want you to know that I know that I'm focusing on the absolute essentials about something that's really very complicated. But I'm focusing in a way that's helpful, without neglecting the impactful issues. That's because I have the experience of a lot of people who've been in your situation to help me.

And if I listen carefully to them and to what they've said over a period of years, this is the question that comes up:

Diagnostic question #28. Whatever was done that caused hurt and betrayal, do you have the sense that the pain and damage has lessened with time?

Notice that this question doesn't ask how bad a thing was done in the abstract. This isn't a court of law. There's no Book of Hurtful Deeds where you can look up some action and find it written whether it's a relationship buster or not. In fact, even in ancient times the crime of adultery was only recognized if the hurt spouse wanted to make a big deal of it. In relationships, the meaning of "crimes" is always determined by what happens between the two partners and in their individual psychologies.

An Affair, for Example

I realize that question #28 might be hard to answer. To help you with it, let's go through an example.

Suppose that the thing one of you did to cause hurt and betrayal was have an affair. Okay. I know there was a lot of anger and pain. I know that if this were a physical wound there'd be a lot of blood all over the place. But some wounds are very bloody and there's not much real damage, and other wounds are fatal without much blood at all. So focusing on this affair we're using as an example, whenever it happened, a year ago or ten years ago, the question is: is the sense of grievance less now than it was when you or your partner first found out about it?

Time Makes a Difference. Of course, healing depends on how long ago an affair happened.

If the affair was only, say, a year ago, that's not a lot of time in relationship years and it's certainly possible that not a lot of cooling off will have happened. So, in this example, if the affair has only been a problem between you for a year, then you've got to look closely to see if there's been a slight lessening of the sense of grievance. After only a year, a slight lessening is all you need to be able to say that the damage can be healed. What you have to avoid is being misled by how little cooling off there's been into thinking there's been no cooling off.

But suppose that the affair has been an issue between you and your partner for, say, ten years now. Now time can be confusing in a different way. The everyday details of life and the inevitable changes in your living patterns can make it seem as though you're going for weeks without a hint of the memory of the affair. Denial is easy and attractive. And yet, in some cases, if there's the slightest tension or irritation between you, the affair can still leap out of the box you've put it in as fresh as if it had just happened yesterday. What you have to avoid here is being misled by how seldom the issue of the affair comes up into thinking there's been any cooling off at all.

In other words, when one person in a relationship does something to cause a lot of hurt and anger, there are two completely opposite kinds of reactions that even after all my years of clinical work still impress me:

1. The utter violence and craziness of people's responses (particularly in the short run)
2. People's total capacity for complete denial or avoidance (particularly in the long run)

Keeping this in mind, here's the guideline. But let me point out that there's some explanation following the guideline you must pay attention to.

GUIDELINE #28

If, according to the following timetable, there continues to be a lessening in the sense of pain and hurt and fear and anger after the "crime" you or your partner committed, then there's a good chance that your relationship can heal the damage caused by this "crime." In that case, if this was the main reason you were thinking of leaving the relationship, the odds are in your favor that it's too good to leave. *Quick take:* Time heals all healable wounds.

Here's the timetable for measuring whether there's been a healing of the damage:

- *The first month.* Any slight hint of cooling off at all in the first month is a good sign. This could include moments when you can talk about something other than the "crime" without tears or anger, even though you're still guarded. It could even include an inner feeling of hope that the two of you can get beyond this. The avoidance of hysterical, acting-out reactions that actually make things worse is another good sign.
- *After the first month.* Any small or temporary reestablishment of your prior relationship is a good sign, combined with the ability to take the first steps toward dealing productively with what happened. Some examples of healing to look for after the first month are that you begin to talk for several minutes about what happened before you get upset again; you find yourself falling into your old intimacy patterns for a day or so at a time; you begin to entertain the possibility of one day trusting each other again; there's simply less emotional pain coming up spontaneously with the thought of what happened.
- *After the first year.* It's a good sign when there are periods as long as two or three months in which your relationship is on its old footing, combined with periods equally as long when the "crime" isn't foreground. The

mention of people, places, and events associated with the "crime" is less upsetting. You can listen to your partner's explanation of what the crime meant to him without getting very upset. You can talk about what happened without feeling the same degree of pain you first felt and without spiraling into hurt and anger.

- *After the first five years.* It's a good sign if you've arrived at some sense of exactly where your relationship was damaged and if it seems as though this specific damage is significantly healing; if you don't avoid talking about what happened but actually bring it up; if the issue of trust and what's needed to rebuild it has been brought out into the open and you're making progress toward regaining trust.

By the time five years are up, you should be able to formulate what you learned from your mistakes and what you can do to prevent them in the future. Each person should be able to take responsibility for what he did without there being a sense of blame. The two of you should be able to start feeling good about yourselves as a couple in spite of what happened.

This framework is rough. Individuals will vary. A happy-go-lucky person with a generally positive outlook might heal faster. Someone who'd suffered a number of personal disasters or losses in the past might heal much more slowly. The point, though, is to look for some healing overall, as measured by

- A less painful wound between you in the short run
- A resumption of ordinary relationship activities in the medium run
- The ability for both of you to deal productively and nonavoidantly with the wound and what caused it in the long run

Guideline #28 is important because people often don't even know how to begin to think about what a "crime" really means to their relationship. But merely because something bad happened is not a sign that the relationship is too bad to stay in. If you can see that healing is happening, then you can feel comfortable knowing that you're going through a healing process and that you'll survive the wound intact.

STEP #29: IS FORGIVENESS POSSIBLE?

But what does it mean if your answer to question #28 was no; if, depending on where you are in the timetable, there's been no healing yet? That's important, but all by itself it doesn't tell you if you'll be happier if you leave. It's true that healing hasn't happened yet. But the question now is whether the two of you have the *capacity* to heal a wound like yours.

And that depends on your answer to the following question:

Diagnostic question **#29. Is there a demonstrated capacity and mechanism for genuine forgiveness in your relationship?**

What I'm asking is whether the person who's been injured has actually ever forgiven her partner for anything. After a period of hurt and anger, did she actually let go of her sense of grievance? Was the forgiveness genuine, and not merely words? And, equally important, did the other partner, the one who needed the forgiveness, willingly perform any act of restitution or atonement or healing? And did this act make a difference?

Genuine forgiveness is both a psychological capacity and an interpersonal talent. You have it *in* you to give and you know *how* to give it. It's also a mechanism that some relationships have, just the way some relationships have a mechanism for preparing a party without having a fight. If there is this possibility of genuine forgiveness, then wounds can heal.

The Ingredients for Forgiveness

When I've seen people forgive each other through the years, even for inflicting the deepest wounds, I keep seeing three ingredients for forgiveness. As long as you have these three, the capacity for healing is there.

First, and most basically, the aggrieved person simply reaches the point where she doesn't need to hold on to her bitterness and hurt and fear and loss. You can't forgive your partner when you're more emotionally invested in holding on to your feeling devastated and beating your partner over the head with it.

Second, the aggrieved person actually has forgiven her partner for things in the past. If you're in a relationship with someone who's always held on to every other grievance, however minor, why would she not hold on to this one? If your partner's only rarely and only reluctantly and only slightly forgiven you when you've apologized in the past, why would she forgive you now? But if you actually felt forgiven for hurts you inflicted in the past, then the capacity for forgiveness has been demonstrated and you can be forgiven again. Yet the possibility of forgiveness *between* you and your partner doesn't only depend on whichever one of you needs to do the forgiving.

So, third, forgiveness is made possible if the other person's genuinely sorry for what he did. It's not just a matter of words. You've got to feel that he truly is remorseful and isn't just sick and tired of your being pissed off at him. One way you can test for the difference between genuine sorrow and phony get-off-my-back sorrow is if you see that your partner really feels the true impact of what he did. He sees exactly how and why you were hurt. He appreciates how and why he'd be hurt if you'd done the same thing to him.

You'll know it's genuine sorrow only if the partner who committed the injury does something concrete to re-balance things. The fact is that if you've suffered a hurt, you've suffered a loss. In the law they talk about being made whole again. That can't happen in a relationship, but something like it can come close to happening. I've seen people say something like, "Look, you suffered that, so I'll suffer this," or "Look, you lost that, so I'll give

you this instead." It's why people who screw up buy their partners flowers. But it's got to be a real act, not an empty, mechanical gesture.

Here then is the guideline:

GUIDELINE #29

If there's a demonstrated capacity for genuine forgiveness, including the ability to let go of anger and hurt, the
ability to feel forgiveness, and the ability in the other person to show that he feels sincerely sorry, then this relationship can survive an injury that would otherwise make
it too bad to stay in.

But if not, and, based on guideline #28, if there's also
been no healing over time, then the damage was probably so great and the capacity for healing is so small that
this relationship is too bad to stay in. In such a case, most
people are happy they left and unhappy they stayed.
Quick take: If you can't find your way back to forgiveness,
you can't find your way back to each other.

The key to this entire issue is signs that natural healing is happening. Some hurts are deep and permanent. And if there's no
change over time and no forgiveness, then the relationship is a
corpse. But improvements over time and the slow but awesome
power of forgiveness are the keys to signs of healing. As long as
healing is happening, it's a mistake to give up on a relationship
just because there's been damage.

16
I Can't Get No Satisfaction

Issue: Getting Your Needs Met

How many needs have to go unmet before it makes sense to leave? How much bitter struggle do you have to put up with to get your needs met before it makes sense to leave? That's what we'll deal with here.

WELCOME HOME

A relationship is supposed to be a kind of home within the home, an inner sanctum, a refuge. It's supposed to be the unique place where you and that one special person can find peace and get the things you really want in life that mean the most to you—that's the vision of a relationship we look forward to when we fall in love.

This vision isn't only about the relationship, it's also about the other person. Part of falling in love with someone is having the feeling that in some special way he or she has something to offer above and beyond what anyone else could offer for meeting your needs and creating safety.

And most of us actually experience this vision when we're first with our partner. It's part of what enables us to go forward with the relationship, the evidence that someone could meet needs that have never been met and could offer safety we've never found before.

So it's a terrible shock for all of us when this special refuge turns into a place of strife and deprivation, where things we want we simply can't get, or we get them only after a painful fight, or we fight and we still don't get them. Probably no experience is more common and more central in turning a relationship we're content with into one we're thinking of leaving than the experience of constant fights and unmet needs.

"All we do is fight these days." "She never does what I want." "He always does the same thing and I can't get him to stop." These are the most common complaints therapists hear from people at the beginning of couples therapy.

Worse Than Fighting

But this isn't the worst. You fight because you hope you can win. But when things get really bad, you give up. Worse than fighting is a kind of cold, distant politeness, an emptiness, a cold war where it's clear to both of you that if you're going to get anything you want you're going to have to get it outside of the relationship.

And like in most cold wars, there's a ton of covert action, secret underground battles and sabotage where you both struggle for the slightest advantage while still trying to avoid the knock-down-drag-out fight you now know is a waste of time.

Fighting in Perspective

If you're feeling ambivalent about your relationship and are agonizing over whether to stay or leave, you've got a special problem with all this. Your problem isn't how bad it is. It's how common it is. Sure, you hate what you're experiencing. But even the most ancient forms of cultural understanding show marriage as a place of strife and unmet needs.

For example, in the *Iliad*, the very first work of Western literature, Zeus and Hera, the top god and goddess, fight like the old married couple they are and complain constantly about each other, just like Ralph and Alice on *The Honeymooners.* What image of marriage in popular culture, from Homer through Shakespeare through Dickens through every radio and TV sitcom isn't filled with people fighting to get what they want and somehow always losing?

The shortest joke in the history of the world, complete in four words, is Henry Youngman's "Take my wife, *please.*" What better testimony to the universality of strife in relationships? But when do you say enough is enough if you're faced with a universal condition? The subtleties and complexities of this issue explain why, in spite of its importance, it comes so late in the diagnostic journey we're making together.

STEP #30: THE ABILITY TO NEGOTIATE SOLUTIONS

The people who've said they were happy they left their relationship, as well as the people who said they were unhappy they stayed, were not babies. They didn't have unrealistic expectations about being in a relationship with someone without having fights. They didn't expect they'd always get everything they wanted and always be able to do whatever they wanted to do. They understood that there's no long-standing relationship without conflict and disappointment.

But they had to deal with something a lot worse than this. The next question points to what they had to deal with:

Diagnostic question #30. **Is it likely that, if you have a reasonable need, you and your partner will be able to work out a way for you to get it met without too painful a struggle?**

In other words, it is actually true for you that, "It's just too hard to get my needs met"?

Do you remember when we talked about power people? The

diagnostic question in the "You've Got a Hold on Me" chapter was about your needs being obliterated, as if you were somehow not allowed to have needs in that relationship. Question #30 is different, and perhaps more difficult to answer. The focus isn't on unmet needs but on unrewarding struggles. It's not so much that none of your needs are met, as that you keep having the sense that it's just not worth struggling to get your needs met. Too much fighting with too little to show for it.

To answer question #30, I think it will help if I lay out the four most important ways our partners make it hard for us to get our needs met without a too-painful struggle.

1. "I Can Do Whatever I Want, Right?"

Here's one way your partner can make the relationship a place where it's just too hard to get your needs met: doing what he wants when he wants it by himself without talking to you about it. It's like the philosophy in the Nike commercials: Just do it. Instead of your partner having a big fight with you because he thinks it's time the two of you got a new car and you don't, he just surprises you one day with the car. It's his way of saying, I don't want to negotiate with you, and I'm not interested in our solving our problems together.

But that's not like his going out one day and getting a haircut without talking about it with you. You had plans for the money he spent on the car, too. You had needs you wanted to get satisfied with that money, too, even if your need was only to know that the money was being saved for a rainy day.

In all my years of working with troubled couples, I see few things more destructive to relationships than people's tendency to make "unilateral moves." This is the expression for doing what you want when you want it without any prior discussion, although there's usually a lot of angry discussion afterward. Someone who constantly makes unilateral moves is typically someone we think of as selfish or immature: "You never think of anyone but yourself," we say.

Someone who makes unilateral moves will often invite you to

do the very same thing: "Hey, I'm not saying you can't do what you want. We should both be able to do what we want. I just don't want to have to talk about it," and he rolls his eyes.

You can see from this example how very different this issue is from power. Power people never say, "Let everyone do what they want." But whether we're talking about power people or people who make unilateral moves, you still end up not getting your needs met.

But as I made clear in the example of the guy who goes and buys a car, resources are limited and more often than not his getting his needs met without any prior discussion means you won't get your needs met. And anything a person does can be a unilateral move, including pressuring you into having sex or insisting you talk about something you don't want to talk about or showing up unannounced with a friend or relative for dinner or accepting a promotion at work that involves massive new responsibilities that you don't even know about.

If your partner makes unilateral moves like these all the time and if you've talked to her about it and she won't stop, then this is going to make it a lot less likely that you'll be able to get your needs met.

2. "It's Such an Ordeal Talking About the Littlest Thing"

Here's another way people can't get their needs met without too-painful struggles. It's the problem that every how-to-have-a-happy-marriage book or workshop focuses on and what I've spent a lot of time helping couples with: how to sit down together and discuss needs openly and easily until you arrive at creative, commonsensical solutions that are good for everyone. If you can do it, it means you never have to say you can't get your needs met.

It's also something, like simultaneous orgasms, that's a lot easier in theory than in practice. What you have to watch out for is when negotiating solutions together is virtually impossible. Here's what makes it impossible:

You can't negotiate if *you can't listen to each other or understand what the other is saying.*

One reason you and your partner might not be able to listen to each other is that you feel furious and deprived. How can you listen to what someone wants or what they need in order to give you what you need, if you feel like strangling them because you have so little or because they've taken so much from you?

Another reason you can't listen is that your partner is a bad communicator. One guy I worked with is so boring and so long-winded and so overintellectual when he opens his mouth, you want to run screaming from the room. Someone else was so confused and diffuse and unfocused that you'd never know what in the world she was talking about. It doesn't have to be this bad, either. It might simply be that no matter how long your partner talks you never figure out exactly what he's asking you to do.

Another reason you can't listen is that you're exhausted and overwhelmed. It may be that you've been listening to people tell you what they want all day—customers, colleagues, bosses. Then the kids are babbling on and on. When your partner opens his mouth you're already on overload.

> You can't negotiate if *you're scared to death
> you're going to lose.*

One reason you would be afraid of losing is that he's a dirty fighter. So when you have to negotiate something he'll call you names, he'll throw your past in your face, he'll threaten you, he'll make it seem as though it's costing him the agony of death to give up the slightest bit, he'll lie about how little money he has, he'll start screaming—you get the picture. He's just got more weapons than you have, and he's more willing to use them.

Another reason you would be afraid of losing is that your partner's limited. She might simply have nothing to give. If she's tired all the time, then you can't have more sex and you can't go out more often and you can't talk about all the things you want to talk about and you can't do any of the things exhaustion prevents people from doing. Or he might simply be stupid. Stupid people can't "get" the idea of negotiating solutions, where you try to find new and better ways for the two of you to satisfy both of your needs. All they can think of is that you want X and they don't have X in that moment and in that way, and so negotiation is impossible.

You can't negotiate if *you're afraid of being attacked*. You have to feel safe putting your needs out there.

One reason you would be afraid of being attacked is that your partner's what I call a "historian." Everything you bring up hooks into the past. If you want to spend some money now it hooks into ways you've spent money foolishly in the past or ways you've been stingy yourself in the past. If you want to have sex more often, it hooks into all the times you said no to sex in the past or all the sexual problems there've ever been between you in the past.

Another reason you'd be afraid of being attacked is that you feel criticized. Every need you bring up is an occasion for your partner to tell you what's wrong with you for having that need. What! You want him to help around the house more? That just means that you're small-minded and obsessive. What! You want her to stop criticizing you so much? That just means you're weak and defensive and unwilling to grow. And if people like this don't criticize you for having your need, they criticize you for the way you bring up your need, so that you end up feeling like someone who has terrible timing or who's terribly insensitive.

You can't negotiate if *you're afraid of conflict and struggle*.

One reason you'd be afraid of this is that every negotiation in the past has ended in disaster. If your idea of negotiation is a calm discussion but for your partner it's an opportunity to get passionate, then you'll quickly spiral into a huge disappointing fight every time one of you brings up a need. Sometimes two people in a relationship are simply both hard bargainers with a total win-lose approach to every negotiation, and so every negotiation is a disaster because no one wants to lose.

Another reason you'd be afraid of conflict and struggle is that, without getting too technical about it, your partner's a nut. The stress of negotiation throws her into a deep depression every time. Or the slightest impasse makes him feel he's got to threaten to leave the relationship.

Another reason you'd be afraid of conflict and struggle is that there are these stumbling blocks lurking in your relationship that you bang into two minutes into any negotiation. For example, the two of you don't have a lot of money, certainly not compared to your bills and expenses, and so even a discussion about how you can have more fresh vegetables in the house bangs into this where's-the-money? stumbling block. Or it could be there's an ongoing fight between you about one of you being too strict and the other being too permissive when it comes to the kids, and even a simple statement of your need to pay more of the bills more on time immediately falls into this strict versus permissive battle.

All these realities I've listed are things that turn negotiating needs from the hassle they are for everybody to the ordeal they are for some people. And if these realities are so powerful and the ordeal they create is so terrible, then this is going to make it a lot less likely that you'll be able to get your needs met.

3. "You Never Do What You Say You're Going to Do"

If you think the negotiation from hell is a problem—and it is— watch out for the negotiation that's "like butter." Few things make it feel harder to get your needs met than the partner who agrees to what you want but then just doesn't keep agreements. *This* is where the issue of trust comes up in relationships. You trust people who do what they say they're going to do. When they don't, the relationship is not only a place of fighting and deprivation, it's a place of betrayal. Not only are you not safely at home there, but you're in a scary alien world.

It might sound hard to believe, but broken trust can all too often lurk undetected. Let's say that after a fight—which is what we're really talking about here when we refer to a negotiation— your partner says he's going to start taking out the garbage every week without having to be reminded. Sounds good so far. And he does take it out for the first week or so. It's after that that things fall apart. One week he "forgets" but he was very busy so you let it go. The next week he looks as though he's going to forget again and so you remind him, and there you are back to where you started.

It's easy to make excuses in a situation like this but the reality is that trust has been broken. If all we're talking about is taking out the garbage, it's no big deal, but a pattern of easily over-looked broken trust is just as deadly to your sense that you can get your needs met as a huge betrayal that slaps you in the face.

There are actually a lot of ways people have of breaking agreements. We just touched on one: forgetting. You've got to be careful with this. You and I lead such incredibly busy lives that we desperately feel we'd love to get some leeway. So I'd love to be allowed to forget things without getting in trouble for it. And that means it's very hard for us to get tough with a partner who's indulging himself with the very thing we want. We identify with him!

But a pattern of constantly forgetting agreements can be toxic and deadly. If your partner always ends up forgetting the agreements he's made, maybe not immediately, but eventually, then before you know it you can find yourself completely with-drawn from this person. Then you don't make love because you're too angry. You don't do anything together because you can't count on your partner being there. You can't talk about any-thing because what's the point if any real conclusion and decision will end up being forgotten. Memory keeps things real. Forget-ting turns things into air. Forgetting in a relationship turns the relationship into air.

And you can't allow yourself to be made the bad guy just be-cause your partner presents his forgetting as a way of being relaxed.

Another way people have of breaking agreements is that they don't think keeping the agreement matters. This can be amazing to you if you've worked hard to set up the agreement in the first place. Finally, after weeks of fighting, the two of you agree that your partner will stop spending money unless he talks about it with you first. Then the very next day, seemingly deliberately, he goes out and buys himself a Burberry raincoat without discussing it first.

And guess what happens to make him think the agreement

doesn't matter to you? He walks in the door and you tell him how nice he looks. Maybe you forgot the agreement. Maybe you're afraid of seeming petty. Maybe after all the fighting that went into setting up the agreement you're sick at the thought of fighting to keep the agreement.

Maybe there are no consequences to keeping the agreement because every single time there are so many "exceptions" that the agreement never quite applies. Your partner promised he'd spend a full twenty minutes with foreplay every time you make love. And he's telling you he's actually keeping the agreement even though he's never kept the agreement. And that's because one night it's late and you're both tired, and the next time you're rushed because you're afraid the kids are going to wake up, and the next time he's just so horny he can't help himself, and on and on.

The point is that without consequences agreements don't matter. And if you're sick of fighting to set up an agreement in the first place, then you're not going to fight to make sure that the consequences happen if the agreement is broken and so there won't be any consequences when the agreement is broken and the agreement will make no difference and you won't get your needs met.

Another way agreements get broken is through misunderstandings. "I didn't realize that when you said twenty minutes of foreplay that didn't include my getting on top of you and putting my penis in your vagina." "I thought when you said we had to discuss the money I wanted to spend that didn't include, you know, spending money on necessities or stuff for the house or the kids or sums less than five hundred dollars or . . ." "I didn't realize that when you said you wanted me to take out the garbage without your reminding me that you meant every single time."

Surely these are not the kinds of things you end a relationship over, are they? Not one at a time. But they are the kinds of things that destroy a relationship when they happen over and over, and form a pattern, and make you feel that having needs, much less thinking of getting them met, is a waste of time.

4. "We're Very Polite with Each Other"

Here's another sign that it's just too hard to get your needs met. I don't want to knock politeness. It's missing from too many relationships. Politeness can be heaven. But it can be the very stuff out of which relationship hell is made, too.

What do you think happens to people in a relationship when they're furious and exhausted from pointless fighting, broken agreements, and unmet needs?

You just stop trying to arrive at agreements. It looks like politeness but it's really despair wearing the mask of politeness. He does whatever he wants with money and you don't say anything. You hate him more than ever, but it might look to an observer as though things were better than ever. Your needs don't get met when it comes to sex, but it's been so hard to talk about it, and the talk never adds up to anything anyway, that you are led to a situation where you politely refrain from sex. And since it's rude to argue over garbage, you just take it out yourself, and feel you're trapped in a relationship with someone who's destroyed your dreams.

So if your despair over negotiating solutions is so great that your relationship has been turned into an empty desert of politeness, where you're unwilling to even ask for what you want, then you already see how unlikely it is that you can get your needs met.

When Enough Is Enough. These then are the four mechanisms that make people feel it's just too hard to get their needs met. Let me briefly summarize them:

1. *"I can do whatever I want, right?"* Your partner's making unilateral moves: doing what he wants when he wants it by himself without talking to you about it.
2. *"It's such an ordeal talking about the littlest thing."* This is when negotiating solutions together is virtually impossible. Here's what makes it impossible:

- You can't listen to each other or understand what the other is saying, because you feel furious and deprived or because your partner is a bad communicator or because you're exhausted and overwhelmed.

- You're scared to death you're going to lose, because your partner's a dirty fighter or because your partner's limited.
- You're afraid of being attacked, because your partner's a "historian" and hooks everything you bring up into the past or because you're constantly criticized when you have a need.
- You're afraid of conflict and struggle, because every single negotiation in the past has ended in disaster, or because your partner's a nut and the stress of negotiation either depresses her or makes her feel she's got to threaten to leave or because there are specific stumbling blocks that you bang into two minutes into any negotiation.

3. *"You never do what you say you're going to do."* This is where the issue of trust comes up in relationships. When people make agreements and then break them, the relationship is not only a place of fighting and deprivation, it's a place of betrayal.

4. *"We're very polite with each other."* This is what happens to people in a relationship when they're furious and exhausted from pointless fighting, broken agreements, and unmet needs. There's no fighting, there's just despair.

If the four mechanisms I've just outlined exist in your relationship, then it's likely that guideline #30 does apply to you.

GUIDELINE #30

If you've lost hope that you'll be able to get a reasonable need met without a too-painful struggle to arrive at a solution, then I feel comfortable saying you'll be happy if you leave and unhappy if you stay. *Quick take:* Frustration, fear, and deprivation are nature's way of telling you that this relationship is not your home.

The four mechanisms listed before this guideline show you what would bring you to the point of losing hope that you can get reasonable needs met or do so without a too-painful struggle. What you have to do is see whether these need-destroying mechanisms actually exist in your relationship and then determine for yourself whether you've actually given up hope. That's the key to this guideline.

The fact that you've stayed in an iffy relationship only means you've accommodated to whatever level of deprivation exists. You can't look at the fact that you've stayed and assume that that by itself means you still have hope. Don't let your actions mislead you about what you really feel. What looks like an action might only be inertia.

But it takes a lot to kill hope. With the four mechanisms I provided I've given you a chance to see what's real in your relationship, and if seeing what's real means that you still have realistic hope that it won't be too hard to get your needs met, then you can't say your relationship is too bad to stay in.

What About Fighting?

Notice I haven't talked about how much fighting there'd have to be before leaving makes sense. That's because when people complain that "all we do is fight" they're really complaining about bloody destructive fights that lead nowhere and get no needs met. That's what guideline #30 talks about. The issue is unmet needs, not fights. The issue is fights that don't lead to solutions, not fights that give you a chance to work things out.

Sometimes people fight and arrive at real solutions to real problems. And people in that situation don't say they're sorry they stayed in the relationship. It's not the fighting in itself but the *unmet* needs and *fruitless* fighting that mean it's time to leave.

STEP #31: GETTING THE BIG NEED MET

Sometimes someone in a relationship says, "We don't fight very often and I get most of my needs met in this relationship, and if there's a problem we can usually talk about it and come to some kind of solution. The problem is there's this *one big need* I have that's very important to me and it's really the only need that's not satisfied in this relationship, but I just can't get it satisfied with my partner." And then he goes on to talk about how his partner either refuses to meet this need or is incapable of meeting it.

Of course we're all grownups and we all understand that you don't get everything you want in life. You might complain about a relationship because some important need isn't getting met, but that doesn't automatically make it too bad to stay in. So where do you draw the line? Where do you stop telling yourself you're being a baby and start giving yourself permission to think that it's worth leaving this relationship to satisfy this need?

Obviously I'm talking about something you need in your life that's so important to you that not getting it changes the meaning of your life. I'm not talking about just another unmet need, I'm talking about an unfulfilled life. Here's a story that makes clear the kind of thing I'm talking about.

Bernie's Story

Bernie loved his life with Sandy. He loved their house, he loved their kids, their friends, their vacations. He even loved the *idea* of going to work every morning and working very hard. And Sandy loved the same things. But he hated his job and he hated himself in it. And what he needed was the freedom and power and sense of owning his destiny that he believed would come with owning his own business.

Bernie was a sales engineer and a manufacturer's rep. He sold a variety of technical instruments of all kinds to a range of industrial companies, large and small. It required a significant amount of technical expertise, because he had to be able to understand and solve their problems with his products.

It bothered him that beneath the technical veneer he was

just a guy with inventory to push so he could meet his quotas, instead of the real engineer he wanted to be. And what killed him most of all was selling products that did a half-assed job of solving his customers' problems when he could easily imagine himself inventing instruments that would do a much better job.

You can guess what Bernie's big need was. He wanted to quit his crazy-making sales job and go after the potential rewards—financial, psychological, and otherwise—of being a freelance inventor. He wanted to go into business for himself. But Sandy wouldn't let him meet his need. She was scared at the thought of his giving up his respectable, highly paid job. She was scared of all the uncertainty they'd face. It's not even that she was afraid of the risk. She just wasn't as confident about his ability to be a successful inventor as he was. So she put her foot down and threatened to leave Bernie if he left his job.

Bernie spent seven years giving up his need. Maybe, he thought, it would just go away. Maybe, he thought, Sandy was right and he'd come to see that what he wanted to do was simply not realistic.

Then one summer during a family get-together he went for a long walk with his sister. He talked about the dream he'd had and how Sandy was against it and he started to put himself down for being unrealistic and immature. But his sister, who'd always liked Sandy, drew him out and it became clear to him that one day he'd be an old man and the entire story of his life would be about whether he followed that dream of his or not, and the thought of letting it go meant letting his life go, and that meant he was faced with a stark choice between getting his need met and staying in the relationship.

So he left his job to become an inventor and, true to her word, Sandy left him. Did he do the right thing? Many of Sandy's predictions came true. His new life was a struggle. Fame and fortune were not waiting just around the corner.

After ten years he hadn't made much money and had built up some debt. Eventually a couple of his inventions clicked, but this didn't make him a rich man. Bernie was a bit disappointed with how his dream had turned out. But this is crucial: he wasn't disappointed that he'd followed his dream. He was proud of himself. He enjoyed the actual work he did every day.

He hadn't wanted the relationship with Sandy to end, not if he could have kept the relationship and kept his new life, too. But forced to choose one or the other, Bernie was glad he'd satisfied the biggest need of his life.

The One Thing You Need

Not everyone has a big need like Bernie's. And most of us who do have big needs in our lives are getting them satisfied the way we're living right now. But if you have an important need that's not getting met, ask yourself this:

Diagnostic question #31. **Is there some particular need that's so important to you that if you don't get it met, looking back you'll say that your life wasn't satisfying, and are you starting to get discouraged about ever being able to get it met?**

What kinds of needs am I talking about? Sometimes what you need is something inside the relationship, something you'd like your partner to give you directly. But as Bernie showed, it doesn't have to be a need for your partner to do something for you. Bernie didn't need anything from Sandy except permission to try to follow his dream. A lot of needs people have are like this: for something that has nothing to do with the relationship but where their partner stands in the way of satisfying their need.

The Need in the Box

On some level the most corrosive thing of all is staying up in the air about a relationship when you could have some kind of peace and clarity one way or the other. Imagine how much better you'd feel if you could just put your need in a box and say to yourself, "It's too bad I'm not getting this need met but *I can let it go* and

I can stop feeling that this relationship is too bad to stay in." Or imagine how much better you'd feel if you could say, "My partner and I need to work on our negotiating skills and *I'll keep trying to get my need met*, but even if I never get it met, I'm still not going to feel this relationship is too bad to stay in." But imagine if you can't say these things. Here's the guideline:

GUIDELINE #31

If you have a need that's so important that, if you don't get it met, looking back you'll say your life wasn't satisfying, and if your partner stands in the way of your getting your need met and you don't believe that you'll ever be able to work out a resolution, then you'll be happy if you leave and unhappy if you stay. *Quick take:* Beware of unmet needs so important they sow the seeds of hate.

What this guideline really says to you is put up or shut up. Look at what you need to be happy in life. Look at what you're doing to get those needs satisfied. If those needs are so important that they'll make all the difference between your being happy in life or not, then either you've got to find a way to get them satisfied in the relationship—and that means learning to negotiate and get whatever other help you need—or you owe it to yourself and your partner to leave the relationship. Otherwise years later you'll find yourself living with someone you hate.

But if those needs are not so all-determining of your future happiness, then work at getting them met by all means, but stop thinking of them as a reason to leave.

Unmet needs are one of the main causes of people being stuck in ambivalence. So face your big needs. See the difference it will make to your happiness if you don't get them met. The guideline is clear. And if you're unsure whether not getting this need met will make your life unsatisfying, then it's not a big enough need to end a relationship over. If not getting it met *will* clearly make your life unsatisfying, you're just condemning yourself and your partner to misery if you do stay.

17

Love To Love You, Baby

Issue: Intimacy—How It Feels to Be Close

Close is what you look for in a relationship. But close is what you've probably found it's hard to get. Close is where you feel good. But close is where you get hurt. This is the promise and problem of intimacy. Let me help you sort all this out.

But it's getting late, isn't it? Here we are, near the end of our diagnostic journey, and if you still haven't gotten the clarity you were looking for, you might be getting nervous, or you might be wondering what's wrong with you.

Don't worry. Even though many people have found the clarity they were looking for by this point, if you haven't yet, there's most likely nothing wrong with you.

The reason you still haven't seen what's best for you to do could be that you simply *won't* find that any diagnostic question points in the direction of your leaving. Not one. And I don't want to give away the punch line, but you'll soon see that if nothing points to leaving, then *that* points to the fact that you'll be happiest if you stay.

It's like when you go to the doctor: if there's nothing wrong that means everything's okay. Not necessarily great. But okay. And that's the kind of clarity you were looking for.

But the reason you haven't found your clarity yet could also be lurking in the complicated area we're about to get into. It's the area where we'll explore how it feels when you and your partner are together, when the two of you get closer and closer to one another. Feeling good and getting close, feeling good because you're getting close, is the essence of what it means to be in a relationship.

But you know why this area is so complicated: You know how hard it is to get close. You know how it's only when you get close that you see how much closer you can get. You know what a cruel, discouraging yardstick it is to apply closeness as the measure of success in a relationship.

If having trouble with intimacy were the cutoff point, we'd all be kicked out of our relationships. So where is the cutoff point? What we'll look at in this chapter is where intimacy hurts, where intimacy doesn't happen, and what makes intimacy special.

STEP #32: WHEN YOU GET CLOSE, YOU GET HURT

When we talk about getting intimate we talk about being vulnerable. Vulnerable literally means "able to be wounded." But what is it exactly about the wounds we incur when we're most woundable that makes some relationships too bad to stay in?

Let's talk about what it means to get close. It means that you show parts of yourself to the other person that you don't show anyone else. And they like what you show them and they like you for showing it. And they let you know that they like it. And then, so that you won't feel stupid hanging out there more psychologically naked than they are, they show parts of themselves to you that they don't show anyone else. And you show them that you like what they've shown you and that you like them for showing it.

Let's call this "mutually appreciative escalating nakedness." And of course it can be nakedness of any kind, physical, psychological, emotional. And while the two of you are getting naked like this and appreciating each other for it, you not only appreciate each other for what you've disclosed but also for the fact that you have disclosed something special between you. And that's where the problems start to come in.

As long as you keep telling each other how wonderful you are with every disclosure—well, you certainly feel appreciated, but you wonder if you've been seen at all. So that you know you've really been seen you need to tell each other a special truth that no one else can tell you. For example, if one of you tells the other something about what it was like for you growing up, and you've disclosed something really personal, you'll know the other has seen your nakedness if they say something about what you told them that no one else would say. Such as, "You've talked a lot about stuff people in your family did to you, but it seems to me that you relished a lot of it and used it as a weapon against them."

And you're hungry to hear that truth until you actually do hear it. Then you aren't quite as happy as you were before. Sure, you've been seen all right, but you're not hearing such nice things. And you don't like hearing such not-nice things, especially when you've taken the risk of getting naked. So you feel rejected instead of appreciated. And then there's a big fight.

Does any of this sound familiar?

And so two people while experiencing mutually escalating nakedness keep bumping into each other like two unrehearsed ballroom dancers stepping on each other's toes.

You're Beautiful When You're Naked

But there's a way of managing this successfully in spite of all the places where we keep stubbing our toes. This is when you manage to convey to each other that—even though you say critical, even rejecting, things, even though you get angry at what your partner reveals in her nakedness, even though your partner gets angry with you for getting angry at what she revealed in her nakedness—you still basically think the other is pretty terrific. That way, even though feelings get hurt, the stage of intimacy doesn't become a place of horror.

But when does it become a place of horror? When does intimacy turn from being a place where feelings occasionally get hurt to being the one place in the world where you feel least at home? Here's the question:

Diagnostic question #32. Given the way your partner acts, does it feel as though in getting close to you what he's most interested in is subjecting you to his anger and criticism?

You know how it is. Some people really seem to want to get close so they can get close. Some people want to get close so they can complain about their lives to you. Some people want to get close so they can have sex. And some people seem to want to get close just so they can hurt you.

Here's an example of what this is like so that you can see if question #32 applies to you.

Theresa's Story

Theresa admired Paul before she loved him. Then she fell in love with him because of how much she admired him. Paul was a psychiatrist unusual for his devotion to working with the poorest, most disturbed people in the community. As someone who worked in a funding agency and was frustrated with trying to help people from behind a wall of ledgers, Theresa saw Paul as a hero.

Both because she wanted to meet him personally and because she wanted to find a way to give him agency money, Theresa arranged for them to have dinner together. Soon they were seeing more and more of each other. They found they shared a wide range of beliefs and attitudes, particularly about the terrible psychological burden of growing up poor in the ghetto and about how important it was to devote resources to helping the people there. They found they liked the same music. They found they liked the same movies and liked seeing them at home on videotape with a pizza. They found they liked the same things in sex.

Speaking of movies, if this were one of those movies from the thirties you could imagine the pages of a calendar slowly flipping one after another to indicate the months passing. And that's because that's how long it took for Theresa to realize that something terrible was happening.

If only her hero had feet of clay for her. But for her he had the cloven-hoofed feet of the devil.

A Wolf in Shrink's Clothing. It all began sadly enough with the very thing that had made Paul a god to her: his insights and his desire to improve things. She praised him so much for this that it was hard for her to see what was happening inside her when he started turning his insights and his desire to improve things toward her. In her love and innocence she laid bare to him all of her faults and fears. After all, doesn't love mean never having to say you're sorry you let your partner see you naked?

And that's where she found he was jumping all over her. It began seemingly gently, with insights alone. He merely "pointed out" things to her. As she later said to me, "You wouldn't believe how many conversations we had where all I said was 'I know' and 'you're right' and 'that's true.' "

"Let Me Tell You What's Wrong with You." At first these insights were relatively neutral—things like his pointing out the connection between Theresa's always putting things off until the last minute and the way her parents had been permissive bringing her up. But once Paul softened her up for receiving his insights they started getting more critical. It wasn't just his saying that she had a tendency to be late, but that she had a lax, lazy, sloppy orientation to life.

It was hard for her to resist even this kind of critical insight, because it would seem as though any attempt at resistance would exhibit the very flaws of laziness and defensiveness that he was criticizing her for. Then, with a well-established basis between them for his telling her what was wrong with her, he started telling her what to do to improve herself in every part of her life.

He told her what she should eat—certainly much less than she'd been eating—and how she should exercise more and more.

He told her how, since she had so many ill-informed, ill-conceived ideas about things, she should study before she offered an opinion about issues she'd felt confident talking about before, and how could she argue with him since he seemed so confident and so right about everything?

He told her that since she was so bad with money—something she didn't see until he'd pointed it out to her—she should give her money to him to invest for her besides tithing ten percent of her money by giving it to charities he worked for on contract.

For a long time, Theresa accepted all this destructive overinvolvement as Paul's way of expressing his love and caring and concern, or at worst as an expression of his perfectionism, which after all led him to accomplish so much, which was why she'd admired him in the first place.

"*I'm Only Doing This Because I Hate You.*" But eventually and with growing shock Theresa came to realize the degree to which the way Paul treated her when they were close was fueled by tremendous anger, if not hatred.

He was cold to her much of the time, she realized. He kept fueling a hunger in her for them to get close again the way they used to. Then he used her hunger for closeness as a way to exact a willingness in her to put up with his harsh judgments of everything about her. He enticed her with a promise of the kind of soft, safe intimacy they'd had at first, but only when she was good again, only when she was perfect.

One weekend she was in bed with a bad cold. She hoped he'd take care of her or at least leave her alone. But Paul seemed to find her pain and vulnerability the perfect opportunity for him to tell her how her cold was a sign of how little she knew about taking care of herself, of all the toxins she'd allowed to grow within her. The only way she could purge herself, he said, was for him to sit there and for her to dredge up every weak or erroneous or evil thought or feeling she'd ever had.

It was, she realized, a kind of brainwashing he was putting

her through. And she was suddenly struck by what seemed obvious the minute it hit her: that he was a man filled with hate and anger and destructiveness. And he loved intimacy only for the opportunity it offered to inflict pain and damage.

Why had it taken her so long to see all this? Partly it was his public role. He really did do good work in the community. Partly it was the gradualness with which he eased into destructive criticism in seeming lockstep with their developing intimacy. And partly it was her hunger for closeness, which made it so hard for her to see the price she was paying for getting close.

Don't Be Cruel

Theresa's story is just an extreme example of the way getting hurt as you're getting close is an essential part of their experience of intimacy for some people, not an accidental part. This was not simply the case of somebody bringing up a deeply personal memory and having their partner misunderstand or fail to respond adequately. This was not just the case of a critical remark uttered during a moment of closeness which turned out to be far more cutting and cruel than the person who said it could have imagined. Intimacy can survive these mishaps.

But Theresa's story illustrates the corner you can turn and that you have to watch out for. There's no objective way to measure when you've turned this corner. But here's the guideline:

GUIDELINE #32

It's normal to get hurt occasionally when you get close to someone, but if you feel that your partner's main interest in getting close to you is making you feel his anger and criticism, then you'll never feel close or safe in your relationship and you'll be happier if you leave than if you stay. *Quick take:* If getting close to your partner feels like you're getting into the boxing ring with him or her, then it's time to end the match.

Here's how to apply this guideline. In our relationships, none of us like to feel constantly criticized and judged and controlled and micromanaged. Most of the time, though, as long as you're not dealing with the kind of power person I described in the "You've Got a Hold on Me" chapter who's mainly interested in obliterating your needs, you can let your partner know that you're starting to feel judged and he'll back off. And most of the time there are safe havens of closeness in your relationship where criticism and judgment drop away and as you get more intimate you're more appreciative of each other.

This guideline focuses on those people who turn this upside down and inside out, who are invested in *not* backing off their criticism and who are eager to get close to you so they can inflict their judgments on you. Instead of providing safety they destroy it. That's when you know you've got to leave.

But I don't want to emphasize the idea of criticisms. This guideline could apply without your partner ever being critical. The key is your feelings. The key is your sense that you're living in a topsy-turvy world with your partner where, for whatever reason, distance feels better than closeness, where distance feels safer than closeness, where instead of seeking out closeness you avoid it as a place where you sense bad things will happen to you.

This guideline does not apply if you're simply one of those people who aren't quite so comfortable with intimacy as other people. Not everyone has to like getting real close. But there is a big difference between preferring a slightly greater distance and fearing (based on experience with this person) that you'll get hurt if you get close.

Holding on to Anger

There's a special case of this that I need to single out. It's when your partner or you hold on to anger and resentment between fights. Then when you relax and get close the anger that had been held back pours out. That could be because with relaxation you lost your tight grip on your anger or because getting close to your partner again restimulated whatever it was that made you angry in the first place.

There's a big difference between someone who seems to purposely store up his anger so he can hit you with it when you get close and someone who doesn't want to be doing this. The difference lies in your partner's willingness to learn and willingness to do something about it. Going back to what we talked about in the "All the Things You Are" chapter, if he's not willing to acknowledge his holding-on-to-anger problem and work on it, and if his saving up his anger makes being close unsafe and impossible for you, I'd feel comfortable saying guideline #32 applies.

STEP #33: LOOKING FOR INTIMACY

Now let's move on to the next step. I've just talked about where to draw the line when intimacy hurts. Now I'm going to talk about where to draw the line when intimacy doesn't happen. It's not that anything bad happens when you get close, it's that you don't get close.

Let me tell you where I'm coming from in my approach to this crucial issue. On the one hand, I know how incredibly important intimacy is to you. On some level intimacy is the big prize in our relationships. We feel happy and successful when we're close; unhappy and unsuccessful when we're not.

On the other hand, I know how tricky intimacy can be. I know there's no anguish like seeking an intimacy that's forever one step beyond your reach. We have as much trouble finding the intimacy we're looking for as we do growing a garden that's not plagued by bugs and weeds and fungus. What's not intimate enough for you may be far too intimate for your partner. You find it's very intimate when you do one thing; your partner may find it's very intimate when you do something completely different.

A very brief, common example. A couple had been in an on-again/off-again relationship for four years. Now they were starting to edge toward a permanent commitment. One huge obstacle was the woman's unhappiness that her partner wouldn't say he loved her. For her, intimacy meant hearing those words. The thought of a lifetime without hearing those words was like the thought of an emotional desert.

But from his point of view the words "I love you" were mechanical and perfunctory. They devalued his true feelings, he said. From his point of view he was being more intimate by not saying those words than by saying them. For him the thought of a lifetime uttering perfunctory sentiments was like the thought of an emotional desert.

Both people were being honest. Where do you draw the line? I suggest you ask yourself this question:

Diagnostic question #33. **When the subject of intimacy comes up between you and your partner, is there generally a battle over what intimacy is and how to get it?**

The mistake people make about intimacy is thinking that their partner doesn't want it. But people almost never say they don't want intimacy. In fact, whenever I've worked with couples and one of the people in the relationship seems uncomfortable with intimacy or afraid of it, I'm generally hopeful. It may be that they've been hurt in the past, or that they just grew up in a family where they never saw much intimacy, or that they're just not good at it. Someone who even goes so far as to say, "I don't want so much intimacy" (and that doesn't happen very often), can meet you halfway because *you* want intimacy.

The problem isn't when your partner doesn't want as much intimacy as you do; the problem is when your partner does want it and has a completely different vision of intimacy from yours. We tend to think of the classic intimacy problem as between a woman and a not-in-touch-with-his-feelings kind of guy. But let me tell you about the worst intimacy problem I ever saw between two people.

Terri and Flo

A lesbian couple, Terri and Flo, were both very comfortable with the idea of intimacy. What's more, they both were therapists and had experienced and promulgated intimacy every day in their clinical work. The problem was how deeply dug in they were with their opposing visions of intimacy.

For Terri, the height of intimacy was revealing the deepest, darkest secrets and emotions. For her, you were intimate when you cried together, when you talked about the things you were afraid of, when you showed yourself as wounded and woundable. You were intimate when you told someone something you would never tell anyone else and when you told it with a depth of feeling you would never let anyone else see. That, for her, was the real thing when it came to intimacy.

For Flo, the height of intimacy was strolling through the streets of a city they'd never visited before, somehow vibrating in wordless unison in their response to this experience. Or it was working in the garden together, their activities and sensibilities meshing as they were busy together creating something that they saw in the same way. Or it was any shared activity where they did something together and meshed well as they were doing it and felt the same way about it.

Tragically for them, intimacy for each was specifically *not* what it was for the other. Flo, for whom intimacy was doing things together, saw Terri's emotional kind of intimacy as a painful waste of time, as making their relationship feel like work. Terri, for whom intimacy was deep emotional sharing, saw Flo's vision of intimacy through joint activity as anti-intimacy—as the kind of thing you do to avoid being close to someone.

Terri and Flo were as motivated and skilled as any two people could be when it came to "working on" their relationship. In the end, though, they were content to end their relationship because they couldn't bridge the difference between them over the meaning of intimacy. Every time I've seen people driven out of their relationship because of intimacy problems and happy they got out, it was because of this kind of situation, where there

are incompatible visions of intimacy that the two people bat-
tled over.

Here's the guideline:

GUIDELINE #33

If you and your partner cannot agree about what intimacy is for the two of you and how to get it, and if holding on to your positions is more important to you than
bridging your differences, then most people in your situation end up not being happy they stayed in the relationship and end up happy they left. *Quick take:* If getting
close drives you apart, you can never get close.

You can test for this. A partner who's had trouble getting close to
you because of his upbringing or whatever can still say, "I understand that what it means to you for us to get close is [whatever
it happens to be for you], and I'm willing to do what I can, or at
least a better job than I have been, in helping us get close in that
way." Maybe you're still far apart, but slowly that distance can
shrink and you can have the experience of that distance
shrinking. But when you have strongly opposing visions of intimacy, the last thing your partner wants is to understand what it
means for you to get close, because from his point of view your
vision is a mistake, a danger even.

In a sense all this says is that people can learn what they
don't know, but to learn what they think is wrong is impossible.

The last two guidelines have something in common. Both focus on ways it's not safe to get close. Guideline #32 focused on
how it's not safe to get close because that's when you get attacked. Guideline #33 focused on how it's not safe to get close
because that's when your vision of closeness gets attacked.

STEP #34: ARE WE HAVING FUN YET?

Let's be clear about why we're talking about intimacy. It's not because you're supposed to live up to some therapist's theory of

what it's like for two people to be together. It's because being together is supposed to feel good. We've talked about intimacy because it's certainly supposed to feel good when you're closest.

It should also feel good the rest of the time. But how good?
And good in what way? And when does not feeling good mean
that the relationship is too bad to stay in?

It should come as no surprise, of course, that the thirty-three
questions you've gone through up until now have eliminated
most of the ways a relationship feels so bad it's too bad to stay in.
So we're in subtle territory here.

And in this territory what people complain about most is
boredom. The deadly dullness and predictability of your interac-
tions from morning till night. Where you know exactly what the
other's going to say and yet you're still ready to scream at the
thought of hearing him say it.

And yet, just the way you've learned to be mature and accept
the fact that a good-enough relationship has fights from time to
time and frustrations over intimacy, so, too, does boredom become an inevitable part of two people growing old together or
even being together for the first six months. And I know very few
divorcing couples where both partners don't envy old bored married couples. At least they're not hating each other. At least their
relationship is enduring. At least they're sharing a history.

Still, you've got to draw the line somewhere. There's some
degree of cold, empty boredom that makes being alone seem attractive. Based on my experience with people wrestling with this
very issue, here's the question to ask yourself:

**Diagnostic question #34. Does your relationship
support your having fun together?**

This doesn't ask if the two of you have a wild fun time every moment you spend together. It doesn't even ask how often you have
fun together. It doesn't even ask how much fun you have when
you have fun together. It just asks whether you feel confident
that, if the spirit somehow moved you and your partner, you

could somehow stimulate and motivate each other into an experience where you had some fun.

Even if you just sit there like two bumps on a log watching television most evenings because you're too tired when you get home from work to do much else, do you still have the fantasy and the belief that with one word from you and another word from your partner the two of you could be laughing and joking and fooling around? Or just walking out of the house and going out and having a good time?

I know you don't feel this happens often enough. But do you feel the potential is there if the circumstances were right?

People in relationships complain about boredom and bickering. But here's the guideline:

GUIDELINE #34

If you feel that you and your partner have turned a corner where having fun together is simply not a possibility at all, and you're living without hope of the two of you having fun together again, then most people in your situation are happy they leave and unhappy they stay. If the possibility of fun between you does seem fully alive, then that's a sign your relationship is too good to leave. *Quick take:* Fun is the glue of love.

Before we go any further, I've got to talk about what it means to have fun. It means, of course, what it means *to you* for you to have fun. You're the standard. If sitting on the porch gossiping about the neighbors as they go by is fun for you, then that's your fun. If tickling each other until your sides hurt is fun for you, then that's your fun. If having long complicated arguments about federal budget priorities is fun for you, then that's your fun. If having sex is fun for you, then that's your fun and your sex all in one.

And people don't only vary in what it means for them to have fun but in their need for fun. Just the way some people need wild, exotic sex three times a day and other people are content having sex once in a while, some people are satisfied with a level and frequency of fun that would seem very gray to other people. I think of myself, for example, as fun loving, and compared to some therapists I know I think I am, but my kids don't think I have enough fun at all.

So you set the standard. I just want you to be able to give yourself permission to see that your relationship is too bad to stay in if it's the case that there's no more possibility for you to have fun in it, as well as realizing that your relationship may be too good to leave if you still can easily have fun together.

Intimacy and Fun

If you want to see how important fun is for the basic satisfaction-producing core of a relationship, you might have noticed I didn't say people were happy leaving when they weren't close. Even though intimacy's important, with time and age a relationship can still feel satisfying without an incredible special closeness between the partners. They might wish they had more closeness, but they're not going to be happy they leave just because they don't have that closeness.

But in some special way the possibility of fun is more important in the long run than holding on to that last degree of closeness. Let me put it like this. People who were close to each other but who'd lost the possibility of having fun together were a lot more unhappy and a lot more content to end their relationship than people who wished they were closer to each other but still felt the possibility of fun was alive in their relationship.

Whatever fun is for you, fun is the orgasm of intimacy.

18

I've Got You Under My Skin

Issue: Feeling You Belong Together

STEP #35: A REASON TO BE TOGETHER

If you remember back to when you were in elementary school, if one of your friends ever thought you liked someone they'd immediately tease you with the poem:

John and Mary, sitting in a tree,
K-I-S-S-I-N-G.
First comes love, then comes marriage,
Then comes Mary with a baby carriage.

Now answer this. Why "sitting in a tree"? How did falling in love put the two of you in a tree?

Because you fall out of trees. And you fall out of love. That's one of the eternal mysteries of love. How you can fall in love and then out of it again?

And in a horribly frustrating way, the strength of your passion (shall we say, the height of the tree your love has allowed you to sit in) is no protection against your falling out of love. Little passions and grand passions are equally likely to dump you on the ground.

Of course by the time marriage and a baby carriage follow love, you're pretty much stuck up the tree and you don't have to worry every minute about falling out of it. Still, you'd like some protection. You'd particularly like this protection if you're someone who's been wondering about leaving your relationship because sometimes it's felt too bad to stay in. What if you're sitting in the tree of love and there's nothing to hold you up? When love itself seems shaky, is there anything else that can hold you together?

There *is* protection for some people and you deserve to know about it. For some people in some relationships there's a kind of superglue holding them up in the tree of love, beyond love itself. It varies widely in its exact form from person to person. But to see if you've got it (and it doesn't mean anything bad if you don't have it) ask yourself this question:

Diagnostic question #35. Do you currently share goals and dreams for your life together?

Before you respond, let me give you some examples of the kind of answers I'm talking about.

- For one couple their mildly retarded, physically handicapped child was their joint project—caring for him, teaching him, and helping him live.
- Another couple was together because of a shared vision of living in the country and building their own house, growing their own food, and supporting themselves by the sweat of their brows, all in the context of being part of a close-knit community.
- For another couple it was both being surfers, and whatever else they did to earn a living really wasn't important as long as they both could get away whenever possible to catch the best wave at the best beach.
- For another couple it was being conservative, born-again

Christians, praying every day, being active in the church, educating their children at home, and working hard through political action to make the country more reflective of their values.

- For another couple it was being artists together. One supported himself painting full-time, and the other taught art for a living, but they mutually supported and stimulated each other.
- For another couple it was their garden. Not just keeping it up the way most people with a house do, but building it into one of the noteworthy gardens in their state.
- For another couple it was building together a stock market portfolio and getting it big enough as quickly as possible to allow them both to live off the income and enjoy themselves.
- For another couple his political career was their joint dream and project.
- For another couple building a computer software company into a nationwide powerhouse within its niche kept them together through years of difficulties.

It doesn't have to be a noble vision or a vision that anyone else would share. But I am talking about couples for whom having a relationship is about more than just having a relationship. One reason so many Hollywood couples break up, even though they're sincerely in love when they come together, is that their focus on their separate careers, while not being bad in itself, means they don't have any shared vision.

At the same time, I don't want to make it sound as though these shared dreams and goals have to be anything extraordinary. For a lot of people it can simply be to own a house and have a family and friends and put aside enough money to enjoy their retirement. It's not an issue of how special the dream is but whether it has special power to hold you together.

Couples who've got this superglue run into difficulties like everyone else. They hurt each other and disappoint each other.

They have trouble communicating and subject each other to their personality defects like everyone else. They're even subject to certain problems other couples don't face, like the discouragement and mutual blame that follow when they run into obstacles pursuing their joint vision. And they even fall into relationship ambivalence like everyone else.

But their joint vision keeps them going and gives them a strength and focus the rest of us lack. Here's the guideline:

GUIDELINE #35

If you and your partner share a goal or a dream for the future, if there's something you organize your lives around and care about more than almost anything else, and if it's something you do together in some way that not only gives you a sense of satisfaction but a sense of meaning, then for most people in your situation what you've got going for you means your relationship is too good to leave. *Quick take:* Sharing a passion makes it easier to share a life.

It Doesn't Have to Be Anything You Do

What I'm really talking about here is people who feel there's a special reason why they're together. It helps if you can point to some project or activity you share, as with so many of the couples I've just listed. But that's not absolutely necessary. Anything that gives you a sense of why you're together qualifies.

For some couples it's a special sense of fit. There's a special way you're weird and a special way your partner's weird and there's something about your joint weirdness that fits perfectly that means you feel you'd be miserable with anyone else. It could be something as simple as loving to stay up all night. It could be a negative, cynical kind of intelligence that takes pleasure in demolishing icons and pretensions. It could even be a strange way one of you is methodical and the other is creative and yet you somehow enhance each other.

As long as it's sincerely and deeply felt, it could even be a semimystical sense that you belong together, that you were meant to be together, that even if you hadn't met the accidental way you did you'd have somehow met some other way.

And what if you don't have any of this? What if you had to say no to question #35? Don't worry about it. People who are up the tree of love without any superglue are just as happy as everyone else. Having a special shared dream or goal doesn't actually make couples happier than couples who don't have it. If you're in love and you like each other and you enjoy each other, who cares if you don't give a damn about anything else?

It's just that for people in an iffy relationship, having a special sense of belonging can be powerful evidence your relationship is too good to leave. If you don't have it, though, it can still be too good to leave.

STEP #36: THE LAST STEP

We're almost done. By now you've seen all the special issues that people have taught me it's important to focus on in deciding whether to stay or leave. This last step, where we are now, isn't really an issue at all. It's just a question, a last important question you need to ask yourself:

Diagnostic question #36. If all the problems in your relationship were magically solved today, would you still feel ambivalent about whether to stay or leave?

Just think about what you're really answering with this question, if you haven't gotten clarity up until now. You've already read through thirty-five guidelines that point to all the important factors that make people happy they stay or leave. Your responses to the questions didn't indicate that you have any of the problems that make people in general happy they left and unhappy they stayed. So if your answer to question #36 is yes, then that really means that even without the presence of the relationship-destroying problems other people face, you still feel iffy. And that's very significant. Here's the guideline:

GUIDELINE #36

Even if there were no problems, if you still don't know whether you want to be in this relationship, then you're indicating a deep discomfort with something about your partner or your relationship. People who felt this way were happy they left and unhappy they stayed. *Quick take:* If you don't know whether you want to stay even if nothing were wrong, then you don't want to stay.

A clear yes means this relationship is too bad to stay in. If your answer's no—"No, if all the problems in my relationship were solved, I'd want to stay in it"—that means this relationship is too good to leave.

That's it. Your answer to this question was either yes or no. You've found the clarity you were looking for.

HOME AT LAST

Well, here we are. That's some journey we've been on together. I'm sure it's been an emotion-filled journey, too. At the beginning you were stuck, unable to decide what to do with your iffy relationship. You were looking for evidence that would show you once and for all whether you should leave or stay. And now you've found it. Depending on your answer to any of the questions, a guideline might have told you clearly that based on your answer you'll be happiest leaving because most people who gave that answer were happy leaving.

If that happened for you at any point in the book, you've found your truth, and it's pointed to the fact that your relationship is too bad to stay in. You wanted the truth, and that's the truth that was there for you all the time, waiting for you to discover it.

Let me be very definite about something:

Your relationship is too bad to stay in as long as your answer to any question produced a guideline that said that most people who gave that answer were happy they left and unhappy they stayed.

If that's the case, you don't need any other information. Just because other questions don't point you toward the exits doesn't change the fact that your answer to this particular question does point you toward the exits. One clear negative sign is all you need, and it doesn't matter what all the other signs say. That's the way diagnostics work to end confusion and ambivalence.

What about clarity on the other side, seeing whether your relationship is too good to leave? The answer is this:

Your relationship is too good to leave if no guideline points to the fact that it's too bad to stay in.

It's as simple as that.

No doubt you'll feel reassured if your answer to one of the questions produced a guideline that said most people in your situation were happy they stayed and unhappy they left. That would be a sign there were special strengths in your relationship, and that certainly would be powerful confirmation that your relationship is too good to leave. But you don't need that confirmation. As long as there were no exit signs, then that definitely says *stay*: you've got a relationship that can give you what you need and feel satisfying to you once you recommit to it.

You probably find this new-won clarity is pretty emotional and a bit breathtaking. For some people it takes a while for it to sink in. That's okay. If you need to, go back through the book to confirm that you would answer all the questions the same way. Give yourself whatever time you need to accept what you've discovered.

Whether your new clarity points to staying or leaving, you're not quite finished with this book yet. I still need to talk to you for a moment about what's ahead for you.

19
Next Steps

Okay. You've found what you were looking for: an understanding of whether you'll be happiest staying or leaving. Either way, you're starting a new life. That's what's good about this kind of clarity. It makes it possible for you to get on with the rest of your life without the wet blanket of ambivalence.

Let me help you get started with the emotional part of this.

IF YOUR RELATIONSHIP IS TOO BAD TO STAY IN

It's very hard to say good-bye to someone who was important to you. But when you make the decision that's right for you, you can feel confident about expecting good things in your future.

You need to know you did the best you could with what you had to work with. It's just that the raw material of this relationship wasn't what you needed to bring forth the happiness you deserve. You could only say you'd failed if you'd planted a seed in fertile soil. But if you dropped that seed on a rock, it's the rock, not you, that prevented the seed from growing. I'm not saying that rock was necessarily your partner; it might just have been the way the two of you fit together.

I understand that you're having many feelings now that go along with acknowledging a relationship is over. And among them is the feeling of sadness. Of course you're entitled to all of your feelings. But it's important that you know what they mean. And what does it mean that you've spent months or years saying, "I just want clarity," and then are overwhelmed with sadness when you finally get that clarity and it points to leaving?

The most important thing for you to know is that *your sadness doesn't mean that the truth you've found isn't your truth.* If it's best for you to leave, then feeling sad at the thought of leaving doesn't change things. Your sadness is not new information about whether you should stay or leave. Instead, it's a natural response to your loss.

So let yourself have your sadness, but don't let it suck you back into the relationship ambivalence you've worked so hard to get out of. Stay clear in your own mind that it's best for you to leave and give your sadness time to subside.

This is a time when you'll be feeling lots of feelings. No matter what you feel—guilt, liberation, rage, hope, disappointment, joy—assume your feelings are normal and natural. Make sure you get the support you need. But don't let any of your feelings take away the clarity you've found.

What's next for you? I'm sure you have hopes and fears for the future. Your hopes are an important source of energy for you. You're probably looking forward to saying good-bye to all the pain and difficulty. And you're probably looking forward to new opportunities in your new life. And you're right to have these hopes.

But you just wouldn't be human if you weren't nervous about what awaits you too. You're probably concerned about what will happen when you tell your partner you want to end the relationship. You'd like to have the breakup occur without all hell breaking loose. And you probably have fears about what awaits you in starting your new life.

For all these concerns, you need to hear what most people have said who've gone through what you're about to go through: it was hard, but it was worth it, and if you use your head you can get through it without your worst fears coming true.

Our work together here is finished, but there are some wonderful books that can help people in your situation. They deal with the emotions that come up in saying good-bye, the emotional and practical realities of unhitching your life from someone else's, the legalities of divorce, and the experience of living on your own. Let me recommend some of these books and leave you in the hands of these fine people to take you through your next steps:

Coming Apart by Daphne Rose Kingma (Fawcett, 1987). This book is good with the emotional part of letting go.

The Good Divorce by Constance Ahrons (Harper Perennial, 1995). If you're going to get a divorce, you might as well do it right. This book will show you how.

Our Turn: The Good News About Women and Divorce by Christopher Hayes, Deborah Anderson, and Melinda Blau (Pocket, 1993). If you're afraid of what awaits you on the other side, there's solid reassurance here.

Uncoupling by Diane Vaughan (Vintage, 1990). This helps with lingering questions of "How did it happen?"

There's no need to limit yourself to these books. Your bookstore and library will probably have others you'll find helpful. And it's important in this next period to get all the help you need.

Looking Forward

Expect good times ahead. Remember: the guideline that pointed you toward the exit said that *most people who answered the question the way you did were happy they left and unhappy they stayed.* I want you to feel the full weight of that. Leaving in itself may be hard, but, having seen your truth you'll be happy you acted on it.

Of course, there are no guarantees in life. People are just too complex for anyone to offer such a guarantee. But happiness was the general outcome for people in your situation and you should expect that happiness will be the outcome for you.

And you're right to expect happiness whether you enter a new relationship soon or you're on your own for a period of time.

Most people look forward to falling in love at some point with the right person. But the truth you discovered about your relationship is such that you'll be happier on your own than if you stay with your current partner.

I don't need to tell you that what lies ahead of you will be an adventure. It might not even be necessary for me to do so: you might be way ahead of me in your sense of excitement and anticipation thinking about your new life. If you're not so sure, listen to people who've been through what you're going through now. The same message keeps coming up over and over:

- "I didn't know if I'd make it, but I'm in a much better place than I was or than I'd ever thought I'd be in."
- "It was hard, but I stayed connected to people and things I cared about and I'm glad I did it."
- "I can't believe how much I've learned about myself and how many new things I've gotten for myself."

And if that's not what you say about an adventure, then I don't know what is.

Good luck and congratulations. Now you finally can liberate yourself from your relationship, free of confusion, free of pain, free at last to get on with a new and better life.

IF YOUR RELATIONSHIP IS TOO GOOD TO LEAVE

Many people have mixed feelings when they discover that they will be happiest staying. On some level, it means recommitting to a relationship that you've thought about leaving. You might be extremely relieved to hear that your relationship is too good to leave, but you might also be afraid of settling for something that was clearly unsatisfactory enough to make you ambivalent about it.

So you may very well be feeling intimidated at the thought of staying. But it's important to understand this feeling. It's not a sign that you've made a mistake in discovering that you'll be happiest if you stay. It's just a natural response any of us have in the face of a difficult task. It's your way of acknowledging the fact that your ambivalence has allowed you to avoid dealing with some of the problems in your relationship. That's one of the things that made ambivalence so insidiously attractive: it got you off the hook.

But all this really means is that you have your work cut out for you: the work that comes from accepting that you can no longer merely wait for things to get better by themselves. This relationship *is* the relationship for you, and like every other thing in your life it will give back to you only what you give to it.

Now it really does make sense for you to work on your relationship. The guidelines that pointed toward staying said that most people who answered the way you did were happy they stayed and unhappy they left. So you will be happy if you stay. There are no guarantees in life, but that's where I'd place my bet.

You'll find your relationship improves faster than you might think when you say good-bye to your ambivalence. Your energy is in a completely different place now. None of it is being used up thinking about whether you should stay. It's as if you've been living in a messy house and had been using all your time and energy looking for a new house. Imagine if that time and energy were now liberated for fixing your house up. It would be a pleasure to live in fairly quickly. In the same way, all the energy you've used thinking about whether you should stay is now available to make your relationship better.

What does that mean in practice? It means being smart and it means being loving. The loving part's not complicated. You're nice to your partner. You do for her the kinds of things you'd want her to do for you. You discover the kinds of things she wants that you might not think of yourself and you do them, too.

Being smart's a little harder, of course. That you've been iffy about your relationship means that there were some problems in it, although not necessarily any more problems than in most relationships. So being smart means addressing those problems and going some of the way toward resolving them.

Let me make a suggestion. Use some of the energy that's been liberated now that you're no longer ambivalent to read *and put into practice* the material in some excellent books on how to make relationships feel better and work better. Here are some books that people find helpful and that I feel comfortable recommending:

Divorce Busting by Michele Weiner-Davis (Fireside, 1993). This book gives you a lot to do, but it's worth it.

Intimate Partners by Maggie Scarf (Ballantine, 1987). This book provides helpful understanding and perspective about what goes on in a relationship.

Lifemates by Harold Bloomfield and Sira Vittese, with Robert Kory (Signet, 1992). There's a lot of practical help here for strengthening relationships.

Love Is a Verb by Bill O'Hanlon and Pat Hudson (Norton, 1995). This book helpfully steers you toward solutions and away from analysis paralysis.

But don't feel you need to limit yourself. Your bookstore and library shelves have plenty of other books you might find useful.

And if you haven't tried couples therapy before, this might be a perfect time to start.

Well, that's it. You're off to live your life and have the relationship you wanted. But now there's a big difference. You know there's a satisfaction-producing core in your relationship that makes it possible for it to give back to you what you give to it. The happiness you were looking for can now be yours.

Congratulations and good luck as you recommit to your relationship, free of doubt, free of holding back, free at last to pour your love and energy into your relationship and get back everything there is to get from it.

Whatever truths you've discovered,
this isn't the end, it's

THE BEGINNING

INDEX

·A NOTE ON THE TYPE·

The typeface used in this book is a version of Caledonia, originally designed by William A. Dwiggins (1880–1956), who also designed Electra. Starting as a grphic artist and book designer (he called himself a "black and white–smith"), he came late to type design, even though he was from his youth an associate of Frederick Goudy, the precminent American type designer of the time. Caledonia was designed on a challenge from Mergenthaler Linotype: to keep the successful aspects of the popular if not very attractive font, Scotch Roman (so called because it was first cut in Scotland)—its large lowercase letters with generous "counters" (internal spaces)—and to rid it of flaws, especially its overly dark capitals. Dwiggins' strategy was to blend it with elements of another "modern," Bulmer, and in the end he created one of the most attractive typefaces in use today